D1410513

PENGUIN BOOKS

THE ROARING NINETIES

Joseph Stiglitz was Chief Economist at the World Bank until January 2000. Before that he was Chairman of President Clinton's Council of Economic Advisors. He is currently Professor of Finance and Economics at Columbia University. He won the Nobel Prize for Economics in 2001. His previous book, *Globalization and Its Discontents*, was an international bestseller.

The Roaring Nineties

*WHY WE'RE PAYING THE
PRICE FOR THE GREEDIEST
DECADE IN HISTORY*

JOSEPH E. STIGLITZ

PENGUIN BOOKS

PENGUIN BOOKS

Published by the Penguin Group
Penguin Books Ltd, 80 Strand, London WC2R 0RL, England
Penguin Group (USA) Inc., 375 Hudson Street, New York, New York 10014, USA
Penguin Books Australia Ltd, 250 Camberwell Road, Camberwell, Victoria 3124, Australia
Penguin Books Canada Ltd, 10 Alcorn Avenue, Toronto, Ontario, Canada M4V 3B2
Penguin Books India (P) Ltd, 11 Community Centre, Panchsheel Park, New Delhi – 110 017, India
Penguin Books (NZ) Ltd, Cnr Rosedale and Airborne Roads, Albany, Auckland, New Zealand
Penguin Books (South Africa) (Pty) Ltd, 24 Sturdee Avenue, Rosebank 2196, South Africa

Penguin Books Ltd, Registered Offices: 80 Strand, London WC2R 0RL, England

www.penguin.com

First published in the United States of America by W. W. Norton and Company, Inc. 2003
First published in Great Britain, with additional material, by Allen Lane 2003
Published in Penguin Books with a new Preface 2004
7

ISBN-13: 978–0–14–101431–9

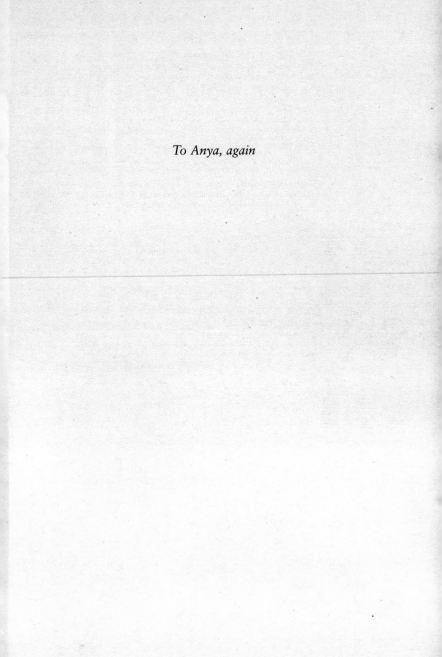

To Anya, again

Contents

Preface

to the Paperback edition

WHEN THE PROBLEMS that I describe in *The Roaring Nineties* as confronting the American economy first rose to the surface, many abroad felt vindicated: they had always been suspicious of American-style capitalism. Many CEOs in Europe and Asia, while they may have envied the fat pay packets of American CEOs, felt that there was something unseemly about their high salaries. The American CEOs didn't seem that much better—if at all—than their colleagues, but America was successful, and perhaps the CEOs were behind this success, and perhaps this might provide some justification. But doubts grew as the pay cheques continued to grow even as America's economy slid into recession and downturn, even as stock prices plummeted. The story changed; now they were to be rewarded not for producing growth, but for preventing decline. Interest in the story of America's failure was as much motivated by an attitude of "I knew something was wrong all along . . ." as it was by a desire to learn from America's experience.

At the same time, here in the United States, the defenders of American capitalism often seemed to take the stance that it was just the press, as always, exaggerating the story of a few firms gone awry—combined with foolish investors who had lost money in the market

looking for someone to blame. The danger, repeatedly emphasized by
the CEOs, was an overreaction, leading to excessive regulation.

In the last year, however, both of these perspectives have had to be
revised. The scandals, the corruption, in America's free market
system were more pervasive than was apparent at the time. And
while the extent elsewhere may be less, each country seemed to have
its own Enron: Parmalat in Italy, Vivendi in France, Ahold in the
Netherlands. Of course, the nature of their sins differed. Parmalat
appeared to be outright, old-fashioned fraud—but whether the large
international banks were incompetent in detecting it, or in fact
conspired with Parmalat in its perpetuation, is still not clear. Each
scandal had a common theme—new techniques combining creative
accounting and creative finance had outpaced whatever advances in
detection had occurred.

As in the case of Enron, bankruptcy proceedings have provided
some of the best insights into malfeasance—a window into the
corporate world that we might not otherwise have had. As I noted
later in the book, it was only by pouring over Enron's records that
lwe finally figured out what had gone wrong in the Californian
electricity crisis—Enron, with other electricity market traders, had
manipulated the market. WorldCom's bankruptcy has provided more
unseemly scenes: its bankers pushing WorldCom bonds on unwary
investors, even as they urged their lending department to cut back on
their own exposure. This provided another example of the playing
out of the conflicts of interest that critics of combining investment
and commercial banks, such as myself, had warned of, but which
were dismissed by the Wall Street lobbyists and sympathetic officials
in the U.S. Treasury.

The image of sophisticated financial institutions exploiting hapless
investors which the analysts' scandal brought to the fore—analysts
privately trashing stocks as they urged their customers to buy these

sure winners—has been further reinforced by the mutual funds scandals. It is easy to make money buying a share at 4.00 p.m. that has gone up since 3.00 p.m., if you can buy it at the price that prevailed at 3.00 p.m. This is a simple variant of the scam called market timing. Market timing sounds like buying a stock at just the right moment, just when it is at a low, through keen insights into stock movements; but economic science has shown that it is virtually impossible systematically to make money by beating the market. The gains made in the market timing scams of the mutual funds came at the expense of others—the other owners of the mutual funds.

With almost every major investment bank, every major accounting firm (and some minor ones), and a large proportion of America's enterprises involved in these scandals, it is no wonder that confidence in these institutions should have faltered. But equally troubling is the unfolding story of the failure of the regulatory mechanisms—not only the checks and balances within firms, what is called the system of corporate governance—but also the public institutions. In the 90s, the Securities and Exchange Commission, whose responsibility it is to make sure that the public retains confidence in capital markets, and that the small investor not be abused, saw some of what was going on. When they tried to do something about it, they were beaten back by those who were profiting from the system. But even they had not fully detected the scope of the problem. In the last few years, it has become increasingly clear that it has not been doing its job—sometimes out of incompetence, but more likely out of a lack of zeal for its task. The business and financial community helped Bush get elected, and they expected a return from at least that investment; so far they have not been disappointed.

As a result, the burden of uncovering the scandals and imposing fines has been left to those responsible for enforcing the law in each of the states—in this regard Eliot Spitzer, New York State's attorney general, stands out. Critics say that he is just doing it for political gain, to advance his career, sliding over the fact that it is his responsibility to enforce the law, and he is simply doing his job.

These critics, including many of the leaders of the financial community, have repeatedly warned of the dangers of going overboard, reflecting that, even with this mounting evidence, there is a reluctance to recognize the depth of the problem. In their minds, the problem is not that they cheated those that they were supposed to serve, but rather that they got caught. They were just doing their job, maximizing their income, and, in doing so, even maximizing shareholder value—though more in the short run than in the long. And isn't that what everyone in the business community does? Of course embezzlement, and outright fraud, raise ethical and moral issues, but, far from taking advantage of unwary customers, *caveat emptor*! These ethical dimensions were brought home by another scandal that broke out shortly after *The Roaring Nineties* was published, involving the New York Stock Exchange and its head, Richard Grasso. With a compensation package in excess of $150 million and total annual compositions almost equal to that of the New York Stock Exchange's net income in 2001, Grasso did not want to be outdone by some of the CEOs whose companies were listed on "his" exchange. Grasso's asking for a $5 million bonus for getting the exchange working quickly again after 9/11—which was, after all, his job—was particularly irksome, in the context of all those firemen and policemen who sacrificed their lives in doing theirs. But the really unseemly side it brought home concerned self-regulation. The New York Stock Exchange not only is a trading forum, but it is supposed to be part of the security market's self-regulating system. The Exchange is supposed to ensure that the companies and the traders comply with certain regulations ensuring a fair and efficient market, and in particular that those who buy and sell get the best price possible. But with those whom one is supposed to regulate voting fat pay packages to the regulator, what confidence does one have that the regulator performs his task with zeal? The fact that Grasso had done little to address one of the major problems of the Exchange—the specialists who make the market—confirmed these worries.

The scandal highlights still more problems. First, when the news of Grasso's pay package was reported in the *Wall Street Journal*, it drew little attention or comment. For the American business community, this was just business as usual. It was only when London's *Financial Times* began putting the story on the front page, months later, that public attention was focused on Grasso's compensation. Had America's business press too come to accept the same ethical norms that guided America's financial firms and corporations? The press is, or should be, an important part of the governance structure, one of the checks and balances that make our system work.

Second; and equally troubling, was the initial response of Grasso and the members of the New York Stock Exchange board who had voted him these packages. They saw no problems with conflict of interest. They saw nothing about which they should be ashamed. For them too, it was just business as usual.

Finally, and perhaps most troubling, were discussions with students at business school—the future leaders of the business community. For them, there was a problem—not what had been done, but how the public relations had been handled. Evidently, they felt that success in the future would mean not changing ethical standards, but making sure that you had better relations with the press, so they could put the right spin on the story!

In short, the problems that I wrote about have not gone away. They appear, if anything, more pervasive, more deep-seated, than I had originally thought.

If those abroad were spared some of the corporate, accounting, and financial scandals, many were not spared the boom-and-bust cycle associated with deregulation and unfettered markets. Those in

Latin America and East Asia suffered particularly, as deregulation and privatization fed an irrational exuberance that led to huge increases in capital, especially short-term capital, which just as suddenly turned into an irrational pessimism.

I wrote this book partly to help Americans so that they would not repeat the mistakes of the past, but also to help those outside America understand what went wrong—and how to prevent it happening to their economies and societies. During the 90s, with America's economy seeming triumphant, others were tempted to follow its lead. As I comment in chapter 9, America went further—it told, coaxed, cajoled others to follow its example, or more accurately, a particular view of American capitalism which differed in essential respects from what was actually going on in America. The U.S. Treasury said, for instance, that others should follow America's lead in corporate governance and accounting. They were correct in advocating good corporate governance and accounting; they were not correct in thinking that we had found the right model. The irony was particularly striking, since they had taken stances that had undermined good governance and accounting.

The tide has changed. The 90s marked the high-water point of finance and market fundamentalism. Those who became wedded to such ideas are often slow to give them up. They say the problem was that the reforms were not carried out with enough vigor. The problem was in their implementation. But fortunately, sanity is gradually returning. The problem is not just with the implementation of the ideas, but with the ideas themselves. If there is a single, simple message to this book it is this: there needs to be a balance between the role of government and the market. A country can suffer from underregulation just as it can from overregulation, from too little public investment just as it can from too much public expenditure; the government can help stabilize the economy—but badly designed policies can make fluctuations worse. The policies of capital market liberalization that the IMF pushed—and the U.S. Treasury continues to push—contributed to the instability of developing countries; even the IMF has finally recognized this.

This broader understanding means that countries should feel greater freedom in their choice of economic policies. There is not one way. There is no perfect system. The story told here exposes some of the flaws in America's version of capitalism, but I have had little to say about some of the more deep-seated problems, the huge inequality, the large numbers of people in prison, the anxiety and insecurity that are felt by so many, including the millions without health insurance, the seeming unconcern about the deterioration of the environment. Other countries may decide to have an economic and social system that pays more attention to these and other dimensions of society, and hence may choose a variant of the market economy that differs from that which is currently in fashion in the United States. In doing so, they should know that other countries, with these variants of the market economy, have been able to achieve societies with less inequality, greater security, better health and education, especially for the poor.

Joseph Stiglitz,
New York, April 2004

Preface

JUST A DECADE ago, I left my quiet life in Stanford as a professor of economics to go to Washington, to serve first as a member, then as chairman of President Clinton's Council of Economic Advisers. I had spent the previous quarter century doing research on economic theory and economic policy. I wanted to see what *really* goes on—to be a fly on the wall. But I wanted to be more than a fly on the wall. I had entered economics in the sixties, the years of the civil rights and peace movements. I wanted, I suppose, to change the world, but I wasn't sure how; as an academic, I needed to understand the world better first.

Little did I know how much I would learn. By the time I left Washington, having served throughout the first Clinton administration and then three years as senior vice president and chief economist at the World Bank, much had changed. These were the years of the tumultuous, Roaring Nineties—the decade of mega-deals and mega-growth. That much is in the public record. But the idea for this book was hatched as I considered stories that were not so widely available, or so well understood. The recovery from the 1991 recession, for instance, seemed to defy what was universally taught in economics courses around the world. The popular version, trumpeted by some within the Clinton administration, claimed that deficit reduction (reducing the gap between the government's expenditures and its taxes) had brought about the recovery, yet standard theory said that deficit reductions worsened economic downturns. To take another example, I had been involved in many battles over deregulation and accounting and thought that particularly with banking deregulation, we pushed too far. We had also missed opportunities to improve corporate accounting. More generally, the decade marked the emergence of the so-called New Economy, with the rate of productivity increases doubling, or tripling, what it had been for the preceding two decades. The economics of innovation had been one of my fields of specialization as an academic, and it was important, I thought, to get a better grasp of what had caused the enormous slowdown in productivity in the seventies and eighties, and the resurgence in the nineties.

But before I could write *that* book, events took over. The economy went into another recession, proving in a stroke that recessions were not a thing of the past. Corporate scandals dethroned the high priests of American capitalism; the CEOs of some of America's largest enterprises seemed to be enriching themselves at the expense of their shareholders and workers. Globalization, the closer integration of the countries of the world as a result of lowering of transportation and communication costs, and the removal of artificial, man-made barriers, which had so shortly before been heralded as bringing on a new world, seemed to be viewed by much of the world with jaundiced eyes. The Seattle, Washington, meeting of the World Trade Organization (WTO) in 1999 was supposed to bring in a new round of opening up of the world under American leadership, a round that would carry with it the name of the city at which it was begun, and would be a permanent reminder of the contribution Clinton had made to globalization. Instead, it ended in riots, as environmentalists, protectionists, those concerned with the sometimes devastating effect of globalization on the poor, and those worried about the undemoc-

Printed in England by Clays Ltd, St Ives plc

ratic nature of the global economic institutions, all joined together in protest. September 11, 2001, showed an even darker side of globalization: terrorism too could move easily across borders. While the roots of terrorism are complex, it was clear that the despair and the high unemployment rate that prevailed in so much of the world provided a fertile feeding ground for it.

The unraveling of the Roaring Nineties came quickly: it began even before the Clinton administration had left office. It provided a new light on what had happened in that decade—and made a reinterpretation of the decade even more compelling.

As it turned out, that project dovetailed with another. One of my abiding concerns has been the appropriate role of government in our society, and in our economy more particularly. A few years before going to Washington, I had written a slim volume called *The Economic Role of the State*, in which I tried to lay out the appropriate roles of the state and the markets, based both on the strengths and failures of markets and those of government. I had tried to identify some general principles for what the government should and should not do. After seeing government at close hand for eight years, I wanted to revisit that subject. A study of the nineties provided an opportunity to do that: the successes of the Clinton administration were, in part, attributable to our doing some things to get the balance right between government and the market, a balance which had been lost in the decade of Reagan and Thatcher; but our failures—some of which only became manifest as the decade came toward an end— were partly attributable to places where we got that balance wrong.

There has been a battle of ideas between those who advocate a minimalist role for the state and those who see the government as playing an important yet limited role not only in correcting failures and limitations of the market but also in working toward greater social justice. I am in the latter camp, and this book is intended to explain why I believe that while markets are at the center of the success of our economy, markets do not always work well by themselves, why they do not solve all problems, and why government will always be an important partner to them.

This book is accordingly not just a rewriting of the economic history of the nineties, though it is partly that. It is as much a story of the future as of the past—it is about where America and the other developed countries find themselves and the direction they should go. Many of the central institutions of our society have had their credibility greatly damaged, irredeemably in some cases, from the church to our CEOs to the judiciary to the accounting profession to our banks. In this book, I look only at our economic institutions, though I cannot help but think that what happens there reflects on, and has very significant consequences for, what happens outside them.

Both the left and the right have lost their bearings. The intellectual foundations of laissez-faire economics, the view that markets by themselves will lead to efficient, let alone fair, outcomes, has been stripped away. As the world went into crisis after September 11, we realized that we had to act together. The corporate scandals that rocked America, and to a lesser extent Europe, made even conservatives realize that there was a role for government. The collapse of the Soviet Union, bringing with it the end of the Cold War, had taken away the economic underpinning of the left: support for socialism, at least of the old-fashioned variety, waned even in those countries where it previously had had enormous strength.

Today, the challenge is to get the balance right, between the state and the market, between collective action at the local, national, and global levels, and between government and non-governmental action. As economic circumstances change, the balance has to be redrawn. Government needs to take on new activities, and shed old ones. We have entered into an era of globalization, in which the countries and peoples of the world are more closely integrated than ever before. But globalization itself means that we have to change that balance: we need more collective action at the international level, and we cannot escape issues of democracy and social justice in the global arena.

The remarkable changes that have confronted our economies, our societies, in the past fifteen years put enormous strains on the balance between state and market; and we have failed to respond appropriately. The problems that have come to the fore in the past several years are, in part, a reflection of that failure. This book seeks to put forward a framework that will help us get the balance back.

There is one more theme behind this book. This was the decade in which finance reigned supreme. Those on Wall Street were making millions, in some cases billions, putting together deals, raising finance for start-ups. The best and the brightest of American youth wanted to join in the excitement. America bought the general line of market economics: compensation reflected productivity. Those who were paid more were contributing more to society. It was natural that young people would be attracted to the frenzy. They could do well for society by doing well for themselves.

Within policymaking circles, there was the same deference to the view of Finance. Central banks, composed mainly of experts from the financial community, were to be left alone to set monetary policy, their steady hand ensuring stable growth without inflation. Bob Woodward's book *The Agenda* (1994) describes in vivid terms how deficit reduction moved front and center in Bill Clinton's agenda. It was not the platform on which Clinton had been elected, but he was persuaded that without deficit reduction, financial markets would punish him, and without the support of finance, he could not accomplish the rest of his agenda. Everything else was put on the back burner—much of it never to be accomplished.

I should be clear: I believe that finance is important. Indeed, my own work in the economics of information helped clarify the relationship between finance and economics. Previously, Nobel Prize winners Franco Modigliani of MIT and the late Merton Miller of the University of Chicago had, for instance, argued that apart from tax considerations, the way firms financed themselves made absolutely no difference. My work on asymmetric information helped explain the central role of finance in a modern economy. But that same work also explained why unregulated financial markets often do not work well, why there was a need for government, and why what was good for Wall Street might not be—and often was not—good for the country as a whole, or for particular groups in the country.

What happened in the Roaring Nineties was that a set of long-standing checks and balances—a balance between Wall Street, Main Street (or High Street, as it is called in the United Kingdom), and labor, between Old Industry and New Technology, government and the market—was upset, in some essential ways, by the new ascendancy of Finance. Everyone deferred to its judgment. Countries, including the United States, were told to accept the discipline of the market. Longstanding wisdom, that there were alternative policies, that different policies affected different groups differently, that there were trade-offs, that politics provided the arena through which the trade-offs were evaluated and choices were made, was shunted aside.

In the Clinton administration, we knew this thinking was wrong. If Finance really did rule supreme, if there was a single set of policies to which all could subscribe, then what would distinguish us from the Republicans was only our greater competence. But a kind of schizophrenia took over. While we believed we were promoting different policies, policies that benefited the poor and middle class more than the policies that the Republicans had advocated, while we knew that there were trade-offs, too many in the administration seemed to accept the notion that the bond market, or financial markets more generally, knew the best way forward. The financial markets, it seemed, represented America's best interests as well as their own.

This seemed like nonsense to me. I believed that we had to recognize that if we did something the bond market or other financial markets did not like, and had to pay a price for it, it might well be a price worth paying.[1] After all, while Finance is important, Wall Street is a special interest group like many others.

I write this book as an American, as someone who has participated in the political discussions within the United States, and who is deeply concerned about the directions in which the country has been moving. But I also write this as someone who has been very much engaged in parallel discussions around the world and in the broader debate about globalization, which has become one of the issues of the day. The failures in America—the boom and the bust, the misman-agement of macroeconomic policy, the excesses of deregulation and the corporate scandals to which that contributed—I believe are of interest not just to Americans. The story which unfolds here is of concern to people throughout the world, and for several reasons.

Globalization has made everyone in the world more interdepend-ent. It used to be said that when the United States sneezes, Mexico catches a cold. Now, when the United States sneezes, much of the rest of the world comes down with the flu. And America's current prob-lems go well beyond sniffles. Any economic analysis of the world's current economic problems, and of the decade that preceded, must begin with a discussion of America.

Moreover, globalization means more than the freer movement of goods, services, and capital across borders. It entails the faster move-ment of ideas. As I noted earlier, in the nineties, America set itself up as the role model for the rest of the world. America was looked to for its views about the right balance of government and the market and about what kinds of institutions and policies are needed to make a market economy work well. American corporate practices became adopted throughout the world, and America pushed its accounting practices wherever it could. Those countries which did not voluntarily mimic America, in the hope that their economy too would experience a boom, including those that thought America had not gotten the balance right, were cajoled, badgered, and, in the case of developing countries dependent on assistance from the International Monetary Fund, effectively forced to go along with what was described as the sweep of history.

Not surprisingly, the problems described here have had their parallels in many countries around the world. The corporate scandals have touched European companies, bringing down the CEOs of giants like Vivendi, and scarring even seemingly staid companies like the Dutch grocer group Ahold. Elsewhere, there may not have been the extremes of corporate executive malfeasance that became evident in America, but the direction of movement was deeply worrying.

Other issues too that are at the center of the American drama have played out, in similar ways, on other stages. In other countries, the deference shown to finance—and its power—is often even greater than in the United States; the views of the financial community dictate policies, and even determine the outcomes of elections. The deficit reduction mantra, combined with an unbridled zeal in fighting the problems of inflation of almost two decades ago, have tied Europe's hands in dealing with the economic downturn that began in 2001. As this book goes to press, the European economies face the fear of deflation and growing unemployment, when earlier action might have arrested the decline into recession. With Japan also in stagnation or worse, the world has been facing the first global downturn of the era of globalization.

Most fundamentally, the battle of ideas between those who advocate a minimalist role for the state and those who believe that there is a greater need for government if we are to achieve the kind of society we would like is being fought in country after country, in the developing world no less than in the developed, on both sides of the Atlantic and the Pacific. The recent American experience carries lessons for all, and I hope the lessons that I draw in the final chapters of this book—and the agenda for the future that I sketch—will be as relevant to other countries as they are to the United States.

This is not a book of investigative reporting. The scandals and other problems I describe are well documented elsewhere.[2] My objective here is *interpretation*, to help us understand what went wrong and how to fix it. As a social scientist, I do not think problems of this magnitude are simply accidents, the result of aberrant individuals. I look for systemic faults—and there are plenty. Interestingly, many of the problems were closely connected with my research agenda of three decades; they relate to problems of imperfect, and particularly asymmetric, information—that is, to situations where some people have information that others do not. Advances in these theories help us understand what went wrong and why. They also help explain why, years before the problems surfaced, I had fought, inside the Clinton administration, against many of the policies which gave rise to them. When these issues were raised a decade ago, they were largely a matter of theory. Today, the evidence is in. Yet in some quarters, resistance to change, to addressing these problems, continues.[3]

In writing this book, as in my previous book, I am deeply indebted to President William Jefferson Clinton, who gave me the opportunity not only to serve my country but to see firsthand the workings of the American government. For a social scientist, it was an unparalleled opportunity.

I am enormously indebted to the president not only for the opportunity he gave me, but for the respect that he showed for the special role that the Council of Economic Advisers plays in our system of government. We had the luxury of not having any constituency—other than the American people, and they paid little attention to what we said or did. That gave us a freedom that is not given to other government agencies, which are constantly subject to pressure from one interest group or another. One of the themes of this book is that individuals respond to incentives: those who misbehaved in the corporate and financial world were not necessarily particularly venal, or more venal than those who occupied their positions in an earlier era; rather, their incentives were different, and their behavior responded to these incentives. By training, we in the Council of Economic Advisers were more attuned to detecting badly designed incentives; but that was our job, and in a sense, we had incentives to detect the problems in incentives—doing so enhanced our standing within our own profession. Similarly, there were strong incentives not to give in to pressure from special interests, for doing so would have detracted from our standing. The members of the Council were, for the most part, drawn from academia, and returned to academia, and it was their standing within this circle that mattered most to them.

The chairmanship of the Council of Economic Advisers not only gave me a ringside seat in government decision making; it also provided me with a unique opportunity to observe the American economy. It was part of my day-to-day responsibilities not just to monitor what was going on, but to think about what might go wrong, and to fix it before it was apparent that it was broken. I could see the American economy from a variety of perspectives seldom available—while we talked to all the leading economists in business, government, and academia, seeking out their different interpretations of what was going on, I also had the opportunity to talk to labor leaders as well as CEOs, to venture capitalists as well as Wall Street financiers. The president worked hard to keep in touch with how the changes in the economy were affecting ordinary Americans; he had regional economic summits, in Atlanta, in Portland, in Columbus, among others. Part of my job was to both listen to their concerns and explain what we were doing, and these frequent forays put me in touch with grassroots in a way that academics seldom are.

One of the major changes in the nineties was a change in the global economic position of the United States, and the two positions, that of chairman of the Council of Economic Advisers and that of chief economist and senior vice president of the World Bank, allowed me to see this change from two quite different perspectives. I could see the impact of the Roaring Nineties in the United States and also abroad. I could see the inconsistency between what we argued for at home, and what we pushed abroad. I could see how those who argued for social justice and democratic values at home, out of a concern for the poor, often seemed much less concerned about these values abroad.

These two positions also gave me a better opportunity to see us—America—and to see the other developed countries, as those in the rest of the world see us. The scientific community has always known no borders and recognized no authority. My students and colleagues have been drawn from all over the world, and I had in fact spent a quarter of my working life abroad. The strong connections I had allowed me an entrée not commonly available to those in public service. And what I saw and felt saddened me: even those who were trained in America, who loved America and Americans, were deeply disappointed by what America's government was doing. Somehow, *collectively*, as a nation, we were so often acting in ways that seemed so different from what we stood for as individuals. In the chapters below, I try to show why there is more than a little truth in these perceptions, and I try to explain, first, how this state of affairs has come about, and second, why the way we have managed our new role in the global economy, after the end of the Cold War, does not serve our long-run interests.

Like *Globalization and Its Discontents*, this is not meant to be a dispassionate look at what happened in the Roaring Nineties and the aftermath. How could it be, given my involvement in so many of the events? But I have tried to make it accurate, to bring together what I know about the events with my understanding of economic and political processes, to provide an interpretation of what happened, and what these events portend for the future. Over the years, my beliefs in democracy have been strengthened, but so too has my belief that if our democracies are to work, citizens must understand the basic issues confronting our societies and the way their government works. And no issues are of more importance for most people than those that surround our economy and the relations between the market and the government.

I am a teacher, and spent most of the last quarter century teaching; every teacher knows that in every class, he or she simplifies—there is no alternative. But I have tried not to *oversimplify*. As I present the narrative of the events of the past decade, I have based my simplified expositions on some quite complicated ideas, which I have presented in detail in several books and dozens of articles. I would like to believe that my simplified exposition of complicated ideas is more persuasive than the simplified articulation of oversimplified ideas that has characterized some of the alternative approaches, and in particular, the simplistic free market ideology. And as a teacher, I tell the story of the events of the nineties not just because they are interesting in their own right—they are undoubtedly of more interest to those of us involved in the events than to anyone else—but because of the general lessons to be learned.

They are lessons that are important for America, but they are lessons that are no less important for those elsewhere in the world. America, as the strongest and most successful economy in the world, is emulated. And America, as the strongest country in the world, pushes a particular view of the role of the state in the economy, especially through the international economic institutions, the WTO, the International Monetary Fund, and the World Bank. One of the central themes later in the book is to show that the ideas America pushes abroad are markedly different from what it practices at home. How we and others interpret our successes (and our failures) has enormous consequences for the choices of policies, programs, and institutions of others. That is why it is so important that the right lessons be drawn.

Some readers of this book, seeing my criticism of the Clinton administration, will come to the wrong conclusions, as some readers of an earlier *Atlantic Monthly* article on the same theme did. If I seem to grade the administration harshly, it is partly because of the high hopes that we had as we entered early in 1993, and how these hopes were in so many ways disappointed. But I should be clear: I am a harsh grader, but in the end, I typically grade on the curve. Looking at what preceded the Clinton administration, and especially what followed it, the grades become almost glowing. The issue, however, is not simply a matter of grading; it is understanding what went wrong, what went right, and why—and most important, how can we construct a future in which economic policy is better managed.

I am enormously proud of what President Clinton and his administration accomplished. Yes, perhaps we could have done more, especially to reshape the global landscape in the aftermath of the Cold War, to make globalization work not just for us but for the whole world. And yes, the country would have been better off had we not succumbed as much as we did to the deregulation mantra. But we took our inheritance—including huge deficits, enormous and growing inequality, and an economy not fully recovering from a recession—and made major strides forward: the deficit was eliminated, the economy did have a robust recovery. Poverty was reduced, the growth in inequality halted, and the expansion of programs like Head Start held out the promise of even more progress on this front in the future. The politics of the moment made it difficult—may have made it impossible—to accomplish much more. But anyone who doubts where I stand on these issues should begin by turning to the Epilogue, in which I contrast what happened during the Clinton years with what has followed. The last two years have been a rude awakening for anyone who says politics does not matter, or that politicians are all the same.

What I am most proud of, perhaps, about the Clinton administration is that, above all, there was a belief in and commitment to democratic values and social justice among virtually all the members of the administration. Rarely has a group of such intelligence and dedication been assembled. There were a few, very few, who from time to time let their egos interfere with their sense of dedication; but one should expect large egos from those who survive the rough-and-tumble to get to the positions that they had attained. I had been warned by friends who served in previous administrations never to turn one's back, lest one be quickly stabbed. In the Clinton administration, though there were the usual tough battles, there was remarkably little back-stabbing. Clinton set a tone of mutual respect. Democracy is more than just periodic elections; it entails ensuring that all voices are heard, and that there is a deliberative process. Each of us in the administration brought to government a particular perspective, a vision necessarily narrowed by our experiences. We deliberated and discussed from early morning into late at night.

I write this book because the battles that I fought will be waged again. In a democracy, these issues are never settled. If we made our mistakes, they can be corrected. But only if we understand why things turned out differently from what we expected, only if we understand where we went wrong. This book is my interpretation. I hope that it will contribute to the deliberative discussions of future administrations who share the values that we espoused.

I have returned to academia, from where I came. When I was fourteen, growing up in the steel town of Gary, Indiana, on the southern shores of Lake Michigan, I had decided that as an adult, I wanted to be a professor, and that, somehow, I wanted to combine that with some form of public service. A few years later, as a student at

Amherst College, having fallen in love with economics, those ambitions took shape: I wanted to understand what caused the poverty, unemployment, and discrimination that I had seen all around me growing up, and I wanted to do something about these problems. Perhaps I have been able to make a small contribution to what are overwhelming problems. Another generation will have to carry on the struggle. My students, with their idealism, energy, and commitment, give me hope.

Acknowledgments

I N   W R I T I N G   A   B O O K   such as this, one accumulates a long list of debts—to my academic colleagues, who helped me understand some of the basic economics underlying the problems discussed here, to those I worked with in Washington and around the world who helped me see the American experience through a different lens, and to those who have helped with the writing and editing. I apologize to anyone who was inadvertently left out of these acknowledgments. Many of those mentioned below may disagree with the interpretations of the events I present; some will disagree with the policy conclusions I reach; and not all share the vision that I present in the final chapters of this book. But, knowingly or not, each has contributed to the perspectives described here.

I have looked at the events of the nineties and the years that followed from a perspective influenced by my research of the past forty years, which focused on information economics, the economics of the public sector, macroeconomics, and finance. I was lucky to have some of the best teachers of the world at Amherst, MIT, and Cambridge: Arnold Collery (who later became dean at Columbia), Jim Nelson, Ralph Beals, Paul Samuelson, Robert Solow, Franco Modigliani, Charles Kindleberger,[1] Nicholas Kaldor, Joan Robinson, and Frank

Hahn. The field of information economics was, in many ways, opened up by Kenneth Arrow, my teacher at MIT and my colleague at Stanford. My first papers were written with my MIT classmate George Akerlof, with whom I shared the Nobel Prize in 2001. I still recall some of our early conversations on the limitations of markets and the problems of imperfect information, almost forty years ago. I also had the opportunity to work with A. Michael Spence (who also shared the prize) when he came to Stanford, where I was then a professor, fresh out of graduate school in the seventies. Problems of incentives and risk, information and decision making, corporate governance and finance, IPOs, and the links between the overall performance of the economy and what went on *inside* firms absorbed me in research projects with Michael Rothschild, Peter Diamond, Richard Arnott, Barry Nalebuff, Sanford Grossman, Carl Shapiro, Ian Gale, Alex Dyck, Thomas Helmann, Peter Neary, Steve Salop, Kevin Murdoch, Andrew Weiss, and Bruce Greenwald. Bruce, while he would not agree with everything I have written here, was particularly insightful in helping me to see the links between the microeconomics of the firm and the macroeconomic performance of the economy and to figure out what was wrong, and right, about the Clinton administration's claim that deficit reduction was responsible for the 1993 recovery.

I should also mention: Michael Boskin, my colleague at Stanford and Chairman of George H. W. Bush's Council of Economic Advisers; David Mullins, who formerly taught at Harvard Business School and was appointed vice chair of the Federal Reserve by President Bush; Mark Wolfson, professor of accounting at Stanford, who played an important role in rethinking accounting by seeing it through the lens of the economics of information.[2]

Columbia has provided a particularly good environment within which I have been able to carry on my work. I want to thank Dean Myer Feldberg of the Graduate School of Business and Dean Lisa

Anderson of the School of International and Public Affairs, and Columbia's new president, Lee Bollinger, for their enthusiastic support, as well as my formidable assistant Maria Kaloudis. The wide range of perspectives at Columbia, not just on globalization but on capitalism more broadly, and the open spirit of debate and discussion, with economists such as Ned Phelps, Robert Mundell, Jagdish Bhagwati, Glenn Hubbard, Frank Edwards, Frederic Mishkin, and Charles Calomiris, encouraged the kind of enquiry that this book represents.

Some of my academic colleagues may have preferred a more analytic book, filled with equations and regressions, "hard evidence" and well-formulated theories supporting the hypotheses I present. That theory and evidence is presented elsewhere. The objective of this book is different: this is a book for general readers who want to learn more about the key economic subjects that affect all of our lives. A well-informed public is the basis of a well-functioning democracy and the object of this book is unabashedly reasoned persuasion: economic policies do matter, and the *right* economic policies are not only likely to enhance growth and stability but to ensure that the fruits of that prosperity are widely shared.

Globalization is an important part of the story told here. There are strong parallels between what went wrong with globalization abroad and went wrong in the nineties in America. This book can be seen as a natural successor to my previous book, *Globalization and Its Discontents,* and many readers of that earlier book saw the parallel and urged me to write this book. I want to acknowledge those who did so, directly and indirectly, through the insights they provided or the opportunities they afforded me to see firsthand what was happening as part of globalization: Jim Wolfensohn, the president of the World Bank, gave me the opportunity to serve that institution as its senior vice president and chief economist, and an enormous number of dedicated and hardworking individuals at the World Bank shared their knowledge and perspectives.[3] Since leaving the World Bank and writing *Globalization and Its Discontents*, I have continued to see firsthand how globalization is affecting all parts of the world and how the ideas that were espoused by America in the Roaring Ninties are shaping, or misshaping, policies elsewhere. Recent visits to Bolivia, Ecuador, Venezuela, Chile, Brazil, Bulgaria, Moldova, and Argentina were particularly instructive. In addition to those acknowledged individually in my earlier book, I want to thank Suppachai Panitchpakdi, the head of the World Trade Organization, for his insights concerning some of the challenges facing that organization, and Presidents Lagos of Chile and Cardoso of Brazil for discussions on the role of government and social democratic ideals in their countries.

Before I went to the World Bank, I was chairman of the Economic Policy Committee of the Organization of Economic Cooperation and Development (OECD), or the "club" of the advanced industrial countries, where I had the opportunity to see American economic policy from quite a different perspective—and to see, at the same time, the influence that American ideas had on economic policy elsewhere. I am indebted to the members of the Economic Policy Committee, to the staff of the OECD, to its director, Donald Johnston, and to the American ambassadors to the OECD, David Aaron and Alan Larsen (now undersecretary of economics for state), who often helped interpret for me the subtext of what was said.

During the nineties, I had the good fortune to work under President Clinton, who assembled a remarkable group of individuals in his administration. Many, like me, came from academia, and sought to base policy on sound analysis. I am most indebted to my colleagues on the Council of Economic Advisers, Laura Tyson, Alan Blinder, Alicia Munnell, and Martin Bailey. We were supported by a first-rate team of economists, mostly academics, citizen-bureaucrats, who took a year or two off from their normal duties to serve in the government. I am particularly indebted to two young economists who combined first-rate economics with a sensitivity to public policy, and both went on from the Council to serve as senior economic advisers inside the National Economic Council: Peter Orszag, now senior fellow at Brookings, and Jason Furman, now completing his doctorate at Harvard. My chiefs of staff, Tom O'Donnell and Michele Jolin, not only made the Council function but provided invaluable insights into the political process. Our macroeconomists, Robert Wescott, Michael Donihue, and Steven Braun, not only provided most reliable forecasts but expressed a deep understanding of macroeconomics and our changing economy. Kevin Murdock, at the time still finishing his graduate studies at Stanford, quickly grasped the importance, and the intricacies, of the stock option issue. Mark Mazur helped analyze the effects of capital gains taxation and worked with me to design versions of the capital gains tax reduction that would have been just as effective, more egalitarian, and would have led to lower deficits in the long run. Over the years, we had an impressive team of international economists—Robert Cumby, Marcus Noland, Robert Dohner, Lael Brainard, Ellen Meade, and John Montgomery; macroeconomists— including Matthew Shapiro, David Wilcox, Eileen Mauskopf, William English, and Chad Stone; and regulatory and industrial organization economists—including Jonathan Baker, Marius Schwartz, and Tim Brennan—all of whom helped shape views, and policies, on the issues which are the subject of this book.[4] Robert Cumby was particularly involved in the effort to help create indexed bonds, which could help protect those saving for their retirement from the uncertainties of inflation and at the same time reduce the government's deficit. Jay Stowsky and Scott Walsten were central in understanding the role of government in promoting technology; David Levine and William Dickens[5] in understanding labor markets—and some of the consequences of the "bottom line" approach to employment relationships that was becoming fashionable during the nineties.

The Treasury, along with the Office of Management and Budget (OMB) and the Council of Economic Advisors, was one of the three agencies most central to economic policymaking, and it was accordingly with members of this agency that we interacted most, including in particular Lloyd Bentsen, Robert Rubin, Frank Newman, Larry Summers, Les Samuels, Jeff Schaeffer, Josh Gotbaum, Brad DeLong, David Wilcox, Roger Altman, Karl Scholz, and Len Burman. While I often did not see eye-to-eye with my colleagues at Treasury, they often marshaled strong arguments in their defense, arguments that forced us to think more deeply about the basis of our beliefs; most important, I believe, they respected the differences in perspective with which we approached a number of the highly contentious issues. At OMB, Sally Katzen, in charge of regulatory policy, and Robert Litan (currently head of the economics department at Brookings) were especially important in providing insights concerning regulatory policy. I am also indebted to Alice Rivlin, who served as the deputy head, then head, of the OMB and later as vice chair of the Fed.

I owe a great deal both to Robert Reich and to the Department of Labor's two chief labor economists with whom I interacted the most, Larry Katz and Alan Krueger, who not only helped me understand the changing structure of the labor market but what was wrong with the simplistic models that had been used in the past to understand those markets.[6] Reich, in particular, was skeptical that all the changes occurring in the economy would redound to the benefit of the average American worker, and shared with me many of his concerns about the Roaring Nineties and the economic policies we had helped put into place.

Overseeing the entire apparatus of economic policymaking was the National Economic Council (NEC)—a Clinton invention, though similar arrangements had existed in other administrations.[7] It was headed at first by Robert Rubin, then by Laura Tyson, and then by Gene Sperling, all of whom attempted to bring the various interests

and perspectives into focus and resolve the conflicts between economics and politics, thus broadening my own perspectives. In addition to Dan Tarullo, Jon Orszag, Tome Kalil, and Kathy Wallman, I
owe an especial debt to Bowman Cutter, the deputy director of the
NEC during the critical first years of the administration, who in the
early days of the administration set up a working group to think
about where the economy was going over the next quarter century
and what we should do to help shape it. As I think about what happened over the succeeding years, about how the imperatives of day-
to-day decision making combined with the force of politics often
seemed to take over, I look back fondly at those early attempts at capturing a vision. The final chapter of this book is my attempt to provide a new vision, partially informed by the events of the intervening
years. I learned much from others at the NEC, including Dan Trujillo,
Jon Orszag, Tom Kalil, and Kathy Wallman.

I also shared a lot of policy concerns with the Office of Science and
Technology Policy (OSTP): for example, a concern over what role the
government should play in promoting technology; a worry about
anti-competitive practices (e.g., in the market for operating systems
for PCs) and their impact on the advancement of technology; and a
sense of responsibility that the intellectual property regime being
pushed by the United States in trade negotiations in Geneva in 1993
be a balanced one, one which would promote economic growth and
research rather than just enhance profits of the pharmaceuticals.
Among those at the OSTP I should mention are the then head Jack
Gibbons, Jane Wales, Skip Johns, and Robert Watson.

The broad range of responsibilities of the Council of Economic
Advisers brought us into frequent contact with those in other government departments and agencies, and discussions both with the
political appointees and the economists within those organizations
provided broad perspectives on what was going on. Particularly relevant for what is discussed in this book were interactions with the

Securities and Exchange Commission, specifically the crusading role of its chairman, Arthur Levitt. I also benefited enormously from innumerable conversations, both during that period and after, with Steve Wallman, then a member of the Commission. One of the major areas of deregulation was telecommunications, and again, I have benefited from conversations with its chairman, Reed Hundt, both during and after the episodes described here, and its chief economists, Joseph Farrell and Michael Katz (who had both been my students). On the broader issues of competition policy, I should acknowledge valuable discussions with the assistant attorney generals for antitrust, Anne Bingaman and Joel Klein, and their chief economists at various times, Rich Gilbert, who had been my student at Stanford, Carl Shapiro, who had been my colleague and co-author at Princeton, and Tim Breshnahan, my former colleague at Stanford. Issues of international economic policy (NAFTA, WTO and the Uruguay Round negotiations, the Free Trade Area of the Americas, APEC, our relationship with Japan and China, dumping, trade restrictions, etc.) occupied much of our time, and beyond the members of the Council of Economic Advisers and the National Economic Council, we interacted extensively with those involved in economic policy at the State Department, the Commerce Department, and the National Security Council. I am particularly indebted to Jeff Garten, now head of Yale's School of Management, and Joan Spero, now head of the Duke Foundation, for their insights and friendship.

On issues of macroeconomic policy, which I focus on particularly in chapters 2 and 3, our regular interactions with the Fed, including its chair, Alan Greenspan, the board members and their staff, were invaluable. Janet Yellen (who had been my student at Yale and succeeded me as chairman of the Council) and Alan Blinder (who had been my colleague and co-author at Princeton and also a member of the Council, and was appointed by President Clinton as vice chair of the board) have provided their own interpretation of the economic recovery, which differs in some important respects from that presented here.[8]

I owe a particular word of thanks to the vice president, Al Gore, not only for including me in two of his most important initiatives, the reform of telecommunications and the "reinventing government," but also for the openness, and the wonderful sense of humor, with which he conducted these complex and often tendentious deliberations, his repeated putting of principle over politics, his constant urging of others to do so, and his support for them when they did.[9] I also am indebted to the members of the vice president's staff, in particular to Greg Simon for the discussions on telecommunications policy. In addition, I want to acknowledge the role of the president's chiefs of staff, Mac MacLarty, Leon Panetta, and Erskine Bowles, who helped make the White House such and exciting and hospitable place in which to work.

Over the past several years, I have had the opportunity to discuss the "social democratic agenda" with a large number of leaders and academics in Europe; some of their ideas are reflected in the concluding chapter of this book. They encouraged me to undertake this task, and I hope I have lived up to their expectations. While there are too many to single out, there are a few that I would be remiss not to mention: George Papandreou, Greece's foreign minister, who organizes a week-long conclave, the Simi symposium, at which many of the broader issues are debated, often passionately; Laura Pennachi, a member of Italy's parliament, who on several occasions has organized discussions there; Leif Pagrotsky, Sweden's minister of trade, a committed advocate of Sweden's economic system; Gregory Kolodko, Poland's deputy prime minister and finance minister, who played a pivotal role in the successful transition from communism to a market economy; and Kermal Dervis, who I first knew at the World Bank, where he was vice president for the Middle East, and later became finance minister of Turkey.

Thanks also to Robin Blackburn, especially for sharing his thoughts on pensions; to Michael Cragg and George Fenn for their detailed commens on several of the chapters; to Sheridan Prasso and Gretchen Morgenson; to Jim Ledbetter for sharing his thoughts on European businesses; to Kira Brunner and James Lardner for help with editing the manuscript; to Anton Korinek for research assistance; to Francesco Brindisi, Anupama Chandrasekaran, Hamid Rashid, and Jayant Ray for fact checking and research; and Ann Adelman for copy editing. At an early stage, Andre Schiffrin, one of America's great editors, provided not only encouragement but his insights on how I could get my messages across more effectively. At Norton, Drake McFeely, my longtime editor, somehow managed to take time away from his responsibilities as president to edit the manuscript, and assistant editor Eve Lazovitz oversaw final edits and production. Stuart Proffitt at Penguin UK bears more than a little responsibility for the book in its current form—a synthesis of rewriting the economic history of the nineties and a vision for the future; his editing helped ensure that the book had a global perspective, and that it did not excessively reflect an American point of view.

And above all, to Anya Schiffrin, who for months lived this book with me, discussing every idea. Once again, she helped shape the entire book—from its organization as a whole to individual chapters, paragraphs, and sentences. If this book is more than a dry academic treatise on how the insights of modern economics help us understand some of the important events of our times, I owe it to her; if this book avoids the hyperbole that these dramatic events naturally lend themselves to—and the accompanying clichés—I also owe that to her. She understood what I wanted to say, and she shared with me a sense that it was important for these ideas to be widely shared, beyond the narrow range of academics which, until *Globalization and Its Discontents,* had been the focus of my writing. I hope what we have produced conveys some of the passion that we feel about these issues.

The Roaring
Nineties

CHAPTER 1

Boom and Bust

SEEDS OF DESTRUCTION

I N   T H E   R O A R I N G   N I N E T I E S , growth soared to levels not seen in a generation. Newspaper articles and experts proclaimed that there was a New Economy, that recessions were a thing of the past and that globalization was going to bring prosperity to the whole world. But toward the end of the decade, what seemed to be the dawn of a new era began to look more and more like one of those short bursts of economic activity, or hyperactivity, inevitably followed by a bust, which had marked capitalism for two hundred years. Except this time, the bubble—the boom in both the economy and the stock market—was greater, and so too were its consequences; the new era was a new era for the United States and the whole world. Thus, the bust that followed was a downturn not only for the United States but for much of the whole world.

This was not the way it was supposed to be. The end of the Cold War left the United States as the sole superpower and it marked the victory of the market economy over socialism. The world was no longer divided on ideological grounds. It may not have been the End of History, but at least it was supposed to be the beginning of a new era—and for a few years that seemed to be the case.

Not only had capitalism triumphed over communism; the American version of capitalism, based on an image of rugged individualism, seemed to have triumphed over other, softer, fuzzier versions. At international meetings, such as the G-7, which brought together the leaders of the advanced countries, we boasted of our success and preached to the sometimes envious economic leaders of other countries that if they would only imitate us, they too could enjoy prosperity like ours. Asians were told to abandon the model that had seemingly served them so well for two decades, involving lifetime job security—and had led to new ways of business that we had imitated, such as just-in-time production—but was now seen to be faltering. Sweden and other adherents of the welfare state appeared to be abandoning their models as well, by trimming state benefits and lowering tax rates. Small government was the order of the day. We proclaimed the triumph of globalization. With globalization came the spread of American-style capitalism to all the reaches of the world.

Everybody seemed to be benefiting from this new world order, this *Economia Americana*, which brought unprecedented flows of money from developed countries to the developing world—sixfold increases in six years—unprecedented trade—an increase of over 90 percent over the decade—and unprecedented growth. The trade and money would, it was hoped, create jobs and growth.

At the center of modern American-style capitalism was what had come to be called the New Economy, symbolized by the dot-coms that were revolutionizing the way America—and the world—did business, changing the pace of technological change itself and increasing the rate of productivity growth to levels not seen for a quarter century or more. The world had experienced an economic revolution two centuries earlier, the Industrial Revolution, in which the basis of the economy shifted from agriculture to manufacturing. The New Economy represented a change of equally momentous proportions: a shift from the production of goods to the production of ideas, entailing the processing of information, not of people or inventories. Manufacturing had in fact by the mid-nineties shrunk to close to 14 percent of total output, and an even smaller proportion of total employment. The New Economy also promised the end of the business cycle, the ups and downs of the economy that had, until now, always been part of capitalism, as new information technologies allowed businesses to better control their inventories. (Excess investment in inventories, which later had to be cut back, had been one of the major sources of economic downturns in the postwar era.)

It was abroad, in Asia, that the first glimmerings that something was wrong arrived—crises in Korea, Indonesia, Thailand in 1997, followed by Russia in 1998 and Brazil in 1999. But it was in the United States, in Seattle, Washington, in December 1999, that the protest movement against globalization broke out with full vengeance: if globalization was benefiting everybody and making everybody's lives better off, many seemed not to know it. Seattle was but a harbinger of what was to come, the protests in Washington, D.C., Prague, and Genoa—indeed, at every major meeting of global leaders. So strong, so intense, was the protest movement that when the leaders of the advanced industrial countries met, they had to withdraw to isolated venues, such as northern Quebec. Clearly, something was amiss.

Four months into the new millennium, symptoms began to show that something was also wrong at home, with the crash of the technology stocks. As the new millennium began, the stock market, that ultimate barometer of the economy, was at an all-time high. The NASDAQ Composite Index, containing mostly technology shares, soared from 500 in April 1991 to 1,000 in July 1995, surpassing 2,000 in July 1998, and finally peaking at 5,132 in March 2000. The stock market boom reinforced consumer confidence, which also reached new highs, and provided a strong impetus for investment, especially in the booming telecom and high-tech sectors.

The next few years confirmed suspicions that the numbers were unreal, as the stock market set new records for declines. In the next two years, $8.5 trillion were wiped off the value of the firms on America's stock exchange alone—an amount exceeding the annual income of every country in the world, other than the United States. One company, AOL Time Warner, took write-downs of $100 billion, an admission that the investments it had made had lost enormously in value. At the beginning of the nineties, there was no firm worth $100 billion, let alone one capable of losing that much value and continuing to exist.

It was not long after the breaking of the tech stock bubble that the fortunes of the real economy went into reverse and America experienced its first recession in a decade. Evidently, the New Economy had not brought an end to the business cycle. If the boom was greater than most of the others of the postwar period, the downturn too was worse. During the boom, we in the Clinton administration prided ourselves on the new records being set: jobs were being created at an unprecedented pace—10 million from 1993 to 1997, and another 8 million between 1997 and 2000. By 1994, unemployment had fallen below 6 percent for the first time in four years, and by April 2000, below 4 percent for the first time in three decades. Though the rich reaped the largest share of the gains, everyone seemed to be gaining. For the first time in a quarter century, those at the bottom saw their incomes begin to grow, with the greatest ever reduction in welfare roles (more than 50 percent in six years) and the largest declines in poverty since records had been kept.

The first two years of the new millennium saw still more records being broken. They weren't the kind to brag about, however. Enron was the biggest corporate bankruptcy ever—until WorldCom came along in July 2002. Stocks fell further, faster, than they had for years—the S&P 500, which provides the best broad-guaged measure of stock market performance, had its worst annual performance for a quarter century. Americans had confidently plowed their savings into corporate equities during the nineties; now, thanks to an $8.5 trillion decline in the market's value, roughly a third of the worth of America's individual retirement accounts, IRA and 401(k) plans, simply vanished. Even with the boom in real estate prices—a precarious boom, which did not necessarily bode well for the future—the third quarter of 2002 alone saw more than $1.6 trillion wiped off household balance sheets. Longtime workers awoke to discover that their retirement calculations no longer added up.

The stock market, of course, doesn't always reflect the broader economic reality. This time, unfortunately, it did. Between July 2000 and December 2001, the nation registered the longest decline in industrial production since the first oil shock. Two million jobs were lost in a mere twelve months. The number of long-term unemployed more than doubled. The unemployment rate jumped from 3.8 percent to 6.0 percent, while some 1.3 million more Americans moved below the poverty line, and an additional 1.4 million found themselves without health insurance.

And before the economy could recover from the recession, America was rocked by the worst corporate scandals in more than seventy years, bringing down mighty firms like Enron and Arthur Andersen, and touching almost every major financial institution. As time went on, it became clear that the problems were not confined to the telecommunications sector, or even high tech. Problems arose in the health sector and even in what had seemed the boring grocery business.

How HAD THINGS changed so quickly—from American capitalism triumphant around the world to American capitalism becoming a symbol of all that was wrong with the market economy? From globalization that brought untold benefits to all to the first recession of the new era of globalization, as downturns in Europe, United States, and Japan each help pull each other down? From a New Economy that promised the end of the business cycle to a New Economy that meant even larger losses?

The turnaround of events raised more questions: in the boom years, credit was shared between the Federal Reserve Board, with its long-serving chairman, Alan Greenspan, and the Clinton administration. Many outside politics, and especially on Wall Street, gave more of the kudos to Greenspan. Yet, not only did he seem powerless to forestall the downturn, but, as the downturn stretched on and on, he seemed powerless to bring about a recovery. Had Greenspan lost his magic touch? Or had he been given more credit than he deserved?

The timing of the downturn, coming on the heels of the change in America's political administration, provides a too-easy answer to the puzzle of the sudden change in circumstances: Clinton and his economic team knew how to manage the economy, George W. Bush and his team did not. But the downturn came too quickly after the turnover of power for this explanation to hold water.

On the other side, we could have taken some solace from the fact that there have always been ups and downs in market economies. Every bubble comes to an end; usually there are internal dynamics which bring about its own destruction. In housing bubbles, for example, high prices lead to more investment in real estate, and eventually the mismatch between increased supply and decreased demand brought on by ever-soaring prices cannot be avoided. The real estate bubbles of the early eighties burst when vacancy rates in Houston had reached some 30 percent. As the prices get higher and higher, it becomes increasingly implausible that the rate of increase can be sustained. So too in this bubble: the higher prices brought forth more dot-coms, more investment in telecoms. When the bubble burst, perhaps 97 percent of all the fiber optics had seen no light—they had simply never been used. We might even have taken pride in the fact that while the average boom in the half century since the end of

World War II had lasted less than five years, *our* boom had lasted longer, much longer.

But Americans should face up to the fact that in the very boom were planted some of the seeds of destruction, seeds which would not yield their noxious fruits for several years. We had not intended to plant these seeds—we had not even known that we were doing so. On the contrary, we believed we were planting the foundations of a prosperity that would continue into the future. And indeed, we had planted many of those as well. Some of the seeds were for slow-sprouting trees—investments in preschool education for the disadvantaged, or in basic science—the fruits of which will not be realized for another generation. Some of those seeds, however—like the budget surpluses in the trillions of dollars, reversing the mounting deficits of the Bush and Reagan years—proved more fragile than even we had thought, as George W. managed to convert what had seemed huge surpluses as far as the eye could see into mounting deficits. But it became increasingly clear that we had also planted some of the seeds of destruction that would underlay the recession that arrived in March 2001. Had the economy been well managed, the recession that followed might have been short and shallow; but President George W. Bush had another agenda, and the consequences for America, and the world, have been serious.

The Seeds of Destruction

What were these seeds of destruction? The first was the boom itself: it was a classic *bubble*, asset prices unrelated to underlying values, of a kind familiar to capitalism over the centuries. In Holland's tulip bulb bubble in the early seventeenth century, the price of a single tulip bulb soared to the equivalent of thousands of dollars; each investor was willing to pay the price, because he believed that he could sell the bulb to someone else at a still higher price.[1] Bubbles are based on a certain *irrational exuberance*,[2] and perhaps not since the days of tulip bulb mania had the irrationality of the market been more in evidence, as investors paid billions of dollars for companies that had never shown a profit—and likely never would.

No one—not the president, or the secretary of the Treasury, or the chairman of the Fed—can be blamed for this irrational exuberance; but they can be blamed for not dealing with the consequences, and in some cases, for feeding the frenzy. In chapter 3, I spell out what could and should have been done by the Fed, which, after a faint effort to let the air out of the bubble, simply added to the hype.

Bad accounting provided bad information, and part of the irrational exuberance was based on this bad information. We knew that the accounting systems had a major flaw, and that the system of CEO compensation provided incentives to take advantage of the limitations in our accounting systems. We knew that those responsible for accounting, the accounting firms, faced conflicts of interest in providing good and reliable information. There were battles—battles waged by Arthur Levitt, Jr., chairman of the Securities and Exchange Commission, which is in charge of regulating securities markets; by the Council of Economic Advisers, a cabinet-level agency within the White House responsible for providing impartial views about the economy; and by the independent Financial Accounting Standards Board—to make sure that better information was provided. But there were powerful forces lined up on the other side, the accounting firms and financial firms, and they looked for allies in the U.S. Treasury, such as Lloyd Bentsen; the Department of Commerce and its secretary, the late Ron Brown; the National Economic Council, then headed by Robert Rubin; and the U.S. Congress, on both sides of the aisle, including Joe Lieberman (D: CT) and Connie Mack (R: FL). The short-term and special interests prevailed over the long-term and general interests. Not only did they stop efforts at improving matters; tax laws and securities legislation actually made matters worse.

In several sectors, America had an outmoded regulatory system, one which had not kept pace with the changes in technology that were transforming the economy, but we were too trapped into the mantra of deregulation, mindlessly stripping back on regulation. It was no coincidence that many of the problems of the Roaring Nineties can be traced back to the newly deregulated sectors—electricity, telecommunications, and finance. Distorted incentives combined with irrational exuberance induced America's new financial behemoths to provide the finance that underwrote the bubble; they made billions from the IPOs (initial public offerings) and the deceptive boosting of their favored stocks, even if their gains had to come at the expense of someone—in most cases, ordinary shareholders. Within the administration, we debated some of the so-called reforms which potentially exacerbated the conflicts of interests; but Treasury took the side of the financial firms, who said, "trust us." They won and the country lost (see chapter 6).

With these ingredients alone, the brew was strong enough. But to add froth to the frenzy, taxes on capital gains (taxes on the increases in the value of assets like stocks between sale and purchase) were cut. Those who earned their money by speculating and winning on the stock market were the heroes of the day, and were to be taxed more lightly than those who earned their bread by the sweat of their brow. With speculation thus especially blessed, more money poured in, and the bubble got inflated ever further.

Why the Failures?

As I look back on the 1990s from our current vantage point, I ask: where did we go wrong? There were, I think, two principal reasons.

Losing sight of the balanced role of government

For twelve years, during the Reagan and Bush I administrations, national economic policy had been shaped by free market ideologues who idealized the private sector and demonized government programs and regulations. Bill Clinton, like many who served in his administration, identified with the so-called New Democrats—a loose group of politicians, academics, and policy wonks who felt that the Democratic Party, in the past, had been too prone to bureaucratic solutions, and too unconcerned about the impact of its policies on business and the marketplace.

At the same time, there had long been a recognition that markets did not always work well, producing too much of some things—like air pollution—and too few of other things, like investments in education, health, and knowledge. They were also not self-regulating; there were enormous fluctuations in the level of economic activity, with extended episodes of high unemployment, during which millions of those willing and able to work could not find jobs. The social and economic costs of these episodes were in turn enormous.

Since World War II, the federal government had recognized its responsibilities to maintain the economy at full employment—by the same act that created the Council of Economic Advisers. And increasingly, it was recognized that government had an important and legitimate role to play in other areas, like curbing pollution.

Conservatives, however, wanted to limit the role of government (except when it came to giving subsidies or protecting businesses, such as steel, aluminum, corporate farms, and airlines). In some cases, they even wanted to roll back government, turning our Social Security system over to the private sector.

Behind this was a belief in unfettered markets. Adam Smith, the father of modern economics, was often credited with this idea (though he himself was more circumspect), arguing in his 1776 treatise *The Wealth of Nations* that the market leads as if by an invisible hand to economic efficiency. One of the great intellectual achievements of the mid-twentieth century (by Gerard Debreu of the University of California at Berkeley and Kenneth Arrow of Stanford, both of whom received Nobel prizes for this achievement) was to establish the conditions under which Adam Smith's "invisible hand" worked. These included a large number of unrealistic conditions, such as that information was either perfect, or at least not affected by anything going on in the economy, and that whatever information anybody had, others had the same information; that competition was perfect; and that one could buy insurance against any possible risk. Though everyone recognized that these assumptions were unrealistic, there was a hope that if the real world did not depart too much from such assumptions—if information were not too imperfect, or firms did not have too much market power—then Adam Smith's invisible hand theory would still provide a good description of the economy. This was a hope based more on faith—especially by those whom it served well—than on science.

My research, and that of others, on the consequences of imperfect and asymmetric information (where different individuals know different things) over the last quarter of a century, has shown that one of the reasons that the invisible hand may be invisible is that it is simply not there. Even in very developed countries, markets work significantly differently from the way envisaged by the "perfect markets" theories. They do bring enormous benefits, they are largely responsible for the enormous increases of standards of living over the past century, but they have their limitations, and sometimes these limitations simply cannot be ignored. The massive amounts of unemployment which appear periodically, demonstrating that markets are not utilizing resources well, are just the tip of a much bigger iceberg of market failure. As the structure of the economy changed—as we moved from an agricultural economy to an industrial economy to the Information Economy—the limitations of markets, especially those related to imperfect and asymmetric information, became increasingly important.

The invisible hand theory was a great relief to CEOs, for it told them that by doing well (for themselves) they were doing good (for society). Not only should they feel no guilt in greed; they should feel pride. But as endearing as CEOs might find the theory, to most others it seemed counterintuitive. This seems especially the case in the aftermath of the corporate scandals that rocked the world at the turn of the century, and to which we turn at greater length in later chapters. These activities of the CEOs did not *seem* to be in the general interest. The critics were right, and the "market failure" theories helped explain why. Among the "market failures" to which our research called attention were those associated with agency problems, where one person has to act on behalf of another. Because of imperfect information, it is often difficult to make sure that an agent does what he is supposed to do, and because of the failure to align incentives, it is often the case that he does not. Especially problematic are situations where there are conflicts of interest, which were so prominent in the corporate scandals of recent years. The CEOs and other executives of corporations are *supposed* to act in the best interests of the corporations, its shareholders and workers; but in the nineties, incentives got badly misaligned. In acting in their own interests, CEOs often did not serve well those on whose behalf they were supposed to be working. The irony was that the changes in pay structure which were at the root of much of the problem were defended as improving incentives.

No one who has watched the corporate scandals, the wasted investments of America's boom, the idle resources of America's bust, can truly believe that markets, by themselves, result in efficient outcomes. There had been, of course, many earlier episodes in which public attention was drawn to the limitations of the market, and following many of these episodes government regulations had been passed to address the problems. When, a century ago, Upton Sinclair wrote his famous novel *The Jungle,* depicting what happened in the stockyards as beef made its way into the American home, the revulsion from the American consumer was strong. The meat industry turned to the government to ensure food safety as the best way of restoring confidence. So too, in the aftermath of the securities scandals of the Roaring Twenties, government regulation was seen as necessary to restore investor confidence, without which people were hesitant to invest their money. They wanted to know that some oversight was being exercised by someone whose incentives were more aligned with theirs.

In several of the earlier episodes, when the economy performed poorly, market advocates tried to find the culprit in excessive or misguided government intervention: it was the Fed, some claim, that caused the Great Depression. I believe the government did not cause the Great Depression, but it was nevertheless culpable: it did not do what it could have done to reverse it and minimize its damage. But whatever one thinks of the Great Depression, it was government doing too little—insufficient regulation, not excessive regulation—that was at the root of the problem in the Roaring Nineties and the recession that followed.

Government regulation can often play an important role in making markets work better, in limiting the scope, for instance, of the conflicts of interest that repeatedly appeared in accounting, business, and finance. When a fire insurance company requires a business that buys insurance from it to install sprinklers, no one criticizes the insurance firm. It makes good business sense, since with insurance, the insured company no longer bears the full cost of a fire and has inadequate incentive to install sprinklers. But in the economy as a whole the government, in one way or another, winds up picking up the pieces when things go wrong. When bank deregulation led to problems in the savings and loan industry in the 1980s, the American taxpayer paid the bill. Much of regulation is directed at protecting America, and American taxpayers, against such risks.

Although government too is faced by limitations of information, the constraints and incentives facing government are different. Government has an incentive to deliver on what it promises: to ensure that food is safe and that banks do not take excessive risks. Of course, government, like markets, have a variety of imperfections, leading to "government failures" that are as troublesome as market failures, and that is why they have to work together, complementing each other, making up for each other's weaknesses, building on each other's strengths.

In fact, there are some things that government may be able to do even better than the private sector: publicly provided airport security seems better than what it replaced; publicly provided annuities— Social Security—not only have much lower transaction costs than those privately provided but also offer insurance against risks of inflation that no private firm provides.

When Clinton entered office, I and many others who came to Washington with him hoped that he would restore balance to the role of government. Jimmy Carter had begun the process of deregulation, in such vital areas as airlines and trucking. But under Ronald Reagan and George Bush, America had pushed deregulation way too far. Our task was find the appropriate middle course and to adapt the regulations to the changes that were going on in the country. We should not have been talking about deregulation so much as finding the *right* regulatory framework. In some areas, we did that; but in others, we were too swept up by the deregulation, pro-business mantra. The New Democrats were right to emphasize that markets are at the center of every successful economy, but there is still a vital role that government has to play. Misguided deregulation and bad tax policies were at the core of the 1991 recession, and misguided deregulation, misguided tax policies, and misguided accounting practices are at the core of the current downturn. American investors had trusted the corporate auditors, and the auditors had betrayed that trust. Similarly, investors had trusted the Wall Street analysts about which stock to buy, and those analysts too had betrayed that trust.

Ideology led to policies that helped generate the bubble that eventually burst; further, free market ideology also prevented actions that might have addressed some of the underlying problems that gave rise to the bubble, as well as other actions that might have diminished the bubble, and let the air out of it more gradually.

Growth on the cheap

Our emerging understanding of the 1990s requires that we admit—to ourselves and to the world—that we were engaged in a misguided attempt to achieve growth on the cheap; though not via the "Voodoo economics" of Reagan, who somehow believed that by cutting taxes you could raise tax revenues, but by the froth of the bubble economy. Instead of curbing consumption to finance our boom, the United States borrowed heavily, year after year, from abroad, at a rate of more than a billion dollars a day. We did this to fill the widening gap between what we were saving and what we were investing—a gap that opened in earnest under Ronald Reagan but grew under George H. W. Bush and Bill Clinton, and has reached new dimensions under the new President Bush.[3]

We made some good long-run investments—both in the private sector and in the public—but too much of our investment went into wasteful private expenditures—the dot-coms that didn't pan out, the fiber optic cables that were not needed. These were just part of the telecom race to achieve early dominance, and the monopoly power that was assumed to come with it. It is still not clear how much of the private so-called investment of the 1990s was sheer waste, but even if we consider that only a fraction of the erosion in stock values is attributable to bad investments, the figure must be in the hundreds of billions of dollars.

By contrast, too little of our investment went to address vital public needs, in education, in infrastructure, in basic research. We provided tax credits and deductions for higher education, but most of the middle-class kids who benefited were already going to college; the credits and deductions did make their parents' lives easier, but it was unlikely to have much effect on enrollments.[4] The money could have been better spent targeting the very poor, for whom money is a real obstacle—whose parents do not pay taxes.

But most ironic, in the age of the New Economy, we also underinvested in research, especially the basic sciences, which underlay the New Economy. We were, in part, living off past ideas, breakthroughs of an earlier day, such as transistors and lasers. We were counting on the foreign students who were flocking to our universities to sustain much of our research capabilities, while our best students were putting together the financial deals. At the Council of Economic Advisers, we did a study showing the very high returns to investments in R&D, but to no avail.

Underlying many of these mistakes was an excessive zeal in deficit reduction. Reagan had let deficits get out of control, risking the long-term growth of the economy, and something had to be done about the deficits. But just as we pushed deregulation too far, we pushed deficit reduction too far. There were accounting problems in the public sector, just as there were in the private, but many of these were biased in the opposite direction to those in the private sector. They treated public expenditures—whether in roads, infrastructure, or science—as if they were ordinary consumption. If we borrowed to finance these investments, the government accounting frameworks recognized the liability, but took no account of the corresponding asset. It was a framework designed to squeeze the government and inhibit long-term investment, and it did that.

Conservatives had argued relentlessly for a down-sized government, less expenditures, fewer government workers, less regulation.

The presumption was that government was *inevitably* inefficient. Even if there were problems, government regulation would *inevitably* make matters worse; the best course was accordingly simply to leave markets to work on their own. The issue was, was this waste and inefficiency inevitable?

The Clinton administration abhorred the wastefulness of many federal programs and the inefficiency of many regulations—and we actually tried to do something about the problem, partly because we believed that unless we could convince voters that the money they paid to government was well used and regulations were well directed, we would lose their support. While Reagan and Bush had railed against the government, public sector employment actually increased during their presidencies. During the Clinton years, the percentage of the national workforce employed by the federal government contracted to levels not seen since the New Deal, a remarkable achievement given the new tasks which the government had undertaken in the intervening seventy years (including Social Security, Medicare, and other programs that touched the lives of every American family). Yet we initiated these reductions, not in order to tear down government, but to reaffirm its role—not just in national defense and homeland security, but in promoting technology and education, providing infrastructure, and enhancing security of all kinds, including health and economic security. By showing that government could be efficient and innovative, we hoped that there would be renewed support for government, and for those endeavors which lie within the responsibility of government.

American Failures Abroad

The boom and bust in the international economy was, if anything, even greater than in America, and the two were inextricably intertwined. With the end of the Cold War and the coming of globalization, we had the opportunity to create a new international order based on American values, reflecting our sense of the balance between government and markets, one which promoted social justice and democracy on a global scale. The Clinton administration had some notable successes in our efforts to create a new international economic order with the North American Free Trade Agreement (NAFTA), uniting Mexico, United States, and Canada in the largest free trade area of the world, and with the completion of the so-called Uruguay Round of international trade negotiations, which created the World Trade Organization to help regulate international commerce. These agreements promised to bring untold benefits to our economy, such as cutting the cost of living, stimulating economic growth, and creating jobs through access to new markets. Plans were made for still more trade agreements—between the nations of North and South America, and the nations of Asia and the Pacific.

But as we look back on these achievements, as we see the protests around the world, as we feel the pulse of anti-Americanism, it becomes clear that something again had gone wrong.[5] Underlying the protests there were deeper symptoms. Globalization had often not produced the benefits that were promised. Except in Asia—which had largely not followed the prescriptions for growth and development the United States had put forth—poverty was up, in some places dramatically so. With growth in Latin America during the reform and globalization decade of the nineties just over half of what it had been in the fifties, sixties, and seventies, no wonder there was dissatisfaction. The gap between the haves and have-nots—both between the United States and the developing world, and between the rich and the poor within the developing countries—was growing. Even many of those who are better off feel more vulnerable. Argentina was touted as the A+ student of reform. Looking at the disaster that befell Argentina, developing countries ask, If this is the result, what is in store for us? And as unemployment and the sense of vulnerability

increase, and the fruits of what limited growth occurs go dispropor-
tionately to the rich, the sense of social injustice increases too.

A decade of unparalleled American influence over the global economy was also a decade in which one economic crisis seemed to follow another—every year there was another crisis. We survived these
crises. We may have even benefited as a result of the lower prices at
which we could buy some imported goods, and our investment banks
may have profited. But they caused untold hardship in the countries
that suffered them. The heralded transition of ex-Communist countries to a market economy, which was supposed to bring unprecedented prosperity, instead brought unprecedented poverty. The
transition turned out to be such a disaster that by the summer of
1999, *The New York Times* was asking, "Who Lost Russia?"[6] And
even if Russia was not ours to lose, the statistics were sobering: with
efficient capitalism replacing moribund and decadent communism,
output was supposed to soar. In fact GDP declined 40 percent and
poverty increased tenfold. And the results were similar in the other
economies making the transition who followed the advice of the U.S.
Treasury and the International Monetary Fund. Meanwhile, China,
following its own course, showed that there was an alternative path
of transition which could succeed both in bringing the growth that
markets promised and in markedly reducing poverty.

Clearly, something was amiss in the way we were leading the
world into the new international order. At the very least, we had not
addressed the fundamental problems of instability. There was enormous talk of reforming the global financial architecture but not real
action. Nor had we convinced many, probably most, in the developing countries that the international economic order that we were trying to create would work well for them.

Again, we needed to ask, what were our mistakes and why did we
make them? We failed in what we did, and what we did not do; and
we failed in how we did what we did.

The international agreements, for instance, reflected our concerns, our interests: we forced those abroad to open up their capital markets, say, to our derivatives and speculative capital flows, knowing how destabilizing they could be. But Wall Street wanted it, and what Wall Street wanted, it more than likely got.

Developing countries were told to open their markets to every imaginable form of import, including the things Corporate America was best at, such as financial services and computer software. Meanwhile, we maintained stiff trade barriers and large subsidies of our own on behalf of U.S. farmers and agribusiness, thereby denying our market to the farmers of the Third World. To a country fallen on hard times and facing recession, our standard advice was to slash spending—even though we had routinely relied on deficit spending to get us out of economic downturns.

These were not the only examples of what struck those abroad as blatant hypocrisy. Even in the budget-balancing nineties, we maintained robust trade deficits even as we preached to others that they should keep their trade deficits down; evidently, it was understandable if the rich could not live within their means; what was not to be forgiven was for the poor to do so.[7]

We scolded the developing nations about their disrespect for intellectual property laws that we, too, had scorned in our days as a developing nation. (The United States didn't get around to protecting the rights of foreign authors until 1891.)

Especially strange was the contrast between the Clinton administration's palliatives abroad and the battles it waged at home. At home, we defended our public Social Security against privatization, lauding its low transactions costs, the income security which it provided, how it had virtually eliminated poverty among the elderly. Abroad, we pushed privatization. At home, we argued strongly that the Fed should keep a focus on growth and unemployment, as well as inflation—with a president elected on a jobs platform, he could do nothing less. Abroad, we urged Central Banks to focus exclusively on inflation.

One of America's great glories had been the growth of its middle class. Still, we almost completely ignored the equity implications of the policies we urged on other nations—and the increasingly inescapable fact that globalization, as it was actually practiced, tended to make poor societies more rather than less unequal.

Some of our problems abroad were caused by *how* we interacted with other countries, especially weaker developing nations. Acting as if we had come up with a unique, guaranteed formula for prosperity, we—sometimes with the assistance of other advanced industrial countries—bullied other nations into doing things our way. Both through our own economic diplomacy, and through the influence of the American-dominated International Monetary Fund, Uncle Sam became Dr. Sam, dispensing prescriptions to the rest of the world: *Cut that budget. Lower that trade barrier. Privatize that utility.* Like some physicians, we were too busy—and too sure of ourselves—to listen to patients with their own ideas. Too busy, sometimes, even to look at individual countries and their circumstances. The economists and development experts of the Third World, many of them brilliant and highly educated, were sometimes treated like children. Our bed-side manner was dreadful; and, as one patient after another couldn't help noticing, the medicine we dispensed abroad was, in important respects, not really the same stuff we drank at home.

Some of our failures arose because we naturally had a focus on domestic politics. Global leadership had been thrust upon us. We in the Clinton administration did not have a vision of a new post–Cold War international order, but the business and financial community did: they saw new opportunities for profits. To them, there was a role for government: helping them gain access to markets. The policy framework that we pushed abroad was the one that would help our businesses do well abroad. At home, there was a check on these policies, caused by our concern for consumers and workers. Abroad, there was none. At home, we resisted pressure for changes in the bankruptcy law that would unduly hurt debtors. Abroad, a primary concern in any foreign crisis seemed the promptest and fullest repayment of debts to American and other Western banks, even to the point of supplying billions of dollars to ensure that that happened. The deregulation mantra that we pushed too far at home we pushed even further abroad.

Not surprisingly, the policies we pushed and the way we pushed them generated enormous resentment. The full implications of this resentment are, at present, very hard to assess. But the already visible results include growing anti-Americanism in Asia and Latin America. Some manifestations are obvious: boycotts of American products, increased protests at McDonald's. Today, in many countries, the endorsement of a policy by the U.S. government is almost certain to lead to its defeat; others, which were obliged, until recently, to heed our advice, like it or not, may begin to ignore us in an equally undiscriminating fashion, citing our failures as an excuse for not fixing their problems. Just because we have a problem with accounting fraud doesn't mean that accounting standards should not be raised around the world; but our Enrons and Arthur Andersens have undermined American authority in such matters. Our hypocrisy on trade becomes a reason to maintain protectionist regimes abroad, even in nations that would truly benefit from lower trade barriers.

The Politics of Failure

When the economic advisers to President Clinton came to Washington, we were well poised to address many of the problems that gave rise to the bubble and its bursting; to restore balance, between the role of collective action and private, between government and the market; to create the foundations for strong, long-term growth. Clinton had been elected on a platform of "putting the people first," not putting financial interests first. We knew that there were conflicts of interests; we knew that markets by themselves often did not work; we knew that there was a role for government regulation. And the broader general interests that most of us came to serve meant that we should not have been seduced by the self-serving arguments of free market advocates. Democrats had long argued against preferential tax treatment of capital gains, and yet here we were, a few years after coming to Washington, advocating it.

Of all the mistakes we made in the Roaring Nineties, the worst were caused by a lack of standing by our principles and a lack of vision. We had principles. As the administration came into office, most of us knew what we were *against*. We were against Reagan conservatism. We knew that there needed to be a larger and different role for government, that we needed to be more concerned for the poor and for providing education and social protection for all, and we needed to protect the environment. The shortsighted focus on finance, on the deficit, made us push this agenda aside.

We stood too for civil and human rights, for a new internationalism, for democracy. In the Cold War, we had befriended ruthless dictators, paying little heed to what they stood for and what they did, simply because they were on our side in the fight against communism. The end of the Cold War gave us more freedom to stand for traditional American values—and we did that. We pushed for democratic governments. AID, the U.S. agency providing international assistance, spent more of its money supporting democracy. But, again under the influence of finance, abroad we pushed a market fundamentalist set of reforms, in any way we could, paying little attention to how what we did undermined democratic processes.[8]

Why did we fail to follow through on our principles? It is easy to blame others—the deficit that we had inherited did circumscribe what we could do, as did the conservative Congress that was elected

in 1994. We were, however, I think, in part a victim of our own seeming success. At the beginning of the administration, the bold, broad-
gauged agenda to address America's problems was put aside in favor
of a single-minded focus on deficit reduction. The economy recovered, and deficit reduction was given the credit, and with that credit,
the credibility of those who had advocated it soared. If they advocated deregulation, we should listen to their wisdom. If they advocated deregulation for their own industry, we should be particularly
attentive—after all, who knows more about financial markets than
the financiers. So enthralled with our seeming success, we put aside
two centuries of experience about problems of conflicts of interest—
let alone the lessons in the recent advances in the economics of asymmetric information.

Politically, the new orientation seemed to serve the Democratic
Party well. The old coalition of southern conservatives and northern
liberals had fallen apart, one couldn't win an election just standing up
for the poor, and in modern America, everyone saw themselves as
middle class. Advocating deregulation distanced the New Democrats
from the New Deal of the Old Democrats.

Moreover, when the Republicans seized control of Congress,
deregulation and capital gains tax cuts provided part of the *common
ground*: an activist president, wanting to place the Democratic Party
in a new centrist position, wanted to find some common ground with
the conservative Republicans.

Lessons

The central lesson that emerges from this story of the boom and
bust—that there needs to be a balance between the role of government and of markets—is one which evidently the world has had to
learn over and over again. When countries got that balance right,
they grew strongly—America through much of its history, East Asia

in the sixties, seventies, and eighties. When countries got that balance wrong, veering either toward too much or too little government, disaster awaited. Although the failures of excessive government—evidenced by the collapse of the Communist system—are the most dramatic, there are failures on the other side as well.

It was too little regulation, not too much, that caused the economic crises in East Asia in 1997. It was too little regulation that gave rise to the savings and loan debacle in 1989, in which American taxpayers paid more than $100 billion bailing out an important part of the nation's financial system. (The only thing that could be said in favor of the bailout was that—given the consequences of excessive deregulation—the costs of not bailing them out would have been even greater.)

If we in the Clinton administration sometimes lost that balance, matters have become even worse during the next administration—with the predictable consequences that our economy's performance has become worse. The challenge today is to regain that balance, to learn the lessons of the tumultuous decade of the nineties and the years that have followed.

MUCH OF THIS book is about domestic American politics and economics, but as the events of recent years have made clear, these issues, and our very well-being, cannot be separated from what happens outside our borders. Globalization may be inevitable, but the way we attempted to structure it—for our interests—was not consonant with our values, and ultimately failed to serve even our own interests. The "globalization" boom, like the stock market boom and the economic boom, was followed by a bust, and partly because, as in the case of those two other booms, they had within themselves the seeds of their own destruction.

Even if our own economy had not faltered, our global strategy was not likely to succeed. It was based on pressuring countries in the Third World to adopt policies that were markedly different from those that we ourselves had adopted—to adopt the market fundamentalist policies that represented everything at home that the Clinton administration was fighting against. It was based on our putting aside principles—principles of social justice, equity, fairness that we stressed at home—to get the best bargain we could for American special interests.

The world has become economically interdependent, and only by creating equitable international arrangements can we bring stability to the global marketplace. This will require a spirit of cooperation that is not built by brute force, by dictating inappropriate conditions in the midst of a crisis, by bullying, by pushing unfair trade treaties, or by pursuing hypocritical trade policies—all of which are part of the hegemonic legacy that the United States established in the 1990s, but seem to have become worse in the next administration.

In the international economic policy of the nineties, America foreshadowed the ideological fervor and the unilateralism of the next administration. The consequences will be part of the heritage with which the administration to follow will have to deal.

We will turn to the boom and bust in globalization in chapter 9. But first, we need to lay the groundwork: the economic recovery of 1993 and the economic boom that followed.

CHAPTER 2

Miracleworkers, or Lucky Mistakes?

SINCE THE BEGINNING of capitalism, there have been booms and busts—the past century saw one of the strongest booms ever, the Roaring Twenties, followed by the worst bust ever, the Great Depression, in which one out of four American workers was without a job, with similar numbers in other industrialized countries. Since World War II, the fluctuations have been more moderate, the booms longer, the busts shorter and shallower. But as we noticed in the last chapter, as the century drew to a close, we experienced the greatest boom in a third of a century—the Roaring Nineties, with growth rates soaring to 4.4 percent,[1] to be followed by one of the most prolonged downturns.

Much of what happens to the economy does not depend on government, but when you join the administration of a newly elected president, you take it for granted that your reputation and job tenure, along with that of your boss, are likely to depend on the economy. And if you're an economist, you know how fickle and even cruel, at times, that form of judgment can be. George H. W. Bush failed to get reelected in 1992, in spite of record poll results in the aftermath of the Gulf War victory, and most pundits ascribed the loss largely to the economy's dismal performance. Bush himself blamed Alan Green-

span, the chairman of the Federal Reserve Board, and his economic
advisers. Greenspan had been slow to lower interest rates, seemingly
believing the economy would recover quickly from the recession of
1990–91, and that lower interest rates would once again ignite inflation. As Bush reflected some years later, "I reappointed him, and he
disappointed me."[2]

Michael Boskin, who had been my colleague at Stanford, headed
George H. W. Bush's Council of Economic Advisers, and felt the full
brunt of Bush's anger. As the president's campaign floundered, Bush
promised to find a new set of economic advisers. The irony was, of
course, that Boskin had been one of the advisers urging stronger
actions, and one of those who shared his boss's frustration with
Greenspan.

Bush was not the first president to flounder on the poor performance of the economy. Ford (whose chairman of the Council of Economic Advisers had been Greenspan) and Carter also went down to
defeat at least partly because of recessions in the economy at the critical time of elections.

Political scientists and economists have shown that the link
between politics and the economy is not just a matter of anecdote.
There is a clear statistical relationship, with the economy providing
as good a predictor of election outcomes as most polls. During the
1996 election, we at the Council of Economic Advisers provided
Clinton with forecasts of the electoral outcome that proved every bit
as accurate as the polls on which he was relying. (We jokingly suggested that had Clinton relied on us, rather than on the pollsters, he
might have been spared the embarrassment of the notorious fund-
raising activities, from the White House coffees to the Lincoln Bed-
room. But, as the 2000 election proved, these statistical models,
which suggested that Al Gore should have won by a landslide, are far
from infallible.)

There is a certain injustice in all of this: many of the major events affecting the economy are not of the president's making, and one of the most important instruments for controlling the economy—monetary policy, which entails setting interest rates and controlling the money supply—is delegated to the independent Federal Reserve. Gerald Ford's economy was ruined by the oil embargo in 1973, which sent unemployment up steeply, though by the time of the election the economy was already recovering. The 1979 recession, which helped unseat Jimmy Carter, was the result of a combined oil price shock and the Fed setting high interest rates.

Economics Moves Center Stage

Economics had never been the elder George Bush's favorite subject. Like many presidents before him, he gravitated toward foreign policy, where the powers of the office are more clear-cut. Bill Clinton, by contrast, made it plain from the outset that domestic policy was his top priority. With his unofficial campaign slogan, "It's the economy, stupid," Clinton invited Americans to use the economy as their presidential scorecard (which they would have done in any case). With his slogan: "Jobs! Jobs! Jobs!" he made his focus clear—not inflation, but employment. He offered a concrete yardstick against which to measure success—8 million jobs in four years. There was boldness in his deficit-cutting plan (which the Republican Party opposed almost en masse). It was only natural, then, that when the economy began to pick up, Americans were more generous than usual in giving credit to the president and his team. Indeed, for all the harsh things that critics would say about Clinton over the course of his two terms in office, the economy remained the unassailable redoubt of his approval ratings. The stock market seemed to be giving him a final salute by peaking in the last year of Clinton's presidency.

As the economy grew, so did the nation's interest in it. Business, technology, and finance began to receive the kind of press attention formerly reserved for sports and show business. Celebrityhood was conferred not only on corporate CEOs but also on the holders of public offices (Treasury secretary and Federal Reserve Board chairman, to name two) who had cut a far lower profile in the past. The media, of course, likes personalities and thus generally prefers to keep their policy analysis on the short and painless side. In newspaper and magazine stories, editorials and op-ed columns, and the round-the-clock reporting of CNN and MSNBC, business journalists rhapsodized over the brilliance and artistry of the Clinton team. The hagiography reached new heights with Bob Woodward's best-selling book *Maestro: Greenspan's Fed and the American Boom*, published just months before the economy began its downward spin. The tone was set with these words from the preface: ". . . the inherited economic conditions [including the projected surplus of at least several trillion dollars] for everyone—from the next president to any citizen—is in many respects the Greenspan dividend."[3] Economic policymaking began to be described almost as if it were a sporting event, with the outcome dependent on the nimble moves and athletic prowess of a handful of superstars, working, it was said, selflessly and harmoniously in the cause of the nation's prosperity.

The truth, of course, was a good deal messier. While all of us involved in fashioning economic policy in those years eagerly claimed whatever credit we could, we had to shake our heads at some of the tales of our prescience and graceful teamplay. Now and then, perhaps, we came close to living up to our notices; but on many occasions, we argued endlessly over elements of what became known (as if it were a seamless whole) as the Clinton administration's "economic program." Far from seamless, it was really a patchwork quilt of decisions, some courageous, some cowardly, some made by consensus, others by a small faction that had temporarily won the president's confidence, some for the best reasons (because we thought the country would benefit), and at least a few for the worst (because a special interest was better represented than the public interest). We certainly weren't gods. We made our share of mistakes. What came to be regarded as our biggest single policy success—cutting the deficit—worked as well as it did for reasons quite different from those advanced by many of its champions. In the end, the record of any administration is largely the consequence of the hand it has been dealt by history, and by events, such as the terrorist attacks of September 11, 2001, beyond its control. And so too for us. Still, choices are made and decisions are taken, which sooner or later have an influence on determining the administration's legacy.

Clinton's Inheritance: Playing the Hand You Are Dealt

When we arrived in 1993, we inherited formidable problems. We found the economy in a weak, "jobless recovery" from the 1990–91 recession, but it had begun to pull out of the recession well before Clinton took office—there had not been a single quarter of contraction in 1992, and the fourth quarter of 1992, the election quarter, showed a robust 4.3 percent growth. Nonetheless, employment in 1992 remained below the level of 1990. We had been left to deal with a deep budget deficit, one that had been widening ever since the folly of the Reagan tax cuts. These tax cuts were supposed to pay for themselves, according to a theory scrawled on the back of a napkin, called the Laffer curve—after Arthur Laffer, who then was at the University of Chicago—which claimed that as taxes got higher and higher, people worked less hard and saved less, so much so that tax revenue actually declined! (This idea comes out of supply-side economics, which emphasizes the limitations on the economy imposed by the willingness of individuals to work and save, as opposed to demand-side economics, which emphasizes the limitations imposed on the economy by demand—that firms would not produce goods if no one would buy them. The overwhelming evidence of this was that tax rates were nowhere near the level at which a reduction in rates would increase revenues.) By 1992, the deficit amounted to almost 5 percent of America's gross domestic product. Exclude the tax revenues that were supposed to go into the Social Security trust fund, and that figure was even higher. These were the kind of statistics commonly associated with the world's poorest nations, not its richest.

America's weak fiscal position was only the most visible sign of the country's problems. America had long prided itself on its technological superiority. Yet test scores in science and math put U.S. students below the newly emerging economies of East Asia, such as Singapore, Taiwan, and South Korea. We turned increasingly to foreign countries for our graduate students in science and engineering, and, teaching at Stanford and Princeton, I saw these foreign students not only come in with higher test scores but outperform their American classmates. Even our technological preeminence seemed to depend on a brain drain—America was taking the best and the brightest from around the world.

The level of crime, and the proportion of people behind bars, which was among the highest in the world, also suggested that something was very wrong. Some states were spending more money on prisons than on colleges and universities. The level of inequality was not as bad as in Latin America, but it was greater than in the emerging countries of East Asia, which had shown that one could combine high growth with greater equity. And for two decades, inequality in the United States had become worse. As much as the Reaganites might have believed in "trickle-down economics"—which argued that growth benefited all (or as it was sometimes put, a rising tide lifts all boats)—the poor were not benefiting from the growth of the eighties. Indeed, since 1973, the poorest people in America had actually become poorer.

Yet, in other ways, we were in luck. Though we lost no opportunity to claim, and sometimes even believed, that the recovery was our own doing, much of what happened in the nineties could be traced to forces set in play well before the Clinton administration appeared on the scene. Investments in high technology, for example, had begun to pay off, yielding increased productivity. In many of America's biggest cities, crime was in a position to begin to fall, partly for demographic reasons and partly because of the waning of the terrible crack-cocaine epidemic of the eighties.

Those of us appointed to help the Clinton administration plot its economic policy were in the right place at the right time: the previous twelve years of economic policies had done much damage, but the situation was not yet irreparable, and there were some forces working in our favor. In fact, even the deficit proved to be a lucky card for us in one sense: it gave us the opportunity, and the political leverage, to do something dramatic. The end of the Cold War meant that if we only brought down military expenditures to a more reasonable level—from the 6.2 percent of GDP that it reached in the peak of the Reagan era to, say, 3 percent, we would have erased more than half of the deficit. Not that any of us had signed up for our jobs out of a deep inner urge to balance the budget. From the president on down, we had come to Washington with a very different set of hopes, reflected in the campaign document *Putting People First*.

But we played the hand we had been dealt. The president was persuaded that there was a task which had to be attended to first—a task which turned out to preoccupy much of the agenda for the next eight years. He had to bring the deficit under control.

That the deficits were not sustainable in the long run was clear. With deficits equal to 5 percent of GDP every year, the national debt was growing—even as a percentage of GDP (since GDP was growing at only around 2.5 percent). With a growing debt, the federal government had to pay higher and higher interest rates, and with higher interest rates and more debt, more and more money simply went to pay interest on the national debt. These interest payments would eventually crowd out other forms of expenditure. So, ultimately, either taxes had to be increased or expenditures reduced. It made sense to face reality soon, rather than wait for the debilitating effects of mounting debts.

The problem was that this was the worst of possible times to have to face this reality. For the economy was still not out of the 1991 recession, and standard economic theory—the theory that had been taught in every course in economics for more than fifty years—said that increasing taxes or reducing expenditures in an attempt to reduce the deficit would slow down the economy. As growth slowed and unemployment increased, so too would welfare roles and unemployment benefits, leading to disappointing tax receipts. Expenditures would increase as tax revenues declined or at least failed to grow as they would with a robust economy. The attempt at deficit reduction would prove quixotic.

In the end, it turned out that Clinton's strategy for deficit reduction worked. Within a few years, the deficits inherited from Bush turned into huge surpluses and the economy recovered, though for reasons that were particular to the 1990s. It is important to understand why the deficit reduction worked then and why that was the exception that proves the rule.

Matters of History

To understand the part played by deficit reduction in the recovery of the 1990s you have to go back to the late seventies and early eighties, when the Federal Reserve Board, headed at the time by Paul Volcker, was worried about inflation and thus raised interest rates to unprecedented levels in an attempt to slow down what it viewed as an overheated economy—corporate bond rates (the interest rates corporations pay on longer-term borrowing) exceeded 15 percent in late

1981 and early 1982. The Fed was proud of its success in bringing inflation down from 13.5 percent in 1980 to a mere 3.2 percent in 1983. Some of the costs of doing so were immediate—unemployment soared to 9.7 percent—a level not seen in the United States since the Great Depression. But it would take more than a decade for the full costs of that effort to be felt, both within the United States and abroad.

Domestically, sky-high interest rates didn't just kill inflation; they devastated the nation's banks, especially its savings and loan associations, or S&Ls, which specialize in home mortgages. Although the interest rates they received on already-issued mortgages were fixed, the interest rates paid to depositors soared, and the S&Ls were effectively bankrupted. This should have been clear by 1985 or so; indeed, the problem might have been acknowledged and addressed at that time, if the federal government had not resorted to a bit of accounting flimflam in order to disguise reality. The Reagan administration decided to save the banks by helping them "discover" billions of dollars worth of hitherto-unsuspected assets. This was accomplished by permitting the banks to assign a hefty value on the current balance sheet to their "goodwill"—their anticipated future profits. But, of course, paper changes do not alter reality: the banks were still obliged to pay out more to their depositors than they were getting from their loans. One more ingredient was required—one which also required faulty accounting. Reagan had been pushing deregulation, and by allowing banks to invest in new and risky areas—even buying junk bonds—there was the hope that the higher associated profits would enable them to climb their way of the hole in which the Fed had left them, pulling themselves back from the brink of insolvency, at no apparent cost to anyone! Of course, with good accounting procedures, the banks would have had to set aside reserves commensurate with the new risks that were being undertaken, reflecting the higher probability of default; but the objective was not good economics, good accounting, or good lending practices, but putting off the day of reckoning to someone else's watch. By "gambling on resurrection"—making high-risk, high-interest loans—they stood a chance of survival.[4]

With their backs against the wall, the S&Ls began throwing loans at the real estate industry. Reagan's 1981 tax "reform" compounded matters, bestowing rapid depreciation allowances and other big breaks on real estate investors, who, shrewdly assessing the new rules as too good to last, decided to take full advantage of them in the here and now. Real estate tax shelters mushroomed, and useless office towers rose in city after city. By the mid-1980s, vacancy rates for commercial real estate in some metropolitan areas were surpassing 30 percent. Then, under mounting criticism for its tax largesse, the Reagan administration shifted course with the 1986 tax reform, which not only took away the huge benefits but imposed tight restrictions on tax shelters.

Just as the 1981 tax law had fed the boom, the 1986 law accelerated the inevitable bust. Without the tax breaks, the real estate bubble burst. Prices weakened, mortgages went into default, and the high-flyers crashed. By 1988, the S&Ls weren't just sick; they needed intensive care. And they got it, in the form of huge bailouts from the government. But President Reagan had accomplished what he had perhaps intended; it took almost a decade for the mistakes of the early eighties—the exorbitant interest rates, the mindless deregulation, and the whimsical accounting techniques—to become fully manifest and need to be dealt with. This was part of Reagan's legacy to his former vice president, George H. W. Bush, who had to bail out the banks, at a high cost to the federal budget—more than $100 billion—and the national economy; for in a slowly unfolding way, it set the stage for the recession that was to follow two years later.

Global impacts of U.S. monetary policy

There was another consequence of the Fed's exorbitant increases in interest rates in its fight against inflation: not only was America's savings and loan industry destroyed but so was much of Latin America. Throughout the seventies, the countries of Latin America had been encouraged to borrow the petrodollars that oil-producing states had parked in banks in the United States and Europe. They borrowed billions. Latin American debt to commercial banks increased at a cumulative annual rate of 20 percent, far faster than GDP, so that by 1981 their total foreign borrowing was almost 40 percent of GDP.[5]

It was no wonder then that when the U.S. Fed raised interest rates to an unprecedented level in 1981, the Latin American nations had difficulty meeting their obligations. Country after country defaulted between 1981 and 1983. One of the Fed governors at the time described to me his dismay at the lack of concern of the Fed for the global consequences of its actions. In its defense, the Fed claimed that its mandate requires that it focus on the consequences for the United States.

But although America may have advanced its own short-term economic interests, our blithe seeming indifference to the impact on Latin America undermined our nation's claim to global leadership. The defaults in Latin America also led to a weakening of America's banking system, and thus to a weakening of the U.S. economy as well.

The 1991 recession

Still, it was the 1988–89 S&L crisis that had the more profound effect on our economy. In the aftermath of that crisis, the Bush administration imposed tight new banking regulations, which discouraged risky investments and, at least in this one area, partially reversed the deregulation of the Reagan era. The result, as intended, was to put the banks back on a sounder footing, reducing the likelihood of another bailout in the future. But there was also a darker consequence—one that few people foresaw. As banks worked to get their balance sheets back in order and conform to the new regulations, they cut back on their lending. The flow of capital dried up—as did, gradually, the U.S. economy itself. By failing to grasp the underlying source of this problem, the Fed made it worse. A subtle mistake in banking regulations—the decision to treat long-term government bonds, highly sensitive to changes in interest rates, as if they were perfectly safe—further encouraged the banks to put their money into these bonds, rather than do what banks are supposed to do: make funds available for business to expand and create jobs.

The Fed's failure to forestall the 1991 recession

As the economy sank into recession, the Fed eventually lowered interest rates in 1991, but not quickly enough. The recession was, in a sense, the final act of a tragedy that originated with the interest rate increases of the early eighties, the tax giveaway of 1981 and the poorly designed financial sector deregulation carried out under Ronald Reagan. And though the recession was described by many as short and shallow, it didn't feel that way to the 3.5 million people added to the unemployment pool between 1990 and 1992, or to the millions more who lost their jobs and eventually found alternative, lower-paying jobs. Indeed, a close look at the data shows that the downturn was serious: measured by the gap between the economy's potential and its actual performance, the 1991 recession was as bad as the average postwar downturn.

Bill Clinton owed his election, in large part, to the faltering economy and the Fed's failure to address it in time. When Clinton took office in January 1993, unemployment was 7.3 percent, while GDP in the first quarter of that year was actually shrinking (at -0.1 percent). Exacerbated by the recession, the budget deficit had swollen to

4.7 percent of GDP in 1992, up from 2.8 percent in 1989. It was clear that the economy had not been managed well.

The Struggle to Reduce the Deficit

President Clinton was persuaded to make deficit reduction his number one priority. This meant, of course, putting aside much of the social agenda that had motivated him and most of his followers. He even put aside qualms about whether the strategy would work: as I've said, standard economics held that deficit reduction would slow down the recovery and increase unemployment. Those of us advising Clinton were, of course, aware that reducing the deficit was traditionally thought to worsen the economy, and if that happened, the whole strategy could backfire: slower growth would lead to even larger deficits. That's why we tried, as much as possible, to "backload" the deficit reduction—to ensure greater deficit reduction in future years. By then, we hoped the economy would be in strong enough shape to withstand the impact.

It was a risky policy, particularly for a president who had been elected on a platform of "Jobs! Jobs! Jobs!" Seemingly, under the pressure of politics and time, the Clinton economists had overturned a half century of economic research. For decades, conservatives had tried to slay Keynes and his call for government intervention in times of economic downturn. Here, in a short span, we band of Clinton economists, the so-called New Democrats, accomplished what the conservatives had for so long failed to do; for the economy did recover, and deficit reduction was given the credit.

Was Keynes really dead? Did the textbooks need to get rewritten? Were smaller government and deficits the key to economic success? If the standard interpretation of history prevails, the answer appears to be yes.

Those committed to deficit reduction came up with a new theory. Deficit reduction, it was hoped, would lead to lower long-term interest rates, and lower long-term interest rates would lead to increased investment, and increased investment would reignite the economy. Our hope was that this time, the way we had carefully structured the deficit reduction, increased investment from lower long-term interest rates would more than offset the direct effect of higher taxes and lower government expenditures.

But there were several problems with this theory, besides the obvious one noted earlier that it flew in the face of theory, evidence, and what was taught in every course in macroeconomics in the world. If the bond markets believed the deficits would decline in the future, interest rates would come down. We had put ourselves at the mercy of the mercurial bond markets, those same people who at times exhibited irrational exuberance, and at others irrational pessimism. Our fortunes would be determined by the judgments of the bond traders—overwhelmingly hostile to Clinton and his tax increases—about whether we would or could carry through on our deficit reduction commitment. This made none of us, including the president, any too comfortable. And if the president had seen the statistical evidence which showed that investment often did not respond much to interest rates—a fact which we saw in 1991, and we have seen in 2001, as the Fed has repeatedly lowered interest rates—he should, and would, have felt even more nervous.

Why deficit reduction worked this time

If deficit reductions in general should have slowed the recovery, to what can we attribute the recovery's vigor? To a sequence of events that was neither expected beforehand nor fully understood as it unfolded. By lowering the deficit, the Clinton administration ended up recapitalizing a number of American banks; it was this inadvertent act, as much as anything, that refueled the economy.

Here is how it worked: Following the savings and loan debacle, new regulations were adopted, requiring banks to maintain adequate capital on which to draw in case their loan portfolios weakened. The amount of capital banks need, of course, is related to the extent of the risk they assume. Economists who were thinking about the problem, including Michael Boskin, agreed that risk, in this context, went beyond the possibility of bankruptcy: there was also the danger of a decrease in the value of the assets. From this perspective, long-term government bonds are risky, even if there is no chance of default, because they can decrease in worth when interest rates rise. But even as the government was imposing tighter standards on banks in 1989, the Fed decided to allow banks to treat long-term government bonds as risk-free. This made the banks happy, of course, for it increased their short-term profitability, since long-term bonds yield high returns. By using deposit funds to purchase long-term bonds, they were able to generate very handsome profits. (In 1991, for instance, long-term government bonds were yielding 8.14 percent. Treasury bills, meanwhile, averaged only 5.4 percent, and rates on certificates of deposit were typically far lower.) But this was a very dangerous strategy. If interest rates had risen—and they might well have done so if the runaway deficits had continued—bond prices could have plummeted, leaving the federal government to pick up the pieces a second time around.

Thus, once again, overaggressive accounting led to deceptive information, faulty decisions, and serious consequences for the U.S. economy. Long-term bonds yield higher interest rates than short-term bonds to compensate investors for the risk of a fall in value. But the Fed had signed off on a mode of accounting and a set of regulations that did not reflect this risk at all. And it was this that made the strategy "profitable." The banks should probably have been forced to continue setting aside reserves in order to protect themselves against the risk of a drop in the price of long-term government bonds, but they were not, and they did not.

Fortunately, owing in part to Clinton's success in cutting the deficit, long-term interest rates fell sharply, from over 9 percent in September 1990 to under 6 percent by October 1994. The price of long-term bonds increased. As a consequence of their risky game, the banks saw a sharp improvement in their balance sheets. And because long-term interest rates were now low, making long-term bonds a less attractive investment, the banks began to look elsewhere for profits. They went back to their real business, which is lending. It was the banks' increased readiness to give credit that made the real difference, and it was the Clinton administration's deficit reduction plan, and its inadvertent effect of recapitalizing the S&Ls, that got the economy back on track.

Deficit reduction might be described, then, as a lucky mistake—a right decision made for the wrong reasons. And its success rested on another lucky mistake—the Fed's failure to jack up interest rates during the early stages of the recovery, as the Fed would surely have done if it hadn't underestimated the recovery's strength, just as it had seriously underestimated the force of the decline that preceded it.

The Confidence Game: An alternative explanation

So deficit reduction worked, but the process was complicated and unexpected—and inconveniently at odds with the beliefs and self-interest of powerful people and institutions, whose true agenda was to overturn Keynesian economics and/or to downsize the government. By cutting the deficit, it was said, the administration had restored the confidence of bankers and investors—a confidence shaken by the government's loose-spending ways. Thus reassured, business went back to investing in growth and innovation, consumers began spending again, and the recovery gained momentum. The agenda of the deficit hawks was clear: keep deficits low (even in recessions) and listen to what the financial markets want—for if you alienate them, you are lost.

There is a kernel of truth in this oft-told interpretation, which focuses on confidence, but the lesson that should be drawn is surely more guarded. We spent much of our time trying to build confidence, or, to put it less politely, "spinning" the statistics to emphasize our policy successes. But it was not the smoke and mirrors of earlier administrations, whose tax cuts were going to pay for themselves, and then some, through the burst of output they would inspire. Our projections were realistic; even so we worked hard to make sure that the economy outperformed these projections. Take the 8 million jobs that Clinton had promised to create, a promise on which he more than delivered—creating 16 million in eight years. We did not create the jobs; the American economy did, and almost any recovery worthy of that name would have met the objective. If the economy failed to generate at least 8 million jobs, unemployment would be so high as to make Bill Clinton all but unreelectable. A benchmark was set that we were almost sure to attain, if we managed the economy well. Still, it was a meaningful benchmark, especially to those who got the jobs—5.5 million new jobs during the first two years of the Clinton administration alone. That exceeded our target by a wide margin and was certainly far better than the more than 2 million jobs lost at the *beginning* of the second Bush administration.

In other ways as well, we worked hard to shape public opinion and market sentiment. As the monthly economic data came out, dramatizing an impressive record of lower unemployment and stable inflation, we used these occasions to help reporters understand just why it was that the economy could now withstand lower unemployment without fueling inflation. We did our best to enable the press to interpret the numbers in ways consistent with our calm view of the inflation threat. Though the setting of interest rates was the duty of an independent Federal Reserve, the Fed, in truth, was fixated on inflation; behind the scenes, we were working to convince the markets and public opinion—and Alan Greenspan—that inflation was well under control. The truth was on our side, which made our task much easier.

That's the all-important point. We would not have been able to convince the people and the markets for long if truth had been against us. Confidence matters, but it can't be whipped up out of thin air. It was the recovering economy that gave confidence, not the other way around. Confidence can be a very useful source of positive "feedback"; but without an underlying basis for recovery—let us suppose, for instance, that the banks had not been recapitalized, that they had not been enabled and induced to lend more, so that the "direct" negative impact of the deficit reduction was not offset by a positive indirect investment effect—no amount of cheerleading can alter reality.

Over the years, I have become convinced that the confidence argument is the last refuge of those who cannot find better arguments: when there is no direct evidence that deficits directly promote recovery or adversely affect growth, then they do so because of confidence. When there is no direct evidence that lower tax rates stimulate growth, then they do so because of confidence. The reason that so many find the confidence argument so attractive is that it is so difficult to refute. We can measure deficits and assess their impact on growth; we can measure tax rates and assess their impact on growth. But confidence is too elusive to measure accurately.[6] Thus, the businessman-turned-politician can assert his firsthand knowledge of how business thinks—and not be challenged.

Deficit Reduction in Retrospect

By now a number of books have described Clinton's courage and discipline in fighting for deficit reduction. He had run for office, he had thought, to make social changes—to reform welfare and the health care system, to improve education and job training, to advance civil rights; but he had succeeded because his focus on the economy had resonated with voters. Deficit reduction was only one of several things that needed to be done to make the economy more vibrant. In spite of the much-vaunted "supply-side" reforms of the Reagan era—the lowering of taxes and deregulation—that were supposed to accelerate growth, long-term growth was still just over half of what it had been in the fifties and sixties. And because what growth had occurred had mostly benefited the richest Americans, while those at the bottom actually saw their real incomes decline, America faced growing inequality.

Inequality and growth were *our* concerns. Fiscal responsibility was supposed to be the province of the conservative Republicans, but after twelve years of fiscal profligacy, a tax cut that Reagan said would pay for itself through energizing the economy but did not, it was left to Clinton to do the dirty work, without the help of the Republicans, who voted unanimously against Clinton's deficit reduction plan. Their opposition confirmed the more diabolic interpretation of the Reagan tax cuts. They didn't really believe in supply-side economics, the theory that the tax cut would spur the economy so much that tax revenues would actually increase. Instead, they knew that there would be shortfalls, and they hoped that the shortfalls would force a cutback in government spending. The true agenda was thus to force large cutbacks in the size of the government—and since Reagan pushed big increases in military expenditures and did little to cut the subsidies for corporations, this meant that there would have to be huge cutbacks in other public services. But having set the process in motion, the Republicans never could follow through with the cutbacks in services so they never brought the deficit under control.[7] Voodoo economics had not worked, and political courage only went so far: it was easier to cut taxes than to cut expenditures. Having tarred the Democrats as "tax and spend" as Clinton took office, it was perhaps the Republicans' hope that they could once again blame the Democrats for the deficits. But Clinton surprised them: he proposed not only cutting expenditures but raising taxes. The cost of adjustment would be shared.

Analytically, reducing the deficit is an easy matter: cut expenditures and increase taxes. But neither is politically palatable. Although Bush's 1992 defeat was largely due to the economy's poor performance, his limited tax increases—after his pledge not to do so—had also been politically costly. Clinton bravely not only decided to cut spending but also to increase taxes—mostly on the rich, who had reaped the lion's share of economic gains over the previous two decades. Even after the tax increase, they would be far better off than they had been a short while earlier, a far cry from the decline in income among the poor. Not surprisingly, the opposition was intense: Republicans insisted that the taxes would put a crimp on economic growth. They didn't; and indeed the rich continued to get richer in comparison to the rest of the population. It was an act of political bravery—a political risk that paid off, but as we have seen, for reasons quite different from those we, and its advocates, thought at the time.

Clinton even proposed a brilliant new idea: why not start taxing "bads"—pollution—rather than "goods"—hard work and savings? But the polluters, those who emitted the greenhouse gases that are leading to global warming, with the resultant erratic weather patterns that have caused such damage in recent years, not surprisingly would have none of that. The energy companies joined with the automobile manufacturers and the coal industry—a broad array of vested interests—to convert what would have been a broad-based tax that would have increased our energy independence and our economic efficiency at the same time that it improved the atmosphere into a puny 4.3 cent gasoline tax.

Deficit reduction gave drama to the early months of the Clinton administration. It was the good guys versus the bad, the fiscally responsible against the fiscally irresponsible. As New Democrats, we felt our political future required that we lay to rest the "tax and spend" image of Democrats—though it did less to change voter perceptions than we had hoped and little to change the Republican rhetoric.

Did we push deficit reduction too far?

Yet, beyond these issues of partisan politics, from today's vantage point, I believe we pushed deficit reduction too far, and unless we understand how to think about deficits, economic policies in the future will be distorted—and economic prosperity will be at risk. As time went on, even the Clinton administration and its Treasury seemed to get more and more muddled about the role of deficit reduction. If deficit reduction had brought us out of our recession, then other countries with recessions should also reduce their deficit, and this was the policy, at our urging, that the IMF imposed on developing countries, with such disastrous results, especially in East Asia and Latin America. But when it came to Europe and Japan—whose growth had an enormous impact on our exports and thus on our growth—we weren't so convinced. I chaired the Economic Policy Committee of the Organization of Economic Cooperation and Development (OECD), the group of industrial countries which got together to share experiences and put peer pressure on each other to undertake "good" economic policies. In the mid-nineties, there was robust growth in the emerging markets, but not in the advanced industrial countries, and America repeatedly urged these countries to undertake more expansionary *macropolicies*. They needed structural reforms, in their labor laws, for instance; but our view was that that was not enough. We repeatedly called upon Japan and Europe to stimulate their economy. America's view was clear: Japan needed more deficit spending, more macroeconomic stimulation.

For an economy facing an economic downturn, the benefit of, say, increasing expenditures enormously exceeds the costs, even if the expenditures are entirely financed by deficits, and that is especially the case when the expenditures are high-return investments. When the economy is operating below capacity—in a recession—$100 billion of increased expenditure will typically give rise to a much larger increase in GDP (this is called the multiplier). For simplicity, assume it is around $200 billion. One of the major lessons of modern economics is that growth begets growth: if the economy is larger today, it is likely to be larger next year, and the year after. Higher growth stimulates more research, more investment. To be conservative, assume that only half of the $200 billion gain is permanent. That means that the $100 billion investment today yields a $100 billion permanent increase in GDP in addition to the $200 billion gained immediately. The country, however, has a higher debt, and for America, that means borrowing $100 billion from abroad, at say 6 percent. In short, we send $6 billion to foreigners every year—leaving us with $94 billion more at home.

It might be useful to run through a thought experiment: what would have happened if we had had a far more modest deficit reduction? In economics, we can't run real experiments, we can't rerun history, so we can never be sure of our conclusions. Yet when we make statements like, "Deficit reduction was critical," what we presumably mean is that matters would have turned out differently—and for the worse—had we done otherwise.

We need to begin with a general lesson often lost sight of in the midst of an economic downturn: every downturn comes to an end. Economic policy does make a difference; it can make a downturn shorter or longer, shallower or deeper. It can make the expansion longer. But economic fluctuations have marked capitalism since the beginning; every boom busts, and every recession is followed by a recovery.

We can thus be confident that had we had less deficit reduction, we would still eventually have had a recovery. We cannot simply observe that the deficit was reduced and the economy recovered, and say that the deficit reduction *caused* the recovery. Deficit reduction accelerated the decline in interest rates, which helped recapitalize the banks. But interest rates would have fallen anyway. They were falling even before Clinton took office. The forces taming inflation—weaker unions, increased international competition, increasing productivity—were already at play, and it was the lower inflation as well as the deficit reduction that lowered long-term interest rates.

These same forces would then have led to the boom that marked the nineties. Maybe the boom would have started a little later, though maybe it would have started a little earlier. But in retrospect, again, a slightly more moderate boom might have stood the economy in good stead in the long run.

The one argument on the other side is related to the mystical word "confidence" discussed earlier. Without deficit reduction, there would be worries that the United States would become another banana republic, a country in which both spending and deficits are out of control. What businessmen in their right minds would invest in such a country?—so the argument went. I find such arguments unpersuasive. One of the richest, and fastest-growing, parts of the world is Northern Italy, a country with a debt to GDP ratio in excess of 100 percent.

While different people find their confidence inspired by different policies—some worry about deficits, some about high tax rates levied to reduce the deficit, some about social unrest that often comes when there is underinvestment in social expenditures—nothing inspires confidence more than growth. If deficits do stimulate the economy, as traditional economics argues, then deficits—moderate and structured to phase out as the economy is restored to health—are the best way to restore confidence.

The technological innovations—the computer revolution—and the process of globalization, changes in the economy that were proceeding before Clinton took office, and that would be little affected by deficit reduction, were making it more attractive to invest in America. It was these *real* changes in the economy, combined with restrained wage growth, that led to high profits and profitability, not some mystical notion of confidence.

If this argument is correct, if the real changes in the economy, the improvements in technology, the opening up of markets in the process of globalization, were what was really driving the recovery, *then the deficit would have been reduced significantly even had Clinton cut back expenditures a little less.*

Assume, for instance, that Clinton had used the additional funds to finance more investments in R&D, technology, infrastructure, and education. Given the high returns for these investments, GDP in the year 2000 would have been higher, and the economy's growth potential would have been stronger.

Of course, our national debt would be higher, but so too would our national assets. The problem is that our accounting framework recognizes our liabilities (our debt) but not our assets. If the returns in these vital investments are as high as calculations suggest they are, the cutbacks in these investments that deficit reduction forced made our country poorer. Wise investors would recognize that *eventually* we would have to make up for our infrastructure deficit, just as *eventually* we might have to pay back any borrowings. They would have recognized that in either case when the day of reckoning came, taxes might be raised. But if the investments yielded a return in excess of the low rate at which government borrowed, and the government could appropriate those returns, taxes on the rest of the economy might actually be reduced.

There were many investment opportunities in the public sector with very high economic and social returns that we had to pass up. I mentioned in the last chapter that we were living off the fruits of earlier investments in basic research. For two decades, the United States has underinvested in infrastructure, to the point where problems in our air traffic control systems, our bridges, and our roads are beginning to turn up. Eventually, such underinvestments in the public sector will hurt returns to investment in the private. So, too, we underinvested in our inner cities. When the Council of Economic Advisers proposed a modest program to improve the dilapidated conditions of some of our inner-city schools, Treasury, with its fixation on deficit reduction, spoke against the idea. Poor schools were contributing to the continuing problems that plagued our inner cities and that get reflected in high crime, which makes investment there unattractive—a vicious circle which has led America to be a world leader (for a country of our income) in so many dimensions about which we should not be proud, such as one of the highest prison populations in the Western world as well as the highest infant mortality rates.

We were tempted to give in to the shortsightedness of the financial markets—and we did. Some of the budget shenanigans would become apparent within years. When we privatized the U.S. Enrichment Corporation (USEC), the corporation which enriched uranium (low enriched uranium is used for nuclear reactors, highly enriched uranium for making atomic bombs), we may have jeopardized our national security, the cost of which is hard to ascertain. But at a far more mundane level, the sale improved the federal budget in the very short term. However, while we added the revenues we received from the sale, we did not make note of the fact that USEC had been turning in a profit of some $120 million a year, and this flow of dividends would disappear once privatization occurred. The long-run budgetary position of the United States was actually worsened. But shortsighted financial markets evidently did not make these calculations; they took the numbers at face value, and according to the deficit reduction mantra, they felt more and more contented as the bottom line *today* looked better and better—no matter what it meant for the future.[8]

But even if the so-called financial experts cannot seemingly understand the failings of the accounting framework, and are sufficiently shortsighted to overlook glaring deficiencies in our educational, research, or physical infrastructure, we should not be so foolish or shortsighted. In the long run, the truth will out. Eventually, deficiencies in infrastructure, in research, or in education cannot be ignored.

There is in this three simple lessons. The first two resonate with themes we will see repeatedly: bad accounting frameworks provide bad information and lead to bad economic decisions; and the so-called wizards of the financial market are remarkably myopic: put too much trust in them at your peril. The third is that deficit reduction is normally not only *not* a solution to a short-run economic downturn; it may even be bad for long-run economic growth. The circumstances of 1992 were unusual; normally, deficit reduction will not lead to an economic recovery.

This latter lesson is of particular relevance to Europe, which has seen its economic policies constrained by the stability pact, limiting the size of government deficits. Deficit hawks have preached the notion that fiscal austerity—cutting back expenditures and raising taxes—will restore confidence, and this in turn will restore economic health. Rejecting the overwhelming evidence that expansionary fiscal policy is the medicine needed in an economic downturn, they have echoed the chorus suggesting that Keynes is dead. Meanwhile, as a result of these doctrines, the economic downturn that began in 2001 lingers on, and as this book goes to press, there appears a reasonable chance that at least some parts of Europe will face recession. Even the European Central Bank has sounded the warnings of deflation. Deficit reduction has not brought recovery to Europe, nor is it likely to.

In the developing world, too, this lesson has enormous resonance. Many developing countries have effectively been forced to engage in deficit reduction measures as they go into a downturn, and repeatedly these measures have only exacerbated the downturns—in Korea, Thailand, Indonesia, and Argentina, to give but a small sample of recent failures. Sometimes, it is the IMF, wedded to pre-Keynesian ideas—and finding support in the Clinton administration's deficit reduction rhetoric—which has forced them to do the opposite of what they know to be in their best interests. Sometimes, it is simply that they cannot get the funds to finance the deficits. Of course, this was why the IMF was founded, under the intellectual aegis of Keynes: to provide countries with the money necessary for expansionary fiscal policy in an economic downturn. But the IMF has forgotten its original mission, and seemingly become more interested in ensuring the repayment of foreign loans than in helping the poor countries sustain their economy at as close to full employment as possible.

Today, we live in an odd world in which supposedly fiscally conservative Republicans are claiming that deficits do not matter—they have become today's Keynesians—while the Democrats, proud of their 1992 victory, are preaching deficit reduction, even in times of recession! Similar debates are occurring in Europe, with the right advocating the breaking of the stability pact, and many social democrats adhering to the budget limits. The Democrats are correct that in the long run, deficits hamper growth, that they can but do not necessarily stimulate the economy in the short run. Bush's 2001 tax cuts provided long-run deficits, but without enough short-run stimulation to restore the economy's strength—thus failing in both the short and the long run. Carefully targeted deficit spending, by contrast, could have stimulated the economy in the short run and strengthened growth in the long run.

CHAPTER 3

The All-Powerful Fed and Its Role in Inflating the Bubble

I T WAS AT a black-tie event in Washington in December 1996 that Alan Greenspan first uttered those attention-getting words, "irrational exuberance." Greenspan had been invited to address a gathering sponsored by the American Enterprise Institute, a conservative Washington think tank, and to receive the Institute's prestigious Francis Boyer Award. It was an impressive, wide-ranging speech, though Greenspan had so trained himself to speal enigmatically like the Delphic oracle—what came to be called "Fedspeak"—that it made the eyes of those untrained in deciphering what he meant, or might have meant, glaze over. One of the topics on which he touched was the sudden plunge in real estate prices that had triggered Japan's descent into a broad state of economic paralysis. It was hard to put a precise value on something like real estate, Greenspan observed, and therefore hard to know when a speculative market might be due for a sudden contraction. It was also hard, he added, to know when such a contraction might prove to be a disaster for the economy at large. Greenspan had no answers that night, only questions; but one of his questions made a memorable impression: "How do we know," he asked, "when irrational exuberance has unduly inflated asset values . . . ?"

As Fed chairman, Greenspan had cultivated the ability to "mumble with great incoherence," as he once put it. He mumbled because his words carried enormous weight, in the financial markets especially. Indeed, Greenspan's "irrational exuberance" comments, vague and timid as they might have sounded to a layperson, set off a minor panic. When I approached him after his speech to discuss several of the ideas that he had thrown out, it was clear that he was fixated on the "irrational exuberance" remark. He knew that the pundits would know that it was the United States rather than Japan that he had in mind. He was worried about the stock market, which was having a blowout year—or so it seemed as the Dow climbed from 5,000 to 6,500 (when it reached 12,000 a little more then three years later, the gains of '96 would no longer be remembered as such a big deal). And if Greenspan was worried, the business and financial world had reason to worry. The following day, stock markets reeled in Tokyo, Sydney, Hong Kong, Amsterdam, and London, as well as New York. Shares of General Motors, IBM, and Dupont all fell by 2 percent or more as investors steeled themselves for a possible interest rate increase.

And then . . . nothing happened. The Labor Department released statistics indicating slow job growth; signs of inflation failed to materialize, even later when unemployment continued its downward march; the Fed did not in fact raise interest rates; and the stock market continued to climb, setting records with almost boring regularity for the next four years, until the bubble burst.

What exactly had Greenspan been up to? If he thought share prices were heading out of control—if he feared the wider effects of a bubble—why didn't he go ahead and *act*? A glimmer of an answer was provided, five years later, by the release of the minutes of a 1996 meeting of the Fed;[1] in conversation with his fellow board members, Greenspan had discussed his bubble-related concerns, as well as his arguments for inaction. Bubbles *are* dangerous, because when they burst—and they *always* do—they can leave havoc in their wake, as Japan so aptly showed. Households, feeling poorer, would cut back on their consumption; some might even be forced into bankruptcy. Firms which counted as part of their wealth investments in other firms would also suddenly find themselves poorer, less able and willing to borrow and invest. The job of the Fed was to stabilize the economy; and unless the air could be let out from the bubble slowly, there was a real risk of a major downturn. The problem was how to let the air out of the bubble—without collateral damage. Higher interest rates, Greenspan had suggested, wouldn't necessarily be an effective response to the problem, and the consequences wouldn't be limited to the stock market, in any case. Higher interest rates could slow down the entire economy—precisely the outcome that deflating the bubble was supposed to forestall.

There was an alternative, far less costly approach: perhaps, merely by speaking out on the subject, he could inspire enough of a market correction to make further measures unnecessary. In short, it seemed he had hoped to tame the bubble—and save the nation from a bubble-bursting—*by words alone*.

As events would, in time, very clearly show, Greenspan had overestimated his influence. Words alone did not do the trick. In fairness to him, however, at the time others, too, seemed to credit the Fed chairman with superhuman powers. The effort to promote Greenspan for economic policy sainthood has lost some impetus in the past few years. With the economy officially declared in recession in March 2001, it became clear that the economic cycle hadn't ended, after all. The Fed was perhaps not quite as masterful as its proponents had claimed. After the boom of the nineties, most of its strong supporters had forgotten its earlier dismal performance in the recession of 1990–91, but once again, in the beginning of the new millennium, it seemed that the Fed had failed to sustain the economy's growth.

This book is not intended to grade our economic leaders, but to

understand how the 1990s set the stage for the bust that followed—
and in the process to explain a little bit about economics, to help us
extract some lessons so that we are not doomed to repeat the failures
of the past. Among those lessons: we put too much faith in words, in
mystical notions of confidence, in the so-called wisdom of financial
markets; we paid too little attention to the underlying *real* economics. We relied more on faith than on economic science, as imperfect
as our knowledge may be. And in doing so, we put some particular
interests over others.

Words versus reality

There were, in fact, three remarkable aspects of the "irrational exuberance" speech and its aftermath. The first is that when the speech
failed—as almost surely could have been predicted—to lead to a
long-term deflation of the bubble, there was no next step, no other
action: the bubble continued to grow unchecked. This is an issue to
which I will return later in the chapter.

The second is, had the speech worked, what its success would have
said about market participants. The image of financial market participants is that they are keen analysts, finely honing their calculations, looking beneath the substance at what is really going on—that
is, at least, the image that they would like to project. But here
Greenspan was saying, in effect, that by just reminding them of the
fact that there are bubbles, they would all of a sudden redo their calculations, reassess their judgments, and decide that Enron or GM or
Amazon was worth less than they had previously thought. Was
Greenspan assuming that *they* assumed that he had so much more
knowledge about the world than they did that a quiet word from him
would lead them to completely redo their calculations? This hardly
seemed plausible. Alternatively, he might have assumed that they
would have thought he was hinting in an even more veiled way than
usual that he might be forced to raise interest rates. But this, too,

seemed implausible—for it was widely recognized that raising interest rates was much too blunt an instrument for letting the air out of a bubble.

Greenspan was conservative, and for a central bank to use interest rate policy to control the stock market would have been truly revolutionary. In a sense, I had a little more confidence in the markets: to me, the quick reaction of the market was not a surprise; they are mercurial; but the fact was that a few days later, *real events*—new data—again dominated the scene. His words had only a fleeting effect. The problem with those who are immersed in the financial market is that a day, or a week, is a long time; they focus on the here and now. Moving the market—if even for a day—is a big deal: fortunes can be made and lost. But for the economist, this is largely (though not entirely) a sideshow. Few real decisions depend on these short-term vagaries of the market. So what if Greenspan moved the market, and the Dow Jones Index had a bad day? A week later, the only legacy was the words themselves, a truly memorable phrase.

Irrational exuberance and market efficiency

Greenspan, like many of his compatriots on Wall Street, has a strong belief in markets. I am not sure that, in emphasizing the market's irrational exuberance (he could have stressed as well its frequent irrational pessimism), he realized the extent to which he had in fact joined some of its most vocal critics.

Prices are critical to confidence in a market economy. They serve as signals guiding the allocation of resources. If prices are based on *information*—information about what is sometimes called the "fundamentals," or basic facts, of a given market (the conditions of that particular sector of the economy, the management of the firms in the sector, the quality of its labor force and their propensity to strike, and so on), then the decisions made on the basis of those prices will be sound ones: resources will be well allocated, and the economy will grow. If prices are basically random, based on the irrational whims of market speculators, changed by a word thrown one way or another by a government official, then investment will go helter-skelter. Here was Greenspan, one of the market economy's strongest advocates, seemingly agreeing with longstanding critics that prices—the prices of the moment, at any rate—were partly, perhaps largely, based on whim.

There had long been a debate within the economics profession about the efficiency of capital markets. Some described the stock market as a rich man's gambling casino. John Maynard Keynes (in an era when the analogy would not have been censored for lack of political correctness) compared it to forecasting the winner of a beauty contest: the object is to choose, not the most beautiful woman, but the woman likely to be declared most beautiful by the judges.[2]

The seemingly random nature of stock markets is, of course, consistent either with very inefficient markets, in which prices just move willy-nilly, say in response to all kinds of extraneous events, or very efficient markets, in which prices reflect all the available information about the fundamentals. For if market prices reflect all available information, they change only in response to what is *unexpected*, to "new news." But you can't predict what the news that will move the markets may be, so the markets are by their nature inherently unpredictable.

One of the commonly observed implications of *efficient* markets in which prices reflect all the relevant information is that you can't beat the market. Mutual funds spend millions on research, but, as study after study has demonstrated, most of them do no better at stock picking than they might by throwing darts at a dartboard.[3] This presents two conundrums: why then do market participants waste money paying people to pick stocks? And if all information is essentially instantaneously reflected in prices, then *rational* investors would never spend money gathering information, and so the only information that would be reflected in the price is that which people happen to come by without spending any money.[4]

Over the years, there is increasing evidence that markets, in one way or another, often do not work well. Even if, over time, share prices stand in some reasonable relation to information—to fundamentals—their ups and downs frequently don't.

Consider October 19, 1987. On that day, the stock market fell by 23 percent; nearly a quarter of Corporate America's capital was erased, in other words. Yet, as Robert Shiller of Yale University, among others, has noted, there was no event, no news, that could possibly account for such a precipitous decline. The market was either wildly overvalued on October 18, or wildly undervalued on October 19 (or conceivably still overvalued on October 19). Something was not right. That time, at least, the volatility of the market was essentially *random*; in the next two chapters, I will talk about *systematic* forces—deliberate decisions made by CEOs and by the government—that sent prices spiraling higher and higher in the nineties. Setting these aside, there are other systemic deviations from rationality, sometimes referred to as market anomalies, that those working in the interstices of economics and psychology have uncovered in the last two decades—for instance, that a large fraction of the annual gains in the stock market used to occur in January (a phenomenon naturally termed the *January effect*), though once discovered, it quickly seemed to disappear.[5]

Some of the deviations from fundamentals can persist for a long time—the bubbles in real estate and most recently in technology. When Greenspan talked of "irrational exuberance," it was with these that he was concerned. The random inefficiencies of the market have high costs: too much investment may go into one firm, too little into another. But the costs of bubbles are of a greater order of magnitude, not only during the bubble but even more in its aftermath. During the bubble, of course, all kinds of resources get wasted—in amounts that are often hard to fathom, and make government waste look small by comparison. Take the real estate bubble of the 1980s. As we saw in the last chapter, it partly led to the collapse of the savings and loan associations, costing the government—the American taxpayer—more than $100 billion. Further costs were borne by banks that did not go bankrupt, and by investors in banks that did. To these costs have to be added the *macroeconomic costs* to society as a whole in the recessions which so frequently follow the bursting of the bubble. Assume, as the result of a bubble, that the economy performs 2 percent below its potential for two years (it looks as though the losses from the dot-com bust will be even greater). In a $10 trillion economy, this means a total dollar cost of the *aftermath* of the bubble in the neighborhood of $400 billion. Even a rich country can ill afford to throw such sums away. Many thought that it was the responsibility of the Fed not only to prevent inflation but to stabilize the economy, and stabilizing the economy meant doing something about the bubble. Clearly, it failed. The failure is all the more puzzling because Greenspan had recognized that there was a bubble in 1996, and seemingly had tried to do something about it. But if there was a bubble in 1996, surely the run-up of the stock market in the final years of the century must have been truly disturbing.

Greenspan rises to his own defense

It was not surprising that in August 2002, with the economy's slump heading into its second year, Greenspan rose to the Fed's defense before an usually friendly audience at the annual meeting of policy-makers and academics in Jackson Hole, Wyoming, sponsored by the Kansas City branch of the Federal Reserve. He recalled that he had considered the problem closely, rejecting action, essentially, for two reasons. In the first place, he hadn't been entirely sure of his diagnosis ("It was very difficult to definitively identify a bubble until after the fact—that is, when its bursting confirmed its existence").[6] In the second place, Greenspan hadn't been sure he possessed an effective remedy. Raising interest rates might well have burst the bubble, but the cost to the general economy could have been huge.

Both halves of this argument are questionable, though they have gone largely unquestioned. To be sure, identifying a bubble before it bursts *is* tricky. If productivity was increasing at an unprecedented rate (as some people argued in the nineties); if it was accompanied by an unprecedented stability in wages and an unprecedented decline in the equity premium (the extra amount that investors demanded to compensate them for the risks of the market—including the risk that prices may be overinflated); then, yes, stock prices might be considered "reasonable," or at least not too badly overinflated. But the longer the boom lasted and the higher prices soared, the less convincing all of this seemed. It is certainly very hard to see how someone who had come close (speaking in Greenspanese) to declaring the existence of a bubble at the end of 1996, when the Standard & Poor's Index stood at 740, could have remained in doubt as late as March 2000, when the S&P hit 1,534. In any case, it was the sort of difficult call that we expect a chairman of the Federal Reserve Board to make.

Greenspan had good reason to be worried that there was a bubble. But contrary to what the Fed chairman said at Jackson Hole in the summer of 2002, there were steps he could have taken to restrain the market without jeopardizing the economy as a whole. Greenspan was probably right to rule out an interest rate increase; but that was never his only option. For one thing, he might have lobbied behind the scenes against the huge capital gains tax cut of 1997, which sent a fresh torrent of investor capital into the markets at a time when a shift in the opposite direction would have been more appropriate.

But Greenspan's authority as Fed chairman gave him another recourse as well: raising margin requirements. Margin requirements govern how much stock people can buy with borrowed money. The present requirements, dating to 1974, are 50 percent: half of any stock purchase can be made with cash, half with credit. If margin requirements are increased, people cannot buy as much stock as they otherwise could. As demand falls, so, under normal circumstances, do prices. Such an action could be expected to dampen a bubble; if done with finesse, increases in the margin requirements might have gradually let the air out of the bubble. As minutes of Fed meetings reveal, this was a possibility that Greenspan himself had raised. As he had said six years earlier, at the September 24, 1996, meeting of the Federal Reserve Board, "I guarantee you that if you want to get rid of the bubble, whatever it is . . . [raising margin requirements] will do it. My concern is that I am not sure what else it will do."[7]

Economies are complicated, and one can never be sure of the full ramifications of any action. But in his Jackson Hole speech, Greenspan offered no explanation for concluding he was wrong in his earlier judgment—that an increase in margin requirements would have been effective—and no hint at what collateral damage might have occurred that could possibly have outweighed the costs which allowing the economy's bubble to run on entailed. Some of those on Wall Street who were gambling with everything they had would have felt the pinch, and perhaps he did not want to hurt them. Perhaps he did not want to be blamed for spoiling the party—there was always the risk that too big an increase in margin requirements would not just have let some of the air out of the bubble, but actually have burst it. Still, the party eventually had to come to an end, and the longer the bubble went on, the more people would be hurt, and the more they would be hurt. (I suspect that there was another reason for his reluctance to use margin requirements. While even most conservatives recognize that markets by themselves often do not achieve macrostability—and agree that the Fed ought to interfere in the economy to do so—they feel uncomfortable when the scope of interventions is expanded beyond its usual instruments. There is no theoretical justification for this position—no reason why interventions should be limited to the banking sector, and indeed some strong arguments why introducing a broader range of instruments and broader interventions in the financial sector would be less distortionary.)

But Greenspan's role may have even been greater: not only did he not speak out against the tax cut that fed the frenzy, not only did he not do what he could have done to tame the market, but after seemingly urging caution, he switched to becoming a cheerleader for the market's boom, almost egging it on, as he repeatedly argued that the New Economy was bringing with it a new era of productivity increases. Yes, productivity was increasing, but was it enough to justify the extent to which stock prices had soared? I doubt whether had he continued to urge caution, it would have made much difference. But clearly, his cheerleading did not help.

Reminiscences

As an economist, I was not surprised at the seeming fallibility of the Fed or its chairman. Indeed, I had been more taken by surprise by the reverence that was accorded to Fed officials during the nineties. These were mortals, being called upon to make very hard decisions, real-time interpretations of a quickly changing economy. We in the Clinton administration prided ourselves on some first-rate appointments: Janet Yellen (who had been my student at Yale), a first-rate economics professor at Berkeley; Alan Blinder (who had been my colleague and co-author at Princeton, and later at the Council of Economic Advisers), one of the country's leading macroeconomists; and Laurence Meyer, of Washington University, one of the country's foremost forecasters. But even if the entire Federal Reserve Board had such credentials, mistakes would have been made. And most of the people who sat and made the critical decisions about whether to raise or lower interest rates simply were not trained to analyze complex economic systems, to use the modern sophisticated statistical techniques to interpret the often hard to understand data, to separate out the ephemeral noise from what was likely to be longer-lasting, though a few without such training developed a remarkable intuitive understanding for the economy.

Economic history is replete with the Fed making not just minor mistakes but major ones. Some economists, such as Nobel Prize winner Milton Friedman, blame the Fed for causing the Great Depression.[8] Whether his judgment is overly harsh or not—and in chapter 1, I criticized his interpretation—there is little doubt that many of the postwar recessions have been caused by the Fed, as it has stepped on the brakes too hard in its fixation that unless it does so, inflation will break out.[9]

Greenspan brought to the Fed enormous talents and experiences, as well as an almost uncanny mastery of data that I saw frequently. There was a monthly lunch with the Fed. Even more important, we in the Council were in charge of transmitting highly sensitive data (on employment, output, wages, etc.) several nights a week from the White House to the Fed. Greenspan often took the time to engage in detailed discussions with us about what he—and we—thought it meant.

Beyond interpreting the data and coming to a conclusion about what he *thought* should be done, Greenspan had to manage a complicated political process. Several on the Federal Open Market Committee (FOMC), the committee of the Federal Reserve System that set monetary policy, were inflation hawks: they always saw inflation around the corner, and were always ready to raise interest rates. Greenspan was far more balanced, and I admired the deftness with which he managed to get his way, even in the face of some hardliners.

I was both fond of and highly indebted to Alan Greenspan. Not long after I assumed chairmanship of the Council of Economic

Advisers, the Republicans, in their budget-cutting orgy, decided to abolish it. Killing us would have done little to balance the budget— our total budget was a few million dollars. But the deficit hawks wanted symbolic victories—a body count of agencies slain. And we were easy prey. After all, we had no vested interests standing behind us. That was why we had been created: an institution inside the White House, staffed neither by politicians nor bureaucrats of the usual sort but citizen–civil servants, people who for the most part had left their jobs at universities and think tanks, who had no incentive other than to serve their country well for a year or two. Fortunately, the Council's institutional credibility, created over the years, served us well at this time of crisis. Senators and congressmen from both sides of the aisle came to our rescue, such as Democrat senator Paul Sar-banes (who later became known for co-authorship of the bill regu-lating the accounting industry in the aftermath of the Arthur Andersen scandal), who had earlier served as counsel for the Coun-cil, and Senator Pete Domenici, the Republican head of the Senate Budget Committee. All of the former heads of the Council rallied, and of these, none was more helpful than Greenspan (who had served as chairman of the Council under President Ford), with his long-standing and deep political connections.

Again, not long after I became chair of the Council, Greenspan passed on to me some avuncular advice one night as he pulled me aside at a Christmas party at my house. It was advice he in turn had received from his mentor, Arthur Burns. Burns had been a professor at Columbia, and became one of the early and powerful chairs of the Council under Eisenhower. Greenspan emphasized that my first and sole responsibility was providing advice to the president, *not* being a public spokesperson for the administration, explaining its position, adding professional credibility to it. He described how Burns had even refused on some occasion to testify before Congress. Of course, much had changed in the almost fifty years since; the field of public relations had developed, and, as I sat in the 7:30 A.M. senior staff meetings, I sometimes reflected on how much of our time was spent trying to manage, and respond to, public opinion. Clinton wanted our advice, but he wanted more than that. Laura Tyson, my predecessor, who had been a professor at Berkeley and went on to become dean of its business school, and still later head of the London Business School, had in fact been a forceful economic spokesperson for the administration. But she maintained, at the same time, her own and the rest of the Council's professional reputation. As we sometimes put it, we spoke the truth, only the truth, but not necessarily all the truth—that is, we felt it more our responsibility to point out the strengths in what we were advocating, not the weaknesses; had we been presenting an academic paper, it would have been incumbent on us to give a more balanced presentation. Greenspan's advice fit in with my perceptions of my relative strengths, and while I spent much time talking and listening to the press, I saw my main role as working inside the White House and with the government agencies, and especially with the economists who had achieved increasing influence in policy.

Greenspan surely knew of the divisions in views that separated me and the Council on the one side, and Treasury, and much of the financial market, on the other. It no doubt served his interests well that I should be in the background. But I took his advice, modified it to our new circumstances, and it served me well: one could often get far more done behind the scenes than out in the public.

The Council was indebted to Greenspan not only for its survival. Most of us were academics, though we had spent much of our lives thinking about public policy issues. But we had much to learn as we came to the practical economics and politics of Washington. We learned, for instance, about "Fedspeak," and even a little about how to manage the press. There were many legendary Greenspan stories, of his working, and getting, his way in Washington, leaving as few fingerprints as possible, enabling him to seem to remain aloof and above politics. In some of the episodes, we had our suspicions, later partially corroborated by others—I say partially corroborated, because the fingerprints were scant; sometimes no one, not even a first-rate investigative reporter like Bob Woodward, could be sure.[10]

Recovery and soft landing

Greenspan-watching was a major activity at the Council and at the White House more generally. Bill Clinton had run for president on a platform of "Jobs! Jobs! Jobs!" But it was clear that this was not Greenspan's major concern; inflation was more his focus.

Deficit reduction was supposed to restore the economy to full employment by leading to lower interest rates, which would stimulate investment. The Fed was supposed to be controlling the interest rates. Why hadn't it continued to reduce interest rates to stimulate the economy? Deficit or no deficit, standard monetary theory tells the Fed to lower interest rates in order to maintain full employment. A higher deficit only means that the level to which interest rates have to be brought to restore full employment is higher than it otherwise would have been. In setting the deficit, the government affects the mix of what the economy produces when it reaches full employment: typically, more government spending leads to less investment by the private sector, and less consumption. There are trade-offs, and hard decisions—for instance, about whether the long returns to investment in basic research by the government are greater than the returns to investment in the private sector—but they're supposed to be left to the political process.

The Federal Reserve's sole responsibility, according to theory, is a technocratic one: to maintain full employment without inflation, or more precisely, to push unemployment as low as possible without igniting increased inflation. That critical level does not depend on the composition of output, and accordingly on whether the deficit is large or small. If the Fed can lower interest rates and if lower interest rates generate more investment, then normally, lower interest rates will lead to more output and lower unemployment. And the lower interest rates would, themselves, contribute to deficit reduction, both because the enormous debt payments of the government would be reduced and because GDP would be higher. So long as unemployment was kept above the critical threshold at which inflation increased, bondholders need not worry about inflation; and indeed, the improved deficit situation combined with the higher levels of investment should make them feel better about the future.[11] Why, I wondered, was the Fed not willing to go ahead and simply lower interest rates still more? Why had economics suddenly been turned on its head, and why could full employment with stable prices only be achieved in a particular way? Why could it only be achieved if Clinton signed on to deficit reduction? I wondered: did the Fed have a political agenda, perhaps the familiar conservative agenda of simply wanting to downsize the government?

As the recovery began, new questions arose. Would the Fed keep interest rates down long enough that there would be a sustained expansion, so that Clinton's promise of 8 million jobs in four years would be fulfilled? I, like others in the White House, worried that the Fed's preoccupation with inflation might lead it to cut the expansion short. While Clinton seemingly had been reined in by his Treasury secretary not to say anything against the bond markets or even to *question* the Fed in public, in the privacy of the Oval Office there was less confidence in both.

As the unemployment rate fell lower and lower, it seemed to me inevitable that the Fed would eventually become worried about incipient inflation. There was a well-established theory which said that there was a rate of unemployment below which inflation would start to increase. The critical unemployment rate was called the NAIRU, the non-accelerating inflation rate of unemployment.[12] At the time, the Fed's econometric models said that the NAIRU was somewhere between 6.0 and 6.2 percent. The models said, in other words, that if unemployment fell below 6.0 or 6.2 percent, inflation would start to rise. As some in the administration argued—and as experience eventually confirmed—rapid changes in the labor market (higher levels of education, weaker unions, a more competitive marketplace, increased productivity, and a slower influx of new workers) had made it possible for the economy to steer clear of inflation while operating at much lower rates of unemployment than in the past. But from our conversations with Fed officials, we knew that they had not fully grasped this—and the evidence was not overwhelming. If one had a single-minded focus on inflation, the risk lay in not doing something as unemployment fell below 6.2 or 6.0 percent. To someone like the president, or me, who worries about jobs, the risk lay on the other side—putting the brakes on the economy before there was firm evidence that inflation was increasing was condemning millions unnecessarily to unemployment, with all the hardships that that entailed.

Unemployment fell through the 6.2 perent barrier, through the 6.0 percent barrier—and the Fed did not raise interest rates. I do not think it was because the Fed had lost confidence in the concept of the NAIRU, or agreed with us that it had suddenly fallen. Nor do I believe it was because the Fed suddenly had a change of heart, and started worrying more about jobs and growth and less about inflation. Rather, given how slow the recovery had been, and even when it did occur, how slowly unemployment had fallen in what was called the jobless recovery, they were taken by surprise by the seemingly sudden turn of events.

If the Fed had more accurately gauged the extent to which lending, and hence economic activity, would pick up, and to which firms, finally convinced that the downturn was over, were finally willing to start hiring workers rather than relying on expensive overtime, it very likely would have tightened monetary policy early on, in order to stop the inflation threat dead in its tracks. And that might have been the fate of the recovery as well. The theory at the time (at the Fed, with some support from Treasury) was that you had to slay the inflation dragon before you saw the whites of its eyes. If it had crept up on you, unbeknownst, so that you could actually feel its breath (or see it in the statistics), it was too late. The damage would be done: not just the direct harm of the inflation, but the further consequences that come when the Fed slams on the brakes.

Underlying this view were four hypotheses, only one of which had any claim to scientific validity; the rest, while widely shared among central bankers, did not stand up to the test of statistical evidence. The first hypothesis, that it takes six months to a year for the full effects of changes in monetary policy to be felt, is true and important. That means that if the Fed thinks there is a robust recovery that will send the unemployment rate below the NAIRU in, say, the summer, it has to act *early*, in the winter or the previous summer.

The second hypothesis is that high inflation damanges long-term economic growth. But this has only been proved in countries with inflation rates far higher than those ever seen in the United States.[13]

With equal conviction, the central bankers contend that inflation, once it gets going, is extremely hard to bring under control. The analogy is often made to an alcoholic who "falls off the wagon": one sip of the nectar of inflation, in other words, and you'll be hooked. The hard statistics do not support this hypothesis; rather, higher inflation one quarter is followed by lower inflation the next. There was—and is—no evidence for the United States that inflation is "runaway."

By the same token, the inflation hawks at the Fed (and at other central banks) claim that they must take anticipatory action because the costs of combating inflation are likely to be high, far outweighing any benefit that the economy might register while it is ramping up growth. Again, the evidence, including studies by the Council of Economic Advisers and the Federal Reserve itself, points to the opposite conclusion.

Early in 1994, the Fed took action before the whites of the eyes of inflation were apparent—but not early enough to stop unemployment falling to new lows, well below what *it* thought the NAIRU was. Its failure to anticipate the pace of the recovery—and accordingly failing to raise interest rates to fully squelch it—redounded to the great benefit of the economy, and the nation.

By May 1994, unemployment was down to 6.1 percent, by August it reached 6.0 percent, by September 5.9 percent: unemployment had clearly crashed through the NAIRU barrier, falling to 5.5 percent in the month of December. Still, contrary to the Fed's model, inflation didn't pick up. Unemployment would eventually fall another 2 percentage points, to a low of 3.8 percent, again without stimulating inflation. To the poor, this lower unemployment was a huge blessing, reducing welfare rolls as much as anything else we did, or might have done. It was our most important anti-poverty program. It played a major role in bringing about other salutary changes—notably a sharp drop in the crime rate.

The Fed had acted early, or so it thought, allowing the federal fund's rate (the rate at which banks borrow from each other) to rise by a quarter percentage point in February 1994, and by a full three quarters of a percentage point by May, to 4 percent. This was in spite of the fact that inflationary pressures appeared very tempered. In fact, the index of employment costs, the most important factor driving inflation, was increasing at a rate of only 0.8 percent a quarter in the last half of 1993 and first half of 1994, lower than it had been in 1992 and the first half of 1993, where it was close to 0.9 percent. Producer prices were actually lower in June 1994 than they were a year earlier. And even the rate of inflation for consumers was falling, from an average of 0.23 percent per month for the first half of '93 to

0.21 per month in the second half of '93, to 0.2 per month in the first half of '94. But even had it not been falling, the rate was low, and the numbers grossly exaggerated the true rate of inflation. (When arguing for a lower rate of increase of Social Security benefits, which increase in tandem with inflation, Greenspan and others suggested that the numbers exaggerated inflation by 1–2 percent a year. In other words, the true rate of inflation, instead of being 0.2 percent per month, might be even lower than 0.1 percent—hardly something to worry about, and certainly hardly something to risk bringing the recovery to an end.)

But to many in the Fed, it was just a matter of time before we had to pay the price of flirting with low unemployment and the attendant risk of inflation. The goal in their minds was a soft landing—gradually increasing the interest rate and slowing growth so that unemployment settled down just at the NAIRU or slightly above, so inflation remained steady, or fell slightly.

The administration was split on the wisdom of the Fed's actions. Treasury Secretary Robert Rubin and his deputy Larry Summers supported the rate increases, Summers arguing that they improved the chances of a soft landing—a smooth transition to a full-employment economy. By raising rates now, the theory went, the Fed would keep the economy from getting overheated, and avoid the need for further increases down the line—say in a year or two, much closer to the election.

The president knew that he would bear the costs if Greenspan's assessments were wrong. He felt strongly that 6 percent unemployment was not good enough; if the economy could sustain a 4 percent unemployment rate without inflation growing, raising interest rates would lead to higher than necessary unemployment, and it would be the poor who bore the brunt. (If inflation picked up, of course, the bonds of the Wall Street traders would decrease in value, and they would be hurt; but who was better able to bear the risk, the bond traders or the workers threatened with unemployment?) Historically, a 2 percent decrease in unemployment translated into a 2–4 percent increase in output (the relationship was called Okun's law, after the former Yale professor and chairman of the Council of Economic Advisers under President Lyndon B. Johnson, Arthur Okun). Unemployment stabilizing at 6 percent would have meant a loss of some $200 to $400 *billion* every year, money that could be used to promote America's growth, reduce our deficit, or increase our expenditures on research, health, and education.

Conflicts between the president and the Fed have been a frequent occurrence of the past—as we have seen, Bush I blamed Greenspan for his defeat, in spite of the fact that Greenspan thought he was doing everything he possibly could *within reason* to resuscitate the economy. But Rubin persuaded the White House not to express their disappointments or frustrations. There were a few exceptions: Chief of Staff Leon Panetta replied to a question on whether the Fed should lower interest rates by saying "it would be nice to get whatever kind of cooperation we can get to get this economy going," and for this, he was strongly and publicly chastised by the Treasury secretary. But in general, the White House maintained a solid phalanx: "We do not comment on the Fed." This stance may not have promoted public discussion, but it didn't get us into trouble.

The president had one other way of influencing the Fed, through the vacancies that occasionally arose. With an impending vacancy in 1996 in the vice chair of the Fed (Blinder, who held that position, had decided not to seek reappointment; though one of the country's leading economists, Greenspan had eviscerated his ability to influence Fed decisions, and he had no desire to remain in a ceremonial post),[14] Clinton looked for someone with stature who shared his views, and he found that someone in Felix Rohatyn, one of the world's best known investment bankers, managing partner of Lazard Frères. Rohatyn had proven his mettle in heading the Municipal Assistance

Corporation, which had rescued New York City from impending bankruptcy. These were impressive credentials—and normally someone with these credentials would not have taken up the post. What swayed Rohatyn was his deep commitment to public service. But he had two strikes against him: he was a liberal Democrat; and he believed that the economy could grow faster, certainly faster than the anemic rates at which it had been growing. A third and perhaps most important strike against him was that he might be able to stand up to Greenspan: he was not just an academic, like Blinder; he was a man of the world, one who had achieved respect in everything he had done. With three strikes against him, it was a matter only of time before he was out. The Senate has to confirm Fed appointments. In this case, the usual deference given to first-rate presidential appointments of this kind was put aside. It was made clear that Rohatyn would not be appointed. It was never proven who had done him in, but there were some obvious suspects.[15]

As the Fed raised interest rates, businesses began to complain about the increased cost of capital, and those in the Clinton camp outside Treasury feared that the brakes were being applied too early and too hard. While jobs were being created, there was concern about whether they were good jobs (they were), and whether the growth would be sustained (it was).

Those early interest rate increases were substantial—federal fund rates went from 3 percent in late 1993 to 6 percent by mid-1995. Nevertheless, the economy continued to grow robustly. The rate of growth of the economy rose and rose. At first, we were just making up for the underutilization of capacity from the recession that we had inherited from Bush, but then it was clear something else was going on, as the growth rate hit 3, 4, and even 5 percent. Meanwhile, unemployment continued to fall, and—here was the real miracle from the Fed's perspective—inflation remained moderate. Even with growth at 5.0 percent in 2000, inflation was under 3.5 percent.

To Greenspan's credit, he eventually got the message that the structure of the economy was changing, that the long-anticipated increase in productivity, resulting from the investments in new technology, had finally occurred; that inflationary pressures had been dampened. As the evidence mounted, he stopped raising interest rates and even allowed them to moderate slightly—indeed, even in early 2000 the discount rate was still only at 5 percent. Greenspan became a convert earlier than many of the other board members, and managed to induce restraint on them.

In retrospect, what is interesting about these early debates is that both sides were wrong. We at the Council were wrong in underestimating the strength of the economy. It withstood the Fed's assault, at a cost. If interest rates had remained lower, unemployment arguably would have fallen faster, growth would have increased earlier. But the Fed and Treasury were clearly wrong to be so worried about inflation and they were wrong in underestimating the economy's potential for growth. So much for the wisdom of financial markets.

Lessons

The lesson of this chapter is not just to avoid making mistakes: mistakes are unavoidable. It is to point out that in the 1990s, there was a systematic pattern to such mistakes. Excessive deference was given to the wisdom of financial markets; the normal checks and balances were put aside. Several potentially dangerous ideas gained ground: that matters of macroeconomic policy were too important to be part of the political process; they should be reserved for public-spirited technocrats, and particularly for the technocrats at the Fed. There was a single set of policies which would advance *all* interests, and in particular, the Fed was right to focus on inflation.

The idea that monetary policy should be delegated to the Fed has, of course, always been popular with financial leaders; with an "independent" Fed typically doing what they wanted, why would they want things any differently? But during the nineties, it gained favor with journalists, ordinary citizens, and, most surprisingly, a Democratic presidential administration.

We liked the non-partisan cover when Greenspan seemingly supported the Clinton deficit-cutting plan. But it was always clear that he was partisan. His "cover" was finally blown in early 2001, as Greenspan suddenly gave up his longstanding credentials as a deficit hawk, and came out in support of President George W. Bush's tax cuts. It was obvious that the Bush tax plan would make a big dent on the surplus, possibly transforming the surplus (the Clinton fiscal legacy, indeed, one of its main legacies) into a deficit. Greenspan could have remained silent, maintaining that just as the executive branch doesn't comment on monetary policy, the monetary authority does not comment on fiscal policy. More responsibly, he could have been consistent with his past, expressing serious reservations about what the tax plan might do to the fiscal prospects and America's national savings rate. Instead, Greenspan essentially endorsed the Bush proposal. The prospective surpluses were large enough to allow for a significant tax cut, he declared. And such a tax cut wasn't merely acceptable, according to Greenspan; it was *necessary*, in order to save the nation from a dangerous predicament: if the surpluses continued, the national debt would eventually be paid off in full. We needed the debt for the management of monetary policy, and at that point we would have to choose between what Greenspan considered two unpleasant alternatives—a large increase in federal spending, or large-scale government acquisition of private assets.

Greenspan did not see fit to explain why it was desirable to cut taxes far in advance of this improbable catastrophe rather than wait for the peril to become a little more imminent—and for good reason: there was no reason. Greenspan, like me, had been chairman of the Council of Economic Advisers, a position in which one is required to make forecasts many years forward. He, of all people, should have known how difficult it is to forecast six months ahead, let alone ten years ahead. He, of all people—having grossly underestimated the economy's growth potential and overestimated the inflationary potential—should have known how quickly the numbers can change. Slight changes in growth rates would have greatly lowered the surplus. Tax revenues were soaring partly because of the huge bonanza from the stock market bubble; but if that bubble burst, tax revenues would plummet. You don't have to be an economist to know that a large budget surplus can become a large budget deficit in a political instant. Indeed, the projected ten-year surplus for the non–Social Security portion of the budget—an estimated $3.1 trillion in April 2001—had become a $1.65 trillion deficit by February 2002. This dramatic, but predictable, reversal was the result of an economic slowdown, a stock market–related decline in capital gains tax revenues, and, of course, the ill-advised Bush tax cut, which the nation could not afford and which Greenspan should never have endorsed.

In this instance, and others, the nation might have been better off if the leader of its "independent" central bank had stuck to managing monetary policy and staving off a recession. And yet, in advancing so far-fetched an argument for the Bush tax cuts, there was an element of consistency with his earlier deficit reduction position. Greenspan revealed himself as an advocate of smaller government: both deficit reductions in the nineties and Bush tax cuts in 2001 would lead to a reduced public sector.

Historically, the Democratic Party has been worried about high interest rates and suspicious of the Fed, and has sought to keep it in check. I recall a number of occasions in the early years of his administration when Bill Clinton worried aloud about a possible interest rate hike and how it might affect the seemingly fragile recovery. Listening to him at such moments, some of us were reminded of the 1896 election, when William Jennings Bryan, running against the gold standard, made his legendary "Cross of Gold" speech. "You shall not crucify mankind upon a cross of gold," was its rousing final line. The gold standard, by definition, meant a limited money supply—so limited that the economy faced a constant threat of deflation in Bryan's day. Year after year, farmers earned less for the goods they sold, and found it harder to repay their debts. Including silver in the money supply promised to reverse the situation, saving millions of farmers from bankruptcy. As beneficial as the gold standard might have been for creditors, it was bad economics—it led to slower growth—as the whole world eventually learned, at great cost, in the Great Depression. But even if the gold standard could have been made to work, the decision to stick with it had enormous consequences for the distribution of the economic pie. It was a matter that was properly debated in the political arena, not just in a room full of technocrats.

Today, the average American is not an indebted farmer but an indebted worker. But many of the concerns are similar. High interest rates, while they may increase the incomes of those on Wall Street who are net lenders, aren't good for wage earners, who lose on three counts. Higher interest rates may lead to higher unemployment. Higher unemployment puts downward pressure on wages. And since on average, wage earners are in debt (today, over a seventh of their income goes to debt service), the higher interest rates mean they have less to spend on everything else.

There are trade-offs in almost everything the Fed does—which is why the responsibilities of the Fed should not simply be delegated to technocrats. Even if there were agreement that the Fed should set the interest rate so that the unemployment rate remained as low as possible without inflation increasing (the NAIRU level), there is uncertainty about what that implies. As we have seen, the Fed has been wrong, in its estimates. Perhaps it could have done better, but that is not my concern here. My concern is that, knowing that there is uncertainty, its decisions impose risk: there is a trade-off between a risk of an increase in inflation and an unnecessarily high level of unemployment. That should be a political decision, not a techno-cratic decision, nor a decision entrusted to a particular vested inter-est group, the financial markets, because there is not a single *right* answer.

The existence of these trade-offs raises questions about the whole idea of an independent—that is, non-political—central bank. At the very least, they suggest a need for some mechanism to ensure that all relevant voices and perspectives are heard. In Sweden, for example, labor is represented at the Central Bank.

America's Federal Reserve Board represents a curious mixture: it is independent; and it is dominated by those from financial markets, and secondarily from business, with the voices of workers or con-sumers barely audible. But its charter obligates it not only to main-tain price stability but to promote growth and employment. Little guidance is given on how to make the trade-offs, and the fight against inflation clearly has long had the upper hand. Yet the Fed has been politically sensitive—as the previous chairman, Paul Volcker, once put it, "Congress created us, and the Congress can uncreate us," and with a politically sensitive chairman, when Congress and an admin-istration are willing to speak out for lower interest rates, proclivities for excessively "tight" money may be kept in check.

In the 1990s these checks were suspended. With Clinton so thor-oughly committed to creating jobs and promoting growth, I think he would have been more willing to bear a modest risk of inflation than were the inflation hawks on Wall Street. But we had swallowed the "no comment"mantra. This was not so much because we believed that monetary policy was simply so important and complicated that it *had* to be left to an independent Fed. The argument that convinced us was that commenting on the Fed could well prove counterproduc-tive—it was as likely to lead to higher interest rates as lower. First, there was the worry that the Fed, to prove its independence in the face of criticism, would have to do just the opposite, no matter what its economic judgments were.

But there was a second argument that those at Treasury put forward: anything that any member of the administration said commenting on Fed policy might "roil the markets," sending interest rates up.

It's ironic that those who ostensibly believed most in markets—in their ability to gauge the fundamentals of the economy—expected them to go haywire if one person spoke out. How much actual roiling would have resulted from a comment or two from anyone in the administration is debatable; on the few occasions (like that cited earlier concerning Leon Panetta, the chief of staff) when someone in the administration acted out of line there was little evidence that it did. What seems clear, on the other hand, is that the net effect of our timidity was to give the financial markets a "free pass," with even more influence over the economy. In the end, we allowed the markets to become pivotal in determining not just the government's fiscal policy—making deficit reduction the first priority—but also the government's monetary policy. The Fed, under cover of its vaunted independence, was largely driven by the views of the financial markets; it gave their inflation-related worries far more weight than labor's unemployment-related worries, in spite of its mandate, which is to focus not just on inflation but on growth and employment.

The U.S. Congress too was providing less of a check than it had in earlier years, and when the Republicans seized control of both houses, there was even an attempt to end what little charade there had been in balancing off inflation, growth, and employment. In 1996, Senator Connie Mack, the Florida Republican, introduced legislation to alter the Fed's charter, pruning its mandate—down to the pursuit of price stability alone. Had this effort succeeded, the Fed would have been legally bound, in all its deliberations, simply to ignore the interests of millions of working Americans. Fortunately, President Clinton took a firm stand against Mack's proposal, which was beaten back in one of the unsung economic policy victories of the Clinton administration. It was easy for the president to squelch the initiative; all he needed to indicate was his willingness to make it a campaign issue. The Republicans knew how voters would cast their ballots.

The dangers of an inflation mandate monetary policy are by no means purely theoretical. Since 1994, fighting inflation has indeed been the exclusive mandate of the European Central Bank. When the European Union (EU) made plans for its common currency, the euro, it worried about the problems of the past rather than the future. In the past, Europe had contended with inflation and large government deficits. Thus, the new continentwide Central Bank was told to make inflation its sole concern. To drive the message home, the individual EU countries were given strict fiscal targets—no more than a 3 percent deficit after 2000, ratcheting down to zero over succeeding years by 2004. As a result, the Central Bank's hands were tied as Europe's economy weakened in 2001. Not only did the bank not lower interest rates, but the various governments were unable to stimulate the economy through tax reductions or increased expenditures—in marked contrast to the United States, where both parties, in the abstract, agreed on the need for stimulus as our economy simultaneously slipped into its own recession.

Interestingly, the Republicans, who nowadays favor tax cuts *even if they result in deficits*, never mention the fact that if their party had had its way, such schemes would be unconstitutional. In the early 1990s, they pushed for a balanced-budget amendment, which would have automatically kept expenditures down to the level of tax revenues; in the 2001 recession, with revenues plummeting as stock prices and incomes fell, the Bush administration would thus have been compelled either to cut back spending or raise taxes. Laura Tyson considers the defeat of the balanced-budget amendment idea to be one of the Clinton administration's major achievements. We fought hard on that front because economic fluctuations have always been a part of capitalism; although we ourselves might be lucky and escape a recession, we knew that our successors might not be, and we refused to tie their hands. (This is another example of a Clinton policy that will benefit the economy in decades to follow, even if it had no effect during the years of the Clinton administration itself.)

The record of the nineties doesn't just raise questions about the Fed's ability to manage the economy; it raises questions about the Fed's *institutional* credibility. Have we arrived at a set of institutional arrangements that serves the economic interests of the entire country? Have we given too much weight, too much influence, to a particular industry or a particular subset of the population? Do we need more democratic accountability? These are hard questions, but ones that every democracy must face, and must address over and over again. Our institutions have served us well, in many ways—but they have also faltered, and we should not be complacent.

When it came to matters of economic policy, during the 1990s, many Americans were persuaded that the age of ideology, of interests and politics, was over. America had entered an era of consensus, when everyone reasonably agreed about the "right" economic policies. It was a nonsensical claim—but a brilliant strategy for those whose interests it served. And it worked, for the most part, remarkably well, in the sense that, with the economy in high gear, Americans became largely sold on it. That includes many who viewed themselves as representatives of those segments of the population whose interests were being systematically overridden.

The Roaring Nineties are now a thing of the past. Our financial leaders were shown to be mere mortals. They made mistakes. Some were lucky mistakes, and as a result, we had a robust recovery. Some were mistakes with little consequences: we weathered the interest rate hikes of the mid-nineties. Some were mistakes that had a high price, a cost which we will be paying for years to come.

CHAPTER 4

Deregulation
Run Amok

THE FED MAY NOT have done everything within its power to keep the bubble from growing as big as it did, but the Fed did not *create* the bubble. Bubbles are simply manifestations of the irrational optimism that sometimes besets an economy—an irrational optimism that is often followed by a no less irrational pessimism. As such, it is often difficult to predict the onset of a bubble, or to know when it will end. There are, however, certain circumstances that make it more likely that economic crises or severe recessions will afflict an economy. In the past three decades, the world has seen close to a hundred crises and many of them were brought on by some form of too-rapid deregulation. Though the economic downturn in 2001 is only a milder form of these more virulent diseases, there is no question that major parts of the downturn resulted from the deregulation of the nineties.

Deregulation of the telecommunications sector paved the way for the overinvestment bubble, which then burst so resoundingly in 2001. Deregulation of the electricity market led to the market manipulation that hurt the California economy, the heart of so much of America's innovation. Deregulation of banking—notably the repeal of the Glass-Steagall Act—opened up new opportunities for conflicts of interest, when what was needed was stronger regulations to address extant and growing conflicts of interest which would eventually do so much to undermine confidence in our securities markets. Lax regulation of the accounting sector provided opportunities and incentives to proffer misleading or wrong information.

Markets are delicate things, and the mistakes have cost a lot, though the United States is wealthy enough that it can bear the costs with relative ease. Elsewhere governments forced to right the mistakes of deregulation, especially in banking and finance, have, in some cases, had to use a significant portion of the GDP. Chile is still paying off the costs twenty years after its banking crisis in the early eighties, and Mexico's banking system is still not fully recovered from its crisis in the nineties. Yet, in spite of countless historical lessons, deregulation was once again the darling of politics in the 1990s. Of course, in some cases deregulation has proved to be a good thing, but it must be handled carefully, and too often that has not been done.

Needless to say, something as complex as a recession has many causes: mismanagement by the Fed may interact with deregulation and tax law changes in the creation and inflation of a bubble which eventually bursts. We saw in chapter 2 that President Reagan's deregulation of the savings and loan associations, in conjunction with the devastation of banks' balance sheets caused by the Fed's raising interest rates to unprecedented levels, contributed to the real estate bubble which, when it burst, not only caused America's taxpayers well over $100 billion but led to the recession of 1990–91.

In some ways, the bubble of the nineties was, however, different from many of the bubbles in the past. There were some fundamental reasons for optimism, perhaps not the unbridled optimism that marked the final years of the boom, or the irrational optimism of the dot-com world, but optimism nonetheless. The investments in research that the country had long been making finally seemed to be paying off. High tech at last was delivering on its promise. Productivity was increasing. Globalization was supplying America's consumers with cheap clothing and electronics, and although more and more manufacturing was being moved offshore, the country was creating new, high-paying jobs, largely in the service sector, to more than offset those lost in manufacturing. Unemployment was falling, but competition was increasing, and so inflation was kept in check. We ushered in a new era, repealing one of the longstanding regularities of economics, that lower unemployment results in higher inflation. There was a downside to this rosy picture: real wages were not increasing as fast as they normally do in a recovery. But consumption, buoyed by higher asset prices, maintained its robust growth. And low wages, high growth, and increasing productivity all meant one thing: higher profits. And higher profits, combined with low interest rates, led to a booming stock market. The economy was truly robust. It was not inevitable, however, that this robust economy would turn into a bubble economy.

If there was ever a time *not* to pursue deregulation, or to manage it particularly gingerly, the Roaring Nineties were it. The Democrats had always provided a check on the mindless pursuit of deregulation. Now, we joined in the fray—sometimes pushing things even further than under the Reagan administration.

The demand for deregulation had long been there. When done in the right way, regulation helps ensure that markets work competitively. There are always some companies that want to take advantage of their dominant position. Ideally, regulation stops firms from taking advantage of their monopoly power when competition is limited because there is a "natural monopoly," a market where there would naturally be only one or two firms, even without anyone doing anything to suppress entry or drive out rivals. Regulations help restrain conflicts of interest and abusive practices, so that investors can be confident that the market provides a level playing field and that those who were supposed to be acting in their interests actually do so. But the flip side of all of this is that regulation restrains profits and so deregulation means more profits. And in the nineties, those who saw the larger profits that deregulation would bring were willing to invest to get it—willing to spend megabucks in campaign contributions and lobbyists. Among the firms spending the most on lobbying in the United States in the late nineties were those working for telecommunications and banking deregulation and against environmental regulation and energy conservation. Efforts to prevent needed regulation were equally energetic: the accounting industry spent $15 million on lobbying between 1998 and 2000, and provided campaign contributions to more than 50 percent of House members and 94 percent of the senators.

The fast-changing American economy did mean that the regulations were increasingly out of kilter with what was needed; and it also meant that the profits to be made from deregulation were increasing. The lobbyists who descended on Washington were not economists, but they did make the standard economic argument that the deregulation they proposed would render markets more competitive and so would benefit consumers and society at large. But this raised a question: basic laws of economics say that competition is supposed to result in zero profits; if the lobbyists really believed their proposals would result in intense competition, why were they investing so much in trying to convince the government to adopt these proposals that would, presumably, wipe away their profits? Such internal inconsistencies little bothered the lobbyists—after all, they were not economists and they may not have believed the economic arguments they put forth.

But while the demand for deregulation had long been there, the politics of the nineties provided the "supply." The New Democrats wanted to differentiate themselves from the Old Democrats, who were seen as pro-regulation and anti-business. They wanted to earn their pro-business stripes by pushing deregulation still farther than it had gone before. They wanted to show that they too believed that the era of big government was over. And with Republican control of Congress in 1994, deregulation became one of the areas in which the New Democrats could join forces with the Old Republicans, to show that we had moved beyond gridlock.

"We are all Berliners" was the sentiment of President Kennedy's declaration. Thirty years later, we were all deregulators. The distinction between the parties lay only in the degree of their enthusiasm: as Professor Paul Starr of Princeton has written, the Republicans wanted to jump off the cliff, while the Democrats wanted to scramble down, preserving just enough rules to ensure some actual (as opposed to potential) competition and a bit of protection for those population groups which might otherwise be mistreated.[1]

By adopting the deregulation language, we had in fact conceded the battle. We seemed to be agreeing that government had become too intrusive in the economy, and that it needed to be rolled back. The world was changing rapidly, and many of the regulations, adopted more than seventy years ago, had to be changed. But for the market economy to function well, there is a need for laws and regulations—to ensure fair competition, to protect the environment, to make sure that consumers and investors are not cheated. What was needed was not deregulation, but *reformed* regulation—stronger regulations in some areas, like accounting, weaker regulation in others. The deregulation of the telecom sector illustrates many of the more general problems facing deregulation.

How Telecom Deregulation Contributed to the Great Bubble

The very word "telecommunications" speaks of boom and bust: in just nine years, from 1992 to 2001, this industry's share in the economy doubled, providing two thirds of the new jobs and one third of the new investment. New fortunes were being created, both by those in the industry and those in finance who were putting the deals together.

But by 2002, the picture looked entirely different. Pundits competed with each other over how to portray the gloomy state of the industry: Half a million people out of work, $2 *trillion* in lost market capitalization. Dow Jones communication tech index down 86 percent. Bankruptcies right and left. Twenty-three telecom companies bankrupt, including WorldCom, the biggest bankruptcy ever. In the phone market, Covad, Focal Communications, McLeod, Northpoint, and Winstar all going bust. ("Raiders of the local loop," Reed Hundt, chairman of the Federal Communications Commission, the regulatory agency responsible for oversight of telecommunications, had called them.)[2] Equipment makers also in trouble: Lucent, Nortel, Motorola, Alcatel, Cisco. Similarly, the cable companies, most notably Adelphia. Wireless companies burned up some $10 billion in cash in 2002 alone, according to Morgan Stanley. Investments of some $65 billion that were poured into the telephone industry between 1997 and 2001 were worth under $4 billion by the end of the period, a magnitude of waste that few governments had managed ever to achieve.

In October 2002, the chairman of the Federal Communications Commission (FCC) provided this concise diagnosis: "Few are prospering. Few are growing. Few are spending. Few are investing. The status quo is certain death." The shriveling of investment played a big role in the economic downturn.[3]

In telecommunications, deregulation unleashed powerful forces, as its proponents claimed. But the forces were not aimed solely at producing better products; they were directed at establishing dominance in one part of the market or another. Deregulation in telecom unleashed a Gold Rush; deregulation in banking allowed the rush to go out of control. Inadequate regulation in accounting allowed the race to go in the wrong direction: in some ways, it became a race to the bottom; those who won in the sweepstakes, at least in the short run, were those who were willing to be less than scrupulous. There was enormous excitement among everyone, everywhere, in government, in finance, in technology, in telecommunications; in the excitement, some things of enormous value were created: telecommunications today are better than they were before, though interestingly, U.S. technology remains behind that of much of the rest of the world. Even emerging markets, like Korea, are a decade or more ahead of us, not only in the sophistication of their cellular technology but also in the penetration of broadband into the home.

The existing body of law, much of it written in 1934, had not been designed for such things as direct-broadcast-satellite TV or cellular telephones, let alone the Internet. Long-distance phone service had been opened to competition in the seventies, but local service remained the exclusive (and closely regulated) province of the Baby Bells—the regional companies spun out of the old AT&T in 1984. Regarded as "natural monopolies," the Baby Bells were, in turn, barred from the long-distance business. On a similar theory, cable TV continued to be subject to price and content regulation, even though the cable companies, as their executives indignantly pointed out, were losing significant chunks of business to companies that delivered TV programming via satellite dishes. On top of everything else, it was possible to foresee a day when both the cable and satellite companies would be able to compete for the telephone business of the Baby Bells, and, indeed, when "video on demand" could be sent into people's homes by way of the phone lines.

The reason that telecommunications deregulation contributed to the bubble—to a Gold Rush—helps us understand both the politics and the economics of telecom deregulation. Those who argued for deregulation said it would produce more competition as different companies vied for market share. But there also was a strong belief in the idea of "first mover advantage," the possibility that the first firm in a particular market might dominate. Companies believed they faced a game of winner take all and so spent furiously to make sure they would dominate. In the end, this frenzied overinvestment helped create the excess capacity that overhung the U.S. economy and brought on the downturn that began in 2001 and lasted for more than two years. Although deregulation advocates argued that with the new technologies, regulation was unnecessary, competition would ensure low prices, they knew that that was not the case: they believed that there were huge profits to be made, and they wanted to make sure that the new regulations were written to enable them to grab them.

Even as the president signed the new telecommunications bill, on February 8, 1996, replacing the old law that had been on the books for sixty-two years, we knew that the road ahead would be bumpy—but few grasped exactly how filled with deep potholes it would be. We in the Clinton administration were just happy that there was a bill at all, and one that embodied much, if not all, that we had fought for. We had been working on this project for two and half years. Al Gore headed the task force, which met once a week for breakfast in the vice president's cramped West Wing office. As the member of the Council of Economic Advisers with the most expertise in regulation, I was asked to take part as a representative of the Council. Bowman Cutter, deputy head of the National Economic Council, who served under Clinton as deputy assistant to the president for economic policy, was another; he earlier served as the associate director of the Office of Management and Budget, which manages the federal budget, in the Carter administration. Cutter had enormous experience in the business community related to the telecommunications and information industry. Others on the task force included Ann Bingaman, the assistant attorney general for anti-trust; Gregg Simon, a telecommunications expert on the vice president's staff; Reed

Hundt, soon to be confirmed as head of the Federal Communications Commission; and a number of experts from the Commerce Department, the White House Office of Science and Technology, and the Office of Management and Budget (OMB).

Telecommunications was an area that had been of concern to the vice president when he served in Congress, and although in the campaign of 2000 he was ribbed for his claims of being the father of the Internet, there was no doubt that he had played a pivotal role in the congressional actions that contributed to its development. Long before it was fashionable, Gore talked of building the "information superhighway." Somehow, he intuited the role that this sector was about to play in the economy.

To all of us, the need for change was indisputable. But the proper direction of change was not so clear. The Clinton administration faced the daunting task of trying to forecast the evolution of a set of fast-moving and interrelated technologies, so that one could figure out just what sort of regulatory structure would best serve the interests of the industry and the public.

The informality of the meeting, the cramped quarters, made it clear: this was not just one of those formal meetings to rubber-stamp some decision that had already been made by some cabal. There were difficult political waters to navigate—how deregulation was done would lead to fortunes being won, and lost, and the market participants knew it. Regulated industries were accustomed to coming to Washington; the possibility of deregulation simply gave them more to fight over.

Deregulation was sometimes sold as "the end of politics," but it more often only changed the nature of the political dialogue, the perspectives and interests of which groups were attended to above others. But whatever could be said for deregulation, the process of deregulating itself was among the most political—and least principled—not surprisingly, given the amount of money at stake. The value that was put on just one piece, cable deregulation, was between $3 and $5 billion *per year*. Whatever the cable companies might have said in public, they didn't believe that competition was sufficiently strong to keep their prices down; with deregulation, prices and profits would go up. Their gains from price increases, of course, would be at the expense of consumers—and the economy more broadly. My expertise was not with this money-driven politics, but with the economic principles.

Our deliberations were frequently contentious. Fierce fights broke out between the advocates of complete deregulation—let the markets take care of everything—and those who sought to retain some role for government. Ann Bingaman and I worried that competition would not be strong enough to dispense with regulation. The other side was more confident that there would be robust competition, if we only got the government out of the way. New technology, they kept assuring us, would render the old safeguards unnecessary. Robust competition was just around the corner; at any rate, it would be, if the government would let it happen. The arch deregulators had a seemingly limitless faith in technology and the marketplace. But from where Ann and I and a handful of other skeptics sat, it sometimes seemed that our adversaries in these debates were not only far more sanguine about the prospects of competition but also far less concerned about the costs to society of the unfettered exercise of market power.

Our discussions often devolved into a debate between those who were basically pushing for the smallest possible government role, and those who believed (rightly, as I think events have shown) that we were talking about industries in which there was still plenty of potential for abuse. For years, the old AT&T had used its exclusive control over the "last mile" of phone service (access to homes and businesses) effectively to squeeze out long-distance competitors. I was one of those who expected the Baby Bells to use similar means to stymie competition in local service. The Baby Bells belittled this concern, insisting that new competition—from cable providers, cell phone companies, and even electrical companies delivering phone services over their wires—would quickly check any such monopolistic tendencies. In that argument, they had the backing of a coterie of economists, political scientists, legal scholars, and others who had made careers out of the deregulation movement; even the *potential* for competition, they contended, would be enough to keep any such tendencies in check. Often, the advocates of deregulation made a simple confusion: they thought that all that was needed for markets to work well was that there be *some* competition, while in fact there can still be large distortions. We believed that potential competition could have some effect in the exercise of monopoly power; but there was still enough monopoly power to be worried about. (Similarly, with cable, satellite TV provided some, but limited, competition; they were far from perfect substitutes, and each household had no choice of cable provider. It was hard to deny that there was a danger from the exercise of market power.)

In the telephone market, AT&T itself shared our fear, as did its assorted long-distance competitors. There were two reasons that I was suspicious of those who simply said, "Let competition reign." The first was alluded to at the beginning of this chapter: everyone talked about the importance of being the first mover into a market. In doing so, they were, in effect, admitting that they did not anticipate *sustained* competition. There would be competition *for* the market, but not competition in the market. That, in fact, was why those who had a head start in the race were lobbying so hard: they thought they had the inside track, and the payoff, if they won, would be enormous. By contrast, we know what would have happened if there were sustained competition *in* the market: competition would have driven profits down to zero. The only "supernormal" profits would be those earned during the entry period, before things settled out. (In winner-take-all markets, there are often large losses, especially associated with excessive investment, before things settle down; the events of recent years clearly support the view that market participants believed these markets were winner-take-all markets.)

But secondly, why, if the local phone companies really thought that competition would break out, were they so resistant to efforts to make sure that there was strong anti-trust oversight? Such oversight might be a little costly, but it surely would not be harmful. Surely, given the dangers of anti-competitive behavior—and the history—subjecting telecom to the same kind of anti-trust scrutiny that almost every other industry faces is hardly onerous.

Congressmen, while they might claim to be looking for the right balance that would best serve the long-run interests of the nation, paid special attention to the perspectives of their constituents and contributors, and in this arena the Baby Bells—especially with their thousands of local employees—were way on top. Repeatedly, as the bill wended its way through Congress, a veto threat—sometimes veiled, sometimes not—would be required to get it back on track. On one occasion, at a critical juncture, as the Baby Bells—hoping that issues of competition in telephones seemed to have gotten submerged in the host of other matters that were involved—succeeded in shaping the bill in their interests, I even weighed into the political fray, letting on to a *Wall Street Journal* reporter that I was prepared to strongly recommend a veto, that I viewed competition as the *central* issue. When the president—who had demonstrated that he was willing to use the veto if necessary, and had done so with remarkable effectiveness in the budget battles—hinted at a veto shortly later, the Republicans in Congress who were doing the Baby Bells' bidding knew they had to move toward greater balance.

In the beginning, the vice president had outlined several issues that were non-negotiable—if they were not contained in the bill, he would recommend a veto. These included giving the FCC powers to bring about competition; not deregulating cable until there was effective competition; and connecting classrooms to the Internet. The Republicans always hoped, and assumed, if there were enough goodies for enough groups, political pressure would make it difficult to veto; especially if there were enough face-saving concessions to what the president wanted. If the lobbyists could persuade Congress that fears of monopoly were greatly exaggerated, they could persuade the public at large, and with all the monopoly profits, they had the means to do so. Thus, cable rates (which had been deregulated under Reagan and re-regulated by Congress in 1992) were set free once again.

In the end, the Telecommunications Act of 1996 required the Baby Bells to "unbundle" their various lines of service and equipment, offering access to competitors at discount prices. We were also successful in maintaining a degree of price control over local service, and in imposing a phone surcharge to support Internet access in schools and libraries, this tiny provision of the law being, essentially, all that remained of a once elaborate structure of subsidies intended to ensure modestly priced phone service for rural areas and the poor.

The Baby Bells, for their part, won the right to go into the long-distance business, and though, in theory, they could expect to face a host of new competitors on their home turf, the FCC's efforts to guarantee that outcome were promptly met by a battery of lawsuits contesting its rules and, indeed, its right to set them.

The FCC's landmark "interconnection" order was essentially a playbook for implementing the 1996 Telecom Act. The order required the local companies—such as the Bells and GTE Corporation—to offer discounts to rivals seeking to use their networks, with much of that pricing jurisdiction going to the FCC and not the states. In their lawsuits, the established phone companies argued that the new rules forced them to give competitors access to their networks at prohibitively low prices. The fees were so low, according to Verizon, SBC Communications, BellSouth, and Qwest, that neither they nor smaller challengers would have a financial interest in investing to build and improve their networks. Smaller rivals argued that formulas proposed by the bigger telecom companies would lead to higher fees, eviscerating the deregulatory goals of the act, and effectively driving them out of business and leaving local markets exclusively in the hands of monopolists.

Although we had realized we were dealing with delicate jurisdictional questions involving state and federal regulators, and what was at stake was not just a matter of economic principles, we had not fully anticipated the legal battles that followed. The Baby Bells knew that they had far more influence over the state regulators (Nobel Prize winner George Stigler described the process by which industries "capture" those they are supposed to regulate). Each side thought it had put enough language in the bill to protect its interests but in fact the bill was unclear, although the U.S. Supreme Court eventually came down on the side of the FCC.

But our most serious misjudgment involved the degree, in each of the markets we were deregulating, of the intensity of the drive for domination.

In the short run, this drive for domination redounded to our favor. It fed the economic boom. By the end of 2001, some $65 billion had been invested in hundreds of new telecommunications ventures,[4] a headlong rush for market share involving taking on enormous debt and raising vast additional sums of money in the capital markets, and, in all too many cases, keeping their investors and lenders happy by cooking the books. The stakes seemed high, and if everybody else is cheating, it's hard not to cheat yourself. The Telecommunications Act—and the FCC's playbook—had been intended, in the words of Clinton's first FCC commissioner, Reed Hundt, to "cause a flood of new investment and innovation that would wash away the advantages of the incumbents—and erode their market capitalization."[5] There was innovation and, certainly, investment aplenty. But it was unsustainable. When the dust settled, America was left with a tremendous amount of excess network capacity, and a marketplace that in some areas was more concentrated than before.

Deregulation Perspective

I have focused on telecom deregulation partly because of the central role it played in the boom of the Roaring Nineties and the bubble that followed; but also because it illustrates nicely many of the issues of deregulation.

Much of the regulatory structure that governed the U.S. economy, not just that of the telecom industry, was first established in the 1930s, in the aftermath of the last grand period of boom—and bust. Dissatisfaction with markets was rife. But the strength of the American economy during the sixties and seventies restored faith in markets. And technology had changed: areas in which earlier, competition had not appeared viable—the so-called natural monopolies, like electricity and telecom, where without government regulation (or ownership) prices would be high—were no longer natural monopolies. Some competition was feasible. This meant that the regulatory structure had to change; but one of the hard questions was, *was it enough,* enough to put aside all regulation?

By the 1990s, the complexities of the new economic world—new technologies, new financial instruments, a more integrated global economy—were putting increasing strains on the old regulatory system. Change was needed. Although President Jimmy Carter had begun with deregulation in transportation (airlines and trucks), allowing firms to set prices and standards on their own and freeing up entry, the far harder tasks of deregulation—in telecommunications, electricity, and finance—were left to the Clinton administration.

Well-funded conservative think tanks had churned out studies documenting the supposedly prohibitive, or at least exorbitant, costs of regulation in one field after another. If the numbers had much credibility, deregulation should have led to a burst of productivity. Unfortunately, productivity growth during the era of deregulation, the Carter-Reagan-Bush years, was far lower than that which preceded it or followed it. In the case of the Clinton years, deregulation led to a burst of activity, though some of it was simply a waste of resources. The deregulation advocates had a Manichaean view of the world: they saw the wonders of the free market, over here, and evils of government, over there, making no mention of the many instances in which the fruitful operation of the market *depended* on a degree of regulation. By the nineties, it had become an article of faith with many Republicans, and quite a few Democrats as well, that the market, by itself, could handle almost any problem—that government, by definition, made things worse.

But by the time Clinton came to Washington, history had made clear that deregulation was not the unmitigated blessing that its advocates claimed. Airline deregulation had led to a burst of new carriers, but most of them did not survive. Deregulation advocates like Betsy Bailey, of the Civil Aeronautics Board, and her mentor, William Baumol of Princeton University, claimed that potential competition would virtually guarantee low prices and efficiency—even if a single airline flew a given route, the fact that another airline might step in would provide strong market discipline.[6] The monopolist would not dare exceed the competitive price, because he knew that if he did, the rivals would descend upon him, possibly in droves, and any ill-gotten gains from the attempt to exercise monopoly power would backfire. These theories proved wrong—in some cases, massively so, and in ways that were not fully anticipated even by the critics. The hub and spoke system that evolved led to strong, monopolylike positions at certain airports—TWA dominated St. Louis, Northwest dominated Minneapolis, American dominated Dallas—and, not surprisingly, the airlines often used this monopoly power to raise prices and increase profits. When new entrants came in—entrants that would have offered lower prices and more frequent service—often the incumbent airlines responded ruthlessly, slashing prices and adding capacity, to drive out the entrant. Even if they lost money in the process, the airlines knew the investment was wise; not only could they once again raise prices and restore profits after the intruder was driven out, but other potential entrants would be put on notice about what was in store for them.

If airline deregulation proved that deregulation did not always bring the full benefits that it promised, banking deregulation revealed an even darker side. America should have learned more than one lesson from the savings and loan debacle discussed in chapter 2. This experience should have taught us, for instance, that deregulation is difficult to do well. And that when it is not done well, the mistake can be extremely costly.

The S&L debacle showed that when incentives go awry, as they do with bad accounting and poorly designed deregulation, dire consequences can follow. Markets, rather than steadily creating wealth, may undertake excessively risky ventures. Without regulation, weak banks worried about their survival, took large risks, and gambled on huge gains, knowing that others would pick up the pieces if the gamble did not pay off. The S&Ls also illustrated the thin line that sometimes exists between ethical and unethical behavior, and that when the payoffs are large enough, there are many within the business community who find ways of overcoming moral compunctions: at best the law is skirted; at worst, it is ignored. Whether from excessive risk taking or straightforward looting, the bankers gained, the American taxpayer lost.

In many, if not most, of the episodes of deregulation, matters turned out quite differently than its advocates had claimed: evidently, large mistakes in judgment were made—and for good reason. Regulations had typically been imposed because of some market failure.

Removing the regulation did not remove the market failure. But too often, the advocates of deregulation had forgotten, or deliberately ignored, the market failures which had originally given rise to the regulations.

Indeed, precisely when deregulation and free market ideas were becoming most strongly advanced within the political arena, they were most strongly being questioned within academia. In the seventies and eighties, economic research revealed a wide range of market failures, instances in which markets fail to perform well, and in which they fail to deliver even the promise of efficiency. The "market failures" included those related to imperfections of competition, missing markets, and externalities (like pollution, where one person's actions adversely affect another person's well-being). The research for which I received the Nobel Prize focused on one set of problems, one such set of pervasive *market failures*, those arising from imperfect and asymmetric information. But well before economic theorists "explained" why markets could not be relied on, the public had recognized that there were important instances of market failure, where government could make a difference.

Without some form of government intervention, when there are *negative* externalities, like pollution, markets produce too much, and when there are positive externalities, as in the case of basic research, they produce too little. Government-sponsored research (much of it at universities) was central to a successful U.S. economy in the nineteenth century—great advances in agriculture were based on government-supported research—and has also proved central in the twentieth and twenty-first centuries. It was the federal government, for example, that built the first telegraph line between Baltimore and Washington in 1844, and it was the federal government that launched the Internet, the basis of the New Economy.

Fannie Mae, the Federal National Mortgage Association, was created in 1938 to provide mortgages to average Americans, because private mortgage markets were not doing their job. Fannie Mae has resulted both in lower mortgage rates and greater home ownership—which has broader social consequences. Homeowners are more likely to take better care of their houses and also to be more active in the community in which they live.

One of the most important market failures—one to which Adam Smith himself called attention—resulted from the striving of businesses to suppress competition. Anti-trust policy arose because of the tendency of firms to engage in non-competitive behavior, to exert market power, to exploit consumers by charging high prices and attempting, through a variety of channels, to deny entry to new competitors. For a hundred years, we have observed example after example: Standard Oil's attempted monopolization of oil, monopolies in tobacco, aluminum, shoes . . . the list in endless. While many thought that with strong anti-trust enforcement, explicit collusion to fix prices was a thing of the past, the Archer Daniels Midland (ADM) conspiracy, with other manufacturers of lysine, a livestock feed additive, and citric acid, a preservative found in soft drinks, processed food, cosmetics, and pharmaceuticals—uncovered in the mid-nineties—showed that such collusion still occurs. ADM was fined a record setting $100 million and several of its officers were sent to prison. The company used a bogus trade association as a cover for illicit meetings to carve up the market. Of course, the most dramatic case is Microsoft, which was found guilty of engaging in a whole variety of anti-competitive practices. While Microsoft monopolized the operating system, it denied equal access to competing producers of applications, thereby leveraging its dominance of the operating system to gain a dominant position in software. It squeezed out innovative competitors like Netscape, even deliberately sending error messages when rival programs were installed to heighten users' anxiety. Under Bush I, and later under Bush II, these problems were largely swept aside; but one of Clinton's achievements was to recognize how important competition is to the economy, not only in ensuring that consumers get low prices but in promoting innovation and the creation of products that meet consumers' needs.

Corporate Welfare and Corporate Hypocrisy

Deregulation may have been motivated more by attempts to increase profits than by a genuine concern for the efficiency of the American economy. After all, much was revealed about those pushing for deregulation and a smaller government when one examined their attitudes toward _corporate_ subsidies and _government_ protection. As chairman of the Council of Economic Advisers, I observed three almost unfailing principles among those who came to us for help:

First, businesspeople generally oppose subsidies, for everyone but themselves. For their own sector, there were always a host of arguments for why some government help was needed. From unfair competition abroad to an unexpected downturn at home, the stories were endless.

Second, everyone was in favor of competition, in every sector but their own. Again, there were a host of arguments for why competition in their sector would be destructive, or why it needed to be managed carefully.

And third, everyone was in favor of openness and transparency, in every sector but their own. In their sector, transparency might lead to unnecessary disturbances, erode its competitive edge, and so forth.

Most businesses thus viewed any subsidies they received or other forms of government intervention as fully warranted (and they didn't feel that they needed to justify these subsidies and interventions in the peculiar language of economists); the Council, however, typically looked askance.

But what might have been simply an academic debate became a highly charged controversy within the White House with the never-ending quest to balance the budget. We had been forced to abandon many of the programs that had been at the center of Clinton's platform, such as investments in education and health and improvements in science that would enable us to maintain our technological lead. The president had emphasized welfare reform, and what most of those in the Clinton administration wanted was a program that would help welfare recipients move to work, and that required education, training, and perhaps even child care, and that required money. Yet facing budget stringency, it became increasingly clear that the welfare reform we would obtain might push people off welfare roles but not into good jobs, and possibly not into jobs at all.

If we were forced to cut back on welfare to the poor, there was an even more compelling case to eliminate welfare to the rich, and in particular to cut back on corporate welfare—subsidies and tax breaks to corporations. While Labor Secretary Robert Reich led the charge for eliminating corporate welfare, the Council undertook the quieter task of drawing up a comprehensive list of corporate tax breaks and subsidies that could not be justified.

The initiative, though, proved highly divisive. The U.S. Treasury violently opposed the whole idea, suggesting that the very vocabulary, "corporate welfare," smacked of class warfare, and that the attack on corporate welfare was inconsistent with the New Democratic pro-business image we were trying to create. I, for one, did not see it that way at all. On the contrary, I saw the attack on corporate welfare as completely consistent with our attempt to forge a new philosophy, in which markets were at the center. It was because I believed in markets that I thought we should be circumspect about subsidizing them. Such subsidies distort the ways resources get used. Reagan's tax subsidies for smokestack America and for real estate had left a weaker country in their wake. We should be trying to create a level playing field—and corporate welfare destroyed that level playing field. New Democrats were not against markets, and were

most certainly not for regulation for its own sake. Markets sometimes failed, and when they did, there was an argument for government intervention. But when they did not fail, there was an argument
for no government intervention.

Try as we might, Treasury's opposition combined with congressional politics made it difficult to do much about corporate welfare,
and little progress has been made since. We did manage to tighten the
belts of the poor as we loosened those on the rich: not only was little
done about cutting out old corporate welfare programs, left over
from the Reagan/Bush administrations; new forms developed and old
forms were altered to keep them alive.

There were a few cases of near successes in curbing corporate welfare, but even when the administration could agree to take on the
political risk, Congress did not go along.

Corporate jets

The first such near success had more symbolic value than economic
consequences—though it turned out to be more political grandstand-
ing than anything else. Corporate jets, which whisk CEOs from one
meeting to the next, and also from their corporate headquarters to
their ski chalets, have long been emblematic of the differences
between the lives of these captains of industry and ordinary mortals,
who must wait in long lines at crowded airports (with budget austerity, it had become difficult to keep up with demand) and wait in still
longer queues for security checks. It was little known, however, that
ordinary taxpayers were, in effect, subsidizing these corporate jets to
the tune of several billion dollars a year. America, like every other
country, has a complicated and expensive air traffic control system—
the traffic cops of the air, supported by computers and radar that
track the planes as they move, who try to prevent the planes from
crashing into each other. Commercial planes pay hefty landing fees to
help support this system, but the corporate jets were not then, and

still are not, paying their way. Yet budget stringency was not only leading to underinvestment in airports but also in the air traffic control system.

Fortunately, most Americans did not know how bad things had become, or they would have become frightened of flying. I did an on-site inspection of the equipment at National Airport, serving the nation's capital. The computers were so old that they still used vacuum tubes that had to be imported from Poland, since almost everyone else had stopped making them. The roomful of out-of-date computers had a computing power less than the laptop on which I am now writing. The backup batteries occupied another room, old-fashioned chemicals with an on-site shower in case any of the acid spilled—but for all the drama, in the event of a blackout, they could last only about a half hour, far shorter than the battery for my laptop.

The budget rules of the game were driving us to some form of privatization[7] in which a new Air Traffic Control Corporation could borrow money to modernize. For the economy as a whole, of course, it made little difference whether the government or this new corporation borrowed to update the ATC system; but the shortsighted financial analysts didn't see things this way. If the government borrowed, no matter how good the cause, it was bad; they simply didn't bother to look at what was *really* going on.

There was, however, another advantage of privatization—anybody facing a bottom line would force the corporate jets to pay their way, eliminating this particularly obnoxious example of corporate welfare. But I should have realized that the corporate lobbyists are smart, very smart—even if the market system compensated these lobbyists well, it was directing their talents in ways that benefited corporations at the expense of the general public. The lobbyists quickly grasped what privatization would imply, so that while they typically championed the private sector and vigorously attacked government doing anything, in this arena they took the opposite position. They opposed the initiative precisely because they knew that it meant the end of their hidden subsidy. And they won.[8]

Spectrum

Sometimes corporate welfare takes the form of a giveaway of our country's rich natural resources. Mining companies can, for instance, take those resources almost for the asking. When early on in the administration we tried to make them pay, we were beaten back, by normally pro-market conservatives. As the urge to balance the budget increased, we turned to selling the electromagnetic spectrum, the right to use the public airwaves. These too are among the resources that the country owns as a whole. While we can't see this particular resource (unlike our billions of dollars' worth of oil, gas, minerals, and timber), it has enormous value, and one of the advantages of budget stringency was that at last we were beginning to try to use these resources for the public good. Historically, up until 1993 we had given away the right to use our airwaves, and the nation's TV and radio stations, our media moguls, made a fortune as a result. Advances in economic theory had shown how we could conduct auctions that would garner to American citizens the value of this resource, which was rightfully theirs. If one believed in the price system, such auctions would, in addition, help ensure that this scarce resource was used in the best way possible; and one could impose "social responsibility" clauses in the auction, for instance, requiring whoever won to provide so many hours of educational broadcasting. We reached an agreement with the Republican Senate Leader, Robert Dole, that would charge TV stations for the use of spectrum, and for an instant it looked as if the deal would go through. But in the end the media reaction against the plan succeeded in killing it off. The media's power comes not just from their campaign contributions, but from their coverage of the candidates and the issues. Politicians offend them at their peril.

This giveaway continues, and the political costs perhaps exceed even the budgetary impact. Had we auctioned the airwaves, we might have insisted not only on children's programming but also on campaign coverage. Such coverage would have reduced the need for campaign contributions, thereby reducing corporate influence. But the media, who have received the use of the scarce spectrum for nothing—and even expanded it as they claimed they needed more for a smooth transition to digital TV—treated their ownership as a right, and resisted pressure for change.

THESE WERE OUR near successes in eliminating corporate welfare. In most of the areas, entailing billions of dollars every year, either of expenditures or lost tax revenues, we did not even propose major cutbacks. We knew the politics were against us. The huge agricultural subsidies continued to go largely to corporate farmers, though in 1995 we did pass a bill to wean them. We promised bigger up-front benefits, in return for a phaseout. They took the up-front money, but as the benefits began to be cut, they demanded that they be restored. Under Bush II, supposedly free market midwestern conservatives supported not only a restoration of those benefits, but an increase.

The most extensive forms of hidden corporate welfare were tax breaks and protection from competition. In the peculiar logic of Washington, giving someone $100 million for doing something was viewed as far worse than saying, if you do the same thing, your taxes will be reduced by $100 million. A check going out was different from a check not coming in. There is a difference: it is easier to see, and therefore to try to stop, the checks going out. Corporate lobbyists know this, which is why they try to get so many of their subsidies through the tax code. It is remarkable how little progress we made in eliminating these tax subsidies, in spite of the pressure for deficit reduction. We had long had multi-billion-dollar tax subsidies for exports, which so infuriated our trading partners that in 1998 they brought action before the World Trade Organization and won. Rather than abandoning the subsidy, we attempted to make it compatible with WTO rules.[9]

Lessons

The changing world meant that America had to change its regulatory structures. There was a need to redefine the role of government. Within the Clinton administration we knew that there were areas where we needed to downsize government—such as reducing corporate welfare. But we also knew that there were areas where the government was still needed, such as welfare for the poor or investments in basic research. We knew that there was a need for regulation—most of the regulations had been put in place for a good reason. We knew too that while markets fail, so do governments, and thus, one had to have careful and limited regulation. Precisely because markets and governments so often fail it is even more important for them to work in partnership. The strengths of each can offset the weakness of the other. But although some in the Clinton administration understood this, in too many instances—in electricity, telecom, and banking—we succumbed to the deregulation mantra, rather than asking what was the *right* regulatory structure, which would have meant more regulations in some areas (in accounting and on secret offshore banking, for instance), less in others. So, too, in light of the history of problems associated with deregulation, we might have been better advised to go about the process of deregulation with greater caution. To be fair to ourselves, even if the administration had designed the right regulatory bills, it is unlikely it could have gotten them through Congress: even today, in the aftermath of the deregulatory disasters, the deregulation mantra remains strong; those who have made their fortunes through deregulation, and managed to keep them, are in a far better position to lobby for even more and faster deregulation than those who have lost.

In each of these areas, the world turned out quite differently from the way the lobbyists—and even many of those with fewer interests at stake—had said it would. But the deregulation lobbyists were saying one thing as those they represented went about their business on quite different premises: the Baby Bells were clearly wrong about the speed with which competition in the "last mile" would develop. It is years since the Telecommunications Bill of 1996 was enacted, and competition is still limited. We were right to be worried about how fast it would come.

Some critics have faulted the Clinton administration for not going far enough in deregulating the telecommunications industry. They complain that the Baby Bells, in particular, have been impeded from offering high-speed Internet access by the obligation to rent network access to competitors at prohibitively low prices. This line of argument, too, ought to have been put to rest by now. While the prices may have been unreasonably low, the fact is, there is nothing like sufficient demand to justify the amount of investment in high-speed access that has already occurred.

Problems of periodic excess volatility and capacity have plagued capitalist economies since time immemorial. Simplistic economic theory envisions the economic system as a self-regulating mechanism: when supply exceeds demand, prices fall, reducing supply; and the converse. But while such adjustments do indeed occur, they do not happen smoothly, nor without costs. In the telecom case, there were misjudgments, an irrational exuberance. Most anticipated a level of growth far greater than has occurred. Direct broadcast satellite (DBS)

services, in spite of capturing some 23 percent of the subscription tel-
evision market, have yet to turn a profit.[10] To compete, cable has
invested $60 billion in the past five years, only to find its stock mar-
ket value drop by 68 percent. Even when there has been growth—100
million new subscribers in the wireless industry—there has been the
decline of plummeting stock prices. Few anticipated the actual
declines, either in revenues of long distance companies, or in the total
number of local phone lines (down 4.7 percent in 2001 alone, the
first decline since the Great Depression), as some 3 million gave up
wired phones for wireless. Yet the failure of the industry cannot be
explained just by irrational exuberance, by misforecasting: it was the
quest for monopoly profits in the new world of deregulation that
drove the system so out of balance, at such great costs, not only to
the investors but the nation as a whole, and contributed to the overall economic downturn.

Over history, booms and busts have sometimes been associated
with overinvestment in new technologies: the telecom bubble of the
1990s closely parallels the experience of the telegraph and telephone
and railroad industries in their early, anarchic days, before they
became regulated monopolies. Booms and busts have also often been
associated with deregulatory initiatives, especially in finance—the
S&Ls being the most recent example in the United States. The Roaring Nineties brought the two together, with unprecedented excitement, and disappointment.

CHAPTER 5

Creative
Accounting

ONE OF THE BIG might-have-beens of the 1990s involved the strange corporate practice of giving corporate executives stock options—the right to buy company stock at below market prices—and then pretending that nothing of value had changed hands. While the option phenomenon did not originate in the high-tech world, they came to use it more than any other, more traditional sector. As far back as the seventies, broad-based stock ownership was one of the defining characteristics of a new West Coast style of business organization—more collegial and nimble than the corporate giants of old. Options were, of course, a terrific recruiting tool for small, profitless start-ups that could never have come up with their equivalent in cash. And soon the old corporate giants had embraced the practice, hoping to bottle some of the vitality of the tech companies and, while they were at it, bring manager and shareholder interests into alignment (which was one of the corporate mantras of the day). But the neatest thing of all about stock options, for tiny start-ups and corporate colossuses alike, was the fact that since no actual stock got issued until they were "exercised" (which might be several years down the road), they didn't have to be acknowledged as an expense—as something the firm had spent, or a liability it had incurred, in order to do business that year. Thus, a company could please employees and bottom-line-conscious investors at the same time.

By 2001, options accounted for an estimated 80 percent of the compensation of American corporate managers, and the impact on the balance sheet wasn't exactly trivial, either. If Microsoft had been required to acknowledge the value of the options it doled out that year, the effect would have been to reduce the company's 2001 profits (officially, $7.3 billion) by a third.[1] The same play had enabled both Starbucks and Cisco, among other companies, to boost profits by 20 percent or more. Intel's profits would have been cut to a fifth, from $1.3 billion to $254 million, and Yahoo!'s losses would have increased tenfold, from $93 million to $983 million.

The stock options controversy was a simple matter of honest disclosure. And through an insidious logic that I'll spell out later in this chapter, stock options played an important part in the spread of other forms of financial chicanery. Enron, WorldCom, and Adelphia were only the most flagrant and well publicized of many companies where the vaunted energy and creativity of the nineties would eventually be directed less and less into new products and services, and more and more into new ways of maximizing executives' gains at unwary investors' expense.

When I first arrived in Washington, the problem was still comparatively contained. Nevertheless, there were people who had seen enough. In June 1993, the Financial Accounting Standards Board (FASB), the little known but important independent body responsible for formulating accounting standards, came out with a draft rule, intended to make companies put a reasonable value on options and list them as an expense. The FASB was a creature of the accounting industry—an example of self-regulation. The "gnomes of Norwalk," as they were known (because their offices were in Norwalk, Connecticut), had a reputation for moving slowly and soliciting the industry's input at every stage, which made their prescient concern about options, and the straightforwardness of their solution, all the more remarkable.

The corporate world, however, wanted no part of the proposed rule. Silicon Valley was predictably adamant, but not alone. If options had to be "expensed," companies would simply stop granting them, and without this motivational elixir, the economy would grind to a halt—that was the essence of the argument advanced by countless executives and lobbyists. In a heated discussion with Securities and Exchange Commission chairman Arthur Levitt, Jr., the chairman of Home Depot, Bernard Marcus, characterized the FASB rule as "a terrible blow to the free enterprise system," which would "make it impossible to start up new businesses."[2]

The opponents took their case not only to the SEC (which worked closely with the FASB) but also to key figures in the Clinton administration and Congress. Treasury Secretary Lloyd Bentsen and Commerce Secretary Ron Brown wrote a letter denouncing the proposal. Similar expressions of sentiment soon came pouring forth from Capitol Hill, where the tech boom was stirring great interest. Connecticut senator Joe Lieberman (who would go on to be Al Gore's running mate in 2000) attacked the FASB and its rule with righteous ferocity. Lieberman was the author of a Senate resolution, approved by a vote of 88 to 9, urging the FASB to back off, and warning of "grave consequences for America's entrepreneurs" if the proposed rule were adopted. It appeared that the consequences for the FASB itself might not be too pleasant, either. With the support of California senators Barbara Boxer and Dianne Feinstein, and Florida's Connie Mack, among others, Lieberman introduced legislation to effectively strip the board of its power—no matter that it wasn't a government agency in the first place.

The elections of 1994, and the elevation of the staunchly pro-tech, anti-regulation Newt Gingrich as Speaker of the House, sealed the FASB proposal's fate. No one worked harder than Arthur Levitt and the SEC to crack down on deceptive corporate accounting practices in the nineties; but it was Levitt who finally got the FASB to adopt a watered-down rule that would merely require companies to report all option grants in footnotes to their financial statements. He later called it the "biggest mistake" of his tenure at the SEC.[3]

Executive pay would become a topic of growing controversy in the latter part of the decade, as stock options enabled the likes of John Chambers of Cisco, Dennis Kozlowski of Tyco, Sanford I. Weill of Citicorp, and David Komansky of Merrill Lynch to pocket millions of dollars. But while there was plenty of outrage over the amounts of money involved—the popular view was simply that these executives were being paid too much—other aspects of the question got slighted.

As a longtime student of the role of information in a well-functioning economy, I read the story a little differently: the executives are being paid too much partly because *it isn't widely known exactly how much they're really being paid*.[4] And if no one knows how much the CEOs are being paid, that means no one knows how much profit (or loss) the company is making. No one knows how much the firm is really worth. Without this information, prices cannot perform the roles they are supposed to in guiding investment. As economists put it somewhat technically, "resource allocations will be distorted."

I first got involved in this issue in 1993, when the administration was called upon to do something about FASB's proposed ruling. Coming from Silicon Valley (I was then on leave from Stanford University), I knew the concerns of these high-tech companies. Perhaps not surprisingly, Treasury, Commerce, and the National Economic Council were all inclined to intervene on behalf of Wall Street and Silicon Valley. The Council of Economic Advisers was asked to take a look, and the closer we looked, the stronger we felt: FASB was right, and we would be wrong to intervene against it. The board was supposed to be independent and free of political influence. I was, of course, sensitive to the issue that the boundary between what should and should not be *independent* was itself highly contentious. As I pointed out in chapter 3, matters of monetary policy cannot, or at least should not, be devolved to technocrats, because they involve trade-offs of the kind that should be addressed within the political process. But the area of concern of the FASB did seem to be one which could, and perhaps should, be assigned to an independent body. Its task was to design accounting systems that would provide reliable, standardized, understandable information to potential investors. Investors could and would have more confidence in the accounting frameworks if they knew that they were created by an independent body, rather than in a political process in which powerful groups might use their influence to have misleading accounting frameworks.

The Council's confidence that we were taking the right position was reinforced as we saw the flimsiness of the arguments made against expensing options. One point we heard again and again was how difficult it would be to put a value on them. But, of course, that was hardly a reason for giving them no value. There are a host of areas where the rules of accounting call for difficult feats of measurement. Providing an accurate estimate of depreciation—the decrease in the value of machines as they age and get used—is much trickier than estimating the dollar value of a stock option. In any case, we pointed out, a value of zero was clearly wrong. People wanted stock options because they had value.

During the stock options debate, we were often assured that everything was explained in the footnotes of companies' annual reports. But even sophisticated analysts sometimes had trouble interpreting that sort of financial minutiae.[5] The whole point of having accounting standards is to make the state of a company's financial affairs easier—not harder—for investors to evaluate.

Opponents of the FASB's proposed rule insisted that its formula for calculating the value of an option was potentially misleading. Most investors, they said, wouldn't have enough sophistication to make the required corrections, if a wrong estimate was made. The same people who made this point, however, would go on to argue that investors didn't have to see the cost of stock options on a company's balance sheet, because the information was "all in the footnotes," and they could easily calculate what that implied. The intellectual inconsistency of their claims was transparent.

Perhaps the worst argument was the one which its advocates took as the strongest argument against the FASB rule. The worry was that if shareholders saw the value of the stock options being given out (or even worse, the value of the options outstanding), the value of many companies would plunge. They were saying, in effect, that if shareholders only knew what was being given to their executives, they would recognize that there was less left for themselves. This was an argument that better information would make a difference—and I thought it was an argument *for* expensing stock options.[6]

Stock options and shareholder value

When executives (or other employees) receive stock options, a company is committing itself to issue new stock, thereby diluting the value of the existing stock. Assume a case in which there are already 1 million shares outstanding, each worth $30; that would make the company's value (or "market capitalization") $30 million. If its executives get, say, an additional 1 million shares free, then the old shareholders will have to share the company's wealth—and future profits—with these "new" shareholders, and the value of each share will fall to $15. Thus, the shareholders effectively pay the executives

$15 million—not straight out of their own pockets, but through the diminution in their share value.

Things work a little differently, but only a little differently, if the executives have to pay a portion of the price for their shares. Assume they pay $10—a bargain price. The company will now have a market value of $40 million (the original $30 million, plus the cash infusion of $10 million), to be divided among the (now) 2 million shareholders. The value of each share is now $20. Again, the shareholders have lost—in this case, a total of $10 million, which is exactly the amount the executives have gained: 1 million shares, each worth $20, but purchased for only $10.

Factor in the tax implications, and the cost to the company is even higher. When someone receives a salary—even if it's based on an incentive scheme intended to reward performance—the amount is deductible.[7] For a company in a 30 percent corporate tax bracket, the cost to the firm works out to just 70 cents on the dollar. If the recipient of the salary is in the 28 percent tax bracket, he receives 72 cents on the dollar. In short, it costs the firm 70 cents to pay the worker 72 cents. Add it up, and you get a negative tax—a government subsidy, you might say. But with a stock option that is never expensed, there is no corporate income tax deduction. When the executive cashes the option, he or she pays a capital gains tax on the excess of the sale price over the purchase price—but the corporation has no tax deduction. The combined taxes of the corporation and the employee were higher under this arrangement; but the advantages that the CEOs saw in distorting information more than compensated.[8]

I once had a chance to meet with a group of senior compensation officers from some of the nation's largest businesses. I took the opportunity to ask them, quite bluntly, why they had structured their pay in this way so that they paid more taxes than they needed to and also misled investors as to the magnitude of executive compensation. Their responses indicated that, for the most part, they had not considered the full tax implications. But even though they now grasped those implications, they still would not change their practices. Their job was to maximize shareholder value and maximizing shareholder value in the short run meant they had to exploit the market's ignorance of the cost of stock options to the companies issuing them.

In less polite circles, we might speak of stock options as corporate theft—executives stealing money from their unwary shareholders. Yet with stocks leaping from $10 to $20 to $30, few shareholders noticed. They felt like winners. It looked like a game in which there were no losers. But, of course, they did lose. Stocks traded at $30 instead of $40, or $20 instead of $30. The very subtlety of the theft was what enabled so many executives to get away with it.

I use strong language, "theft," to describe one of a number of practices that enabled corporate executives to deprive shareholders of what was theirs. Theft—taking something from someone without consent—is exactly what it was. The victims were in no position to give their consent, because, for the most part, they didn't realize that anything had been taken from them. Of course, shareholders were supposed to be the *beneficiaries* of this practice. The use of stock options as a form of compensation grew out of the "shareholder value" movement of the 1980s. Options, it was said, made the interests of managers and the interests of shareholders the same. It was a seductive argument, but, as events proved, a deeply flawed one.

In a stock market boom, most of the increase in the value of stock has nothing to do with the efforts of management. During the nineties, almost every share went up—often by a lot. In such circumstances, there is one way to provide a true reward for performance: managers have to be graded on a curve, with bonuses going to those who do better than average (the average of firms in their industry, perhaps), and with penalties imposed on those who do worse than average. A few firms did adopt such *relative performance compensation schemes*—a very few. In short, from the perspective of economic theory, setting tax considerations aside, stock options should not have been part of a well-designed compensation scheme. For a well-designed scheme maximizes incentives at the same time that it limits risk. Stock options, on the other hand, provided risk without incentives, making executive compensation dependent chiefly on the outcome of the stock market casino.

Most CEOs were too clever to accept a bona fide stock option scheme. When the market went up, they willingly took the bonuses that it brought; when the market went down, they could honestly go to the executive compensation committees and complain that it would be unfair to them to be penalized for a general stock market decline, and their case might be especially compelling if the firm had performed better than average. (They slid over the fact that they should have said the same thing when they were getting their bonanzas.) They asked the executive compensation committees to come up with other forms of reward—a one-time bonus for bringing the company through a period of hard times, let's say, or for handling a tricky restructuring. Or "repricing" their options, so that they still got a good deal when they exercised the options, even at the low price. The committees (over whose membership the CEOs often played a large role) systematically complied. It was a classic heads-I-win-tails-you-lose arrangement. In practice, "incentive pay" was a euphemism for "big pay." A few cases drew widespread public comment because they were so egregious: Cisco's John Chambers voluntarily cut his annual pay to $1 but still received 6 million stock options in fiscal 2001 as his company lost $1 billion and its stock price fell 70 percent. But the practice is so widespread that on average, there appears little relationship between compensation and reward.

The consequence was that during the nineties overall pay of American CEOs began to bear no relationship to the usual economic forces.[9] In the nineties, compensation soared to unheard-of levels, defying all laws of economics. Competitive markets dictate that compensation is determined by demand and supply. If compensation were really determined by competitive forces, compensation would only have increased if there was a large shift in demand or supply. But the number of CEOs on the market didn't suddenly shrink and the productivity or performance of America's CEOs did not rise so much that they suddenly deserved 1,000 percent raises. During the nineties, senior executive compensation rose by 442 percent in eight years, from an average of $2 million to $10.6 million. Compensation of American executives was completely out of line relative to the salaries of middle management, relative to the salaries of workers, relative to anything imaginable. While senior executive compensation rose 36 percent in 1998 over 1997, the wages of the average blue-collar worker rose just 2.7 percent in the same period. And the pattern was repeated over and over again. Even in 2001, a disaster year for profits and stock prices, executive CEO pay increased twice as fast as the pay of the average worker. American executives may be more productive than their European and Japanese colleagues, but even so, their compensation also was markedly out of line with that of those abroad, not only absolutely but relatively. In Japan, for instance, executive pay is typically 10 times that of the average worker; in Great Britain, executive pay is typically 25 times that of the average worker; by 2000 in America, CEOs were getting more than 500 times the wages of the average employee, up from 85 times at the beginning of the decade, and 42 times two decades earlier.

The problems of executive compensation are distinctive to the modern corporation with wide share ownership. If a single individual owns a firm, then if he pays his manager too much, he bears the cost of the mistake. Over seventy years ago, Adolf A. Berle and Gardiner C. Means drew attention to the fact that in the corporations that were emerging, there was a separation of ownership and control.[10] Shareholders *nominally* owned and controlled the firm, but in fact, they had limited information about what the managers were doing, and limited ability to do anything about it if they didn't like what they saw. There were boards of directors, again nominally elected by the shareholders, whose job it was to provide oversight; but often, the board was hand-selected by the CEO, and only with a massive rebellion could shareholders do much to replace the board.

Here again there was another conflict of interest. Boards are supposed to protect the interests of *all* shareholders. But some boards, whose members often receive large fees—$10,000, $20,000, $40,000—for membership and attendance, were frequently more concerned with pleasing the CEO than fulfilling their supposed fiduciary responsibilities. And while advocates of reform of corporate governance emphasize the importance of *outside* directors, that is, directors who are not part of management, outside directors appointed by or suggested by the CEO become in effect insider directors as soon as they take their seat.

After some CEOs persuaded their boards to give them options, then other CEOs could go to their boards and argue that they also deserved them because it was a matter of prestige, credibility, and would affect the ability of the firm to recruit first-class managers. This argument was particularly persuasive when the CEO in question played a large role in the appointments to these prestigious and well-paying board positions. In extreme cases, boards ratified not only stock options but also low-interest loans for board members; it was clear they were not protecting shareholders, but looking for ways in which shareholders would not realize how richly rewarded the CEOs were becoming.

America has long been a source of innovation, its ideas and products exported abroad. So too in the area of corporate deception, much to the chagrin of the Europeans. When the star practitioner of American economic management style in France, Jean-Marie Messier and the Vivendi Universal that he had built out of a French water company, came crashing down, there was more than a little glee in France.

Incentives matter—but it matters what kind of incentives

The irony is that although advocates of stock options talked about incentives, they didn't really care about getting in place the right kind of incentives. Stock options—as actually practiced—did not provide much of an incentive to do those things that would increase the *long-run* value of the firm. Stock options meant that executive pay depended on stock prices in the short run, and in the short run, it was easier to improve the appearances of profits than to increase true profits.

Even in the good times, many corporate executives were not content to float upward with the rising tide. They found ways to boost their earnings—through sham transactions which allowed them to book revenues even if they didn't really have them, or by moving expenses off their books, or by using one-time write-offs (time and time again), to try to give the appearance of robust *normal* profits. Their objective was to create the appearance of alluring success—or, at least, of alluring promise—and cash out before the world discovered the truth. Thus did one form of deception give rise to many others. And investors were by no means the only victims.

When share prices reflect bad information, resources are likely to be badly deployed. In the late nineties, they were very badly deployed. Rising prices say, "invest more." The fast-rising prices of tech and telecommunications stocks led to an enormous overhang of investment in those sectors of the economy. That overhang, in turn, was partly responsible for the long downturn that began in late 2000. And it all started with ill-advised accounting practices.

Not expensing stock options meant that shareholders did not have accurate information about how their shares were being diluted; it also increased incentives to provide more and more pay in this non-transparent way, and with more and more of compensation depending on the short-run stock value, stock options provided more and more of an incentive for firms to pump up their numbers. And pump up their numbers they did, selling shares at fixed prices that were more and more out of kilter with reality, with the result that more and more investment was wasted.

Stock options provide a good example of how accounting can give misleading information. Accounting standards, implemented by *independent* accounting firms, are supposed to limit the extent to which firms can do this—which was why the FASB was so concerned about the treatment of stock options. But changes in the Roaring Nineties—the financial innovations about which so many on Wall Street were so proud—gave firms more and more opportunities well beyond stock options to do so. And changes in the accounting industry changed the incentives for accounting firms: Accounting firms, who were supposed to provide an independent check, increasingly had perverse incentives—an incentive to aid and abet rather than to provide the safeguards that they were supposed to. The magnitude of the distortion in information resulting from not reporting stock options alone is enormous. One estimate has it that in 2001, earnings per share for companies comprising the S&P 500 would have been 20 percent lower if stock options had been treated as an expense.

Deceptive Accounting 101

Corporate financial reports are tremendously complicated. That's why accountants get hired. They're supposed to present profits and losses, and net worth and so on, in standardized ways that can be widely understood. Some argue that capitalism—and the modern corporation—could not have arisen without a reliable accounting industry able to provide a reasonably accurate picture of a firm's net worth and profits. Without that information, how can anyone assess the value of a firm? Equities are supposed to give the stockholder a share of a firm's profits; but if the firm could simply make up any old number, who would buy a share?

Government has always played an important role in setting fraud standards. Fraud can be depicted as providing grossly misleading information. How the government sets these standards—and the consequences it imposes when auditors fail to do their job—has a big impact on the credibility of the corporate numbers, and thus on the strength of the capital market.

Accountants are required in part because shareholders know they can't trust firms—there is simply too strong an incentive, even in the presence of fraud laws, to provide misleading information. There are natural *asymmetries of information*—managers know information which shareholders don't.[11] The accountants are supposed to make sure that the numbers reported accord with certain standards. Good accounting standards and practices reduce asymmetries of information, and help make capital markets work better. In the last two decades, unfortunately, the forces working in favor of accurate information have been systematically undermined.

While accountants have long been the butt of jokes (they are widely considered even more boring than economists), they have a difficult and important task. Their responsibility goes beyond the mechanical application of rules. Consider a relatively simple issue like depreciation. Both for taxes and the company's books, buildings are supposed to be depreciated (that is, a deduction from income is taken to reflect the loss in value of an asset used to produce income) over a period that represents their expected lifetime, say, thirty years. Since walls are part of a building, their costs, too, should be depreciated, and presumably over the same thirty-year term. But what about a *movable* wall? Is it more like a piece of furniture (depreciated over ten years), or more like a building (thirty years)? If a firm wants to reduce its income for tax purposes, it may prefer to characterize the wall as movable. If it wants to bloat its income for investors, on the other hand, the firm may be inclined to claim that the wall is not movable. In the past, such income-bloating maneuvers carried a high cost: they meant higher taxes. But, in recent years, innovative consultants and accountants have found ways to do both at once, by moving the costs off the balance sheet to a special entity created specifically for the purpose of taking advantage of the most rapid tax write-offs possible.

Some of these maneuvers first became fashionable in the early eighties, though the context was different. The ethos at the time was to avoid as many taxes as possible, and the Reagan administration helpfully provided businesses (and affluent citizens) with a host of new tax-dodging techniques. A firm was entitled to an investment tax credit, for example, when it bought a machine. But if that firm had no income to begin with, the credit was of little value. To get around the difficulty, companies resorted to complex lease deals. Instead of buying a machine with money borrowed from, say, GE Credit, a company would have GE Credit buy it, and rent it back to the company. The payments were much the same. But the debt did not show up on the company's balance sheet, and GE Credit got to take advantage of the investment tax credit (which GE could well use, given its huge profits). Such arrangements made the books look better all around. Taxes were lowered, and so were apparent liabilities.

Leases provided further opportunities for discretion, and firms found ways of using the discretion for their short-run advantage. When Xerox leased machines in Latin America, it booked the entire revenue stream that it expected to receive—it treated it almost as if it were a clean sale. But when the global financial crisis struck Latin America, many of the leases were not honored, and the revenues that had already been added in profits—helping to boost Xerox stock— didn't materialize. The magnitudes are not small: Xerox's profits in 1997, 1998, and 1999 had to be lowered by a total of $6.4 billion.

In 2003, the SEC filed a formal complaint against its auditor, KPMG; although this is only the second such complaint against a major auditing firm, put the other way, it means that there are now only three major auditing firms that have not had SEC complaints brought against them.

In succeeding years, ever more complicated devices were invented, partly to take advantage of different tax laws in different countries. It became common for numerous parties to figure in a single transaction—the kind of equipment purchase that, in the past, would have entailed only a buyer and seller, or, at most, a buyer, a seller, and a bank, which lent the money. An American firm might sublease a piece of computer equipment to a foreign firm, created for that express purpose, and the foreign firm might go on to sublease it to another American firm (also created for that purpose), who would make a single up-front payment to the foreign firm, but borrow the money from one branch of a bank and (to make sure the foreign firm didn't run off with the money) immediately deposit it into another branch of the same bank. The foreign firm might then contribute its capital—which consisted of nothing more than the bank account and its pledge to pay the lease payments for which it was obligated—to a partnership. A year later (seemingly by agreement), the partner would buy out the new "partner," recording a loss on its books on the deal. Other firms might be brought into the tax scam. This whirl of mini-transactions was meant to make the mind spin—to obscure the fact that nothing real was going on, and, ultimately, to rob the U.S. Treasury.

Specialists in this sort of accounting wizardry took pride in it. There was no moral compunction about cheating the government— and little risk. At worst, the IRS might disallow the deal, forcing a company to pay the taxes it should have paid in the first place. It was like a loan from the government—sometimes at a rate that was better than the firm could get on the market. The government rarely attempted to collect penalties—and rarely succeeded when it did.

In the late nineties, with the bubble expanding, tax benefits became secondary; for some companies, all that mattered was making the books look good. Techniques that had been invented to deceive the IRS were now employed, with a little modification, to deceive shareholders. Of course, the moral calculations were different. Most corporate managers felt little guilt about cheating the IRS—they might even have said it was their duty to do so, since by doing so they increased share prices. On the other hand, when it came to reporting information to shareholders, they had a duty to report the firm's financial position accurately. After all, the shareholders are the owners, and the managers work for the shareholders. When they provided deceiving information to the market, the managers might salve their consciences, saying that by driving share prices up, they *were* looking out for their shareholders—at least for those who had bought low and managed to sell high. Apparently, they didn't think about what would happen when the truth would come out; they simply assumed that the day of reckoning would be on someone else's watch. They had been told to maximize today's shareholder value, and that they did—even if it meant providing deceptive information. And their incentive plans rewarded them for maximizing today's shareholder value.

As the structure of the economy changed, the problems facing accountants grew, and ever more opportunities were afforded to use what they had honed to a fine art. Over the years, they had devised standard ways for treating items like investments in factories and real estate. But with the rise of the New Economy, the accounting profession had to contend with assets that were sometimes vexingly difficult to value, giving their client companies all sorts of new ways to manipulate the numbers. Companies were sold on the basis of their subscribers—a number commonly treated as a hard asset, even though, as a practical matter, subscribers could disappear quickly. Some firms had attained huge market values without ever turning a profit; and even if profits existed, what was the assurance that they would be sustained? In the steel industry, huge up-front investments made entry difficult. New Economy mavens, as we saw in the previous chapter, spoke of the critical importance of the "first mover advantage." Get into a market first, in other words, and others will have a hard time following. But the New Economy was also a world in which new firms could spring up, and become major players, overnight. All of these were complicated topics for accountants to make sense of.

Derivatives, those complicated new financial products, allegedly gave companies a powerful new tool for sharing and shifting risk.[12] But they could also be a means of moving money off the balance sheets, and, by doing so, concealing enormous risks. Insiders as well as outsiders were sometimes deceived. Over the years, the public watched as mighty firms like Barings were brought down by the derivatives' trading of their own employees, which their own internal accounting systems had been unable to detect. Public authorities, such as Orange County, California, were brought to the brink of bankruptcy. When unwary customers discovered the true risks of these derivatives, as they lost millions instead of gaining the millions they had been promised, huge legal catfights were waged between the financial houses selling derivatives and the companies buying them.

With each instance of misuse of derivatives, there was increasing concern about the risks of derivatives. While I was chairman of the Council, the issue of derivatives came up repeatedly. There was a monthly meeting of key government officials involved in financial markets—including the secretary of Treasury, the head of the Fed, the chairman of the Council of Economic Advisers, the head of the Securities and Exchange Commission. But the bottom line of our discussions was always the same: We were aware of the risks, and we were aware of the benefits. We were aware of the difficulties that derivatives posed in assessing the true financial state of a bank, or for that matter any firm, but we felt there was little we could do, especially in an era in which regulations were being stripped back. In part we trusted the market and so we were ready to keep a careful watch without taking action to safeguard the markets from derivatives. In retrospect, we could have done much more to improve the quality of reporting, and to restrict the extent of risk exposure.

The Securities and Exchange Commission

There was one part of the U.S. government, however, that did not buy into the deregulation mantra, that saw that there were problems in securities markets which had to be addressed if these markets were really to function as they were supposed to, and in the interests of the average investor: the Securities and Exchange Commission, headed by Arthur Levitt (who, incidentally, was confirmed for his position in the same hearings in which I was, perhaps giving us a bond that went beyond the similarity in our views of the role of government).

Levitt understood there was a multiplicity of problems, all of which had to be addressed. He was concerned about the difficulties that the New Economy presented for accountants, and the opportunities for discretion that that afforded the accountants to provide misleading information. But he was even more concerned about incentives: he worried that auditors not only lacked the incentive to do the job that they were supposed to do; they had perverse incentives.

To address the problems posed by the increased difficulty of accounting in the New Economy, Levitt put together a commission to look at valuation in the New Economy on which I was asked to serve. The group was headed by the energetic and thoughtful dean of Yale's School of Management, Jeffrey Gartner, whom I had known as undersecretary of commerce in the Clinton administration. It was a balanced group, including tech-company executives, academics, and accountants. We understood the importance of hearing from people in the New Economy itself: they inevitably had the best view of what was going on. But therein lay a problem. Some on the commission—which included Enron founder Ken Lay as well as others from Silicon Valley who reaped the benefits of stock options—had vested interests. They knew what was going on, but they were profiting from it, and they wanted as little change as possible. They repeated the standard mantra of the day: fear big government, trust the markets to take care of everything. (The market did take care of Enron, but not before many people's jobs and bank accounts had been destroyed.)

Levitt realized that whatever the guidelines provided accountants, whatever the rules, they would have discretion, and they needed to have the right incentives in place to use that discretion in ways that would result in better and more accurate information. The problem was that accountants didn't have the right incentives. There had always been a problem: auditors get paid by the firms they audit, and they naturally want to please their client; after all, it is the company (and its executives) who make the decision about whom to hire as an accountant. But to this potentially troublesome picture, one new ingredient was added.

Over the years, accountants had expanded into two lines of business: consulting and auditing. There were natural synergies: the insights accountants got from perusing the books allowed them to give advice on how a company could increase its profits (or reported profits). But as the consulting end of the business increased, so did the temptation to play fast and loose with the auditing end; an accounting firm making millions as a consultant might look the other way when it came across evidence of a shady accounting practice. To please a client, an accounting firm might even suggest a shady practice—some method of complying (technically) with the law and rules, while presenting a misleading picture of the firm. Derivatives—the great financial innovations of the preceding decades—were a tool well suited to this sort of deception. They could be used, for example, to disguise a loan as a forward sale, receiving money today for something to be delivered in the future, and the whole transaction could be left off the books. Nothing illegal, other than failing to represent the true balance sheet of the firm; and, as defenders of such practices might point out, it would all be there in the footnotes.

Levitt pushed for regulations that would have kept a firm from serving the same client in both capacities. The reply of the accounting firms and their allies was, essentially, "Trust us," and unfortunately they prevailed. In hindsight, Levitt's good judgment is inescapable. Trust can go only so far.

One firm found the temptations particularly hard to resist. Arthur Andersen, which had enjoyed an almost impeccable reputation over most of the years since its founding in 1913, became embroiled in a bitter internecine warfare. As so often happens in professional service companies, different parts of the company insisted that they weren't getting their fair share of the profits. In this case, the consulting branch of the company, which was generating most of the money, considered itself inadequately compensated. Unable to agree on a settlement, the parties entered into a messy divorce. The consulting part became independent; ordered not to use the Andersen name, it developed a new one, along with a new logo and a new brand identity. The resulting firm, which called itself Accenture, thought it had lost something precious; a few years later, however, that legal defeat became a business godsend.

Deprived of the most profitable part of its business, the old Arthur Andersen now resolved to build up a consulting practice all over again—and quickly. Speed meant risks. In economics, we speak of the "franchise value" of a firm—the value of the future profits of an ongoing enterprise. One of the main motivations for a firm to act prudently (or to provide customers with decent service, for that matter) is to maintain its franchise value. With its franchise value already greatly reduced by internecine struggle, Arthur Andersen had weakened incentives to act prudently. It is perhaps not surprising that

Arthur Andersen became involved in a high proportion of the corporate scandals of the nineties—WorldCom and Enron being the most notorious, but the list of cases over the years is long, and includes among others Sunbeam, Waste Management, Global Crossing, Dynegy, Halliburton, Colonial Realty, and Qwest.[13] It was more than just a case of bad luck.

Any incentive scheme involves carrots and sticks. There were plenty of carrots encouraging the accounting firms to look the other way. Traditionally, there had been one big stick discouraging them. If things went awry, they could be sued. In the past, such lawsuits had, in fact, been fairly common. When a company goes bust, those who lose their money look for someone to blame; in America, that means someone to sue. There's no point, of course, in suing a bankrupt company (especially if you're one of its owners). Sometimes, these disgruntled shareholders would sue a company's officers, but the officers soon learned how to protect themselves (by moving their money offshore, among other things). In some cases, they didn't have enough money to make a lawsuit worthwhile. Lawyers always look for deep pockets—and the auditing firms were the obvious candidate. By the middle of the nineties, the rash of suits, especially in Silicon Valley, home of the dot-com and the tech start-up, was proving particularly troublesome. Companies worried that they would not be able to find auditors, or that the auditors would charge exorbitant fees in order to shore up their defenses against litigation. In 1995, Congress adopted legislation intended to limit securities litigation over the veto of the president; in doing so, they provided substantial protection for the auditors. But we may have gone too far: insulated from suits, the accountants were now willing to take more "gambles," and to give more benefit of the doubt to a firm engaged in aggressive accounting practices.

Lessons

In the 1990s, while America sought to export its version of capitalism to the rest of the world, it also trumpeted its accounting systems. In the aftermath of the East Asia crisis, countries were told, you must adopt sound—that is, American—accounting practices. Yet, ironically, if the United States had adopted the accounting standards used in much of the rest of the world, some of our corporate scandals might not have occurred. Although there were similarities between the practices in America and elsewhere, there was one critical difference: Here, auditors were rulebound. They had to follow the rules. Whatever they could get away with *within the rules* was viewed as fine. Indeed, the challenge facing an auditor/consultant was to make the firm look as good as possible while *staying* within the rules. By contrast, the standards used in most other countries required the auditor to certify that the overall accounts presented an accurate view of the company's financial position. Perhaps, at one time, professional standards would have allowed such a judgment to be taken for granted. But in America, in the nineties, it was money and markets that prevailed, and this meant that while the rules were complied with, the overall picture could be—and often was—misleading.

To most Americans, what was so disturbing about Enron and the other scandals was the inequities. The insiders, already richly rewarded, used their information to cash in, even as they encouraged workers to sit tight and keep their retirement money in company stock. Seeking to justify their rich rewards, corporate leaders claimed that they had "created value," and had built the firms into the powerhouses that they seemed to be. But what they had created, in quite a few cases, was a house of cards.

More than fair play was at stake. For a market economy to function well, all the participants must have confidence in it. Investors and potential investors need to believe that there is a level playing field, with accurate information, rather than a rigged game in which insiders are bound to win. In the aftermath of the scandals of the 1920s and early 1930s, the United States passed legislation trying to address the problems that the crash had exposed—regulations covering everything from cornering the market to insider trading. The Securities and Exchange Commission was created in 1934, and, together with other checks and balances (including class-action suits), it helped build a sense of professional ethics among managers, auditors, and other market participants, leading to the creation of a securities market of unprecedented size, with unprecedented participation. At the peak of the market in March 2000, the market capitalization of U.S. stocks (as measured by the Wilshire index) was $17 trillion, or 1.7 times the value of American GDP. Half of all U.S. households owned equities.

The world has changed a great deal, however, over the past sixty years. New forms of deception have been developed. In the go-go environment of the nineties while market values soared, human values eroded, and the playing field became terribly unlevel once again, contributing to the bubble that burst soon after the beginning of the new millennium. The stock option controversy of the early nineties seemed to me to be a hugely significant matter at the time, perhaps because of my own research, which had emphasized the importance of good and accurate information in making a market economy work. But during the boom, it was difficult to arouse interest in the issue from many, other than those who benefited from the bad accounting. It was another instance where we trusted the judgment of the experts, including those in the financial and accounting community, though, given their vested interests, we should have been skeptical. Arthur Levitt was right. There was a need for more and stronger regulation. Although there was no way we could be sure that information would always be accurate, at least we could get the incentives right. Stock options distorted managerial incentives, consulting distorted auditors' incentives. The carrots were now going the other way—undermining incentives for good information—and at the same time changes in the liability laws weakened the "stick." And all of this was happening just as the difficulties in providing accurate information were increasing, as were the opportunities for providing deceptive information.

I began this chapter with the big question: what might have been? Would the bubble have been averted if only we had only supported better accounting of executive stock options? We will never know the answer. But of this we can be sure: combined with the other problems of accounting discussed in this chapter, the bad accounting of stock options clearly made matters worse. And it contributed to the ethos of the nineties, one that inflated the bubble, making the crash all the worse.

The conflicts of interest that we discussed here were bad enough; the consequences were amplified by similar, or even worse, problems in the financial sector, to which we now turn.

CHAPTER 6

The Banks and the Bubble

I N   T H E   G O - G O nineties, many people in the world of business and finance were carried away by making money and lowered their ethical standards as they raced to cash in. But nowhere was this more surprising than in the banking world. After all, bankers had always been viewed as those sober, prudent men in gray suits who kept an eye on the companies they lent money to because above all else, they wanted to be repaid. Bankers didn't like scandals and bad loans, and so the banking sector provided an important check on U.S. corporate activity. By carefully monitoring their loan portfolio they helped prevent bankruptcies and excesses in the business world.

Much of this changed in the nineties: bank analysts touted bad stocks, bankers helped Enron set up the shaky offshore entities that helped the company conceal its liabilities, handed out shares in hot IPOs[1] to their friends, and engaged in all sorts of unsavory activities. As 2001 and 2002 proceeded, many of the major banks in the United States were involved in one scandal after another, including legendary names such as J. P. Morgan Chase, Merrill Lynch, Credit Suisse First Boston, Citigroup and its brokerage arm, the venerable firm of Salomon Smith Barney, Goldman Sachs—culminating in settlement payments of $1.4 billion imposed by New York State's attorney general Eliot Spitzer.[2]

What concerns me is not so much the individual stories and the misdoings of a few greedy analysts but the effect that the transformation of U.S. banking had on the overall functioning of the economy. Traditionally, in the United States there had been two kinds of banks—investment banks, which issue bonds and shares, and commercial banks, which lend out money that has been deposited in them. In the nineties, legislation was passed that allowed mergers between these two kinds of banks, forming financial conglomerates like J. P. Morgan Chase and Citigroup. Most of these banks had, or acquired, brokerage arms, such as Citibank's Salomon Smith Barney. Much of the story told here focuses on investment banking, including the conflicts of interests that arose between that and the other activities in which they were engaged. The profitability of investment banks had traditionally beeen based on information: they had developed a reputation for reliability. But the changes in the economy in the nineties changed their incentives; like the CEOs whose shares they were issuing, they had an incentive to provide distorted information to the market.

For the stock market to function well, there needs to be accurate information about what a company is worth so that investors can pay the right price for its shares. By obfuscating the problems inherent in many of the companies they brought to the market or for which they helped raise capital by issuing shares, the banks contributed to the erosion of the quality of information. They were supposed to provide information to investors, to reduce the disparity between informed insiders and outsiders. Instead, asymmetries of information were maintained or increased; in many cases, bankers and analysts knew the real state of affairs about the companies they worked with but the public did not. Confidence in the markets declined, and when the correct information came out, share prices declined sharply.

Why the bankers and analysts were willing to provide misleading information is related to the question of incentives. They made money from IPOs and other deals, so much money that the rewards for providing wrong information were higher than the rewards for providing accurate information. And while there were plenty of incentives to provide inaccurate information, the counterbalancing incentives were weak or absent, because of what is called the "public good" aspect of firm management: if the firm is managed well, all stakeholders, all equity holders as well as creditors, benefit.[3] If a single shareholder successfully exerts efforts to improve the quality of management, her returns are increased and so are the returns to other shareholders. But since the do-good shareholder receives only a small part of the benefits accruing from her action, she does not have an incentive to make a huge effort to improve things.

There were several changes during the nineties which transformed what had been a latent set of problems into what became for many an economic disaster. Deregulation, which opened up new sources of conflicts of interests, and stock options and other badly designed compensation schemes, which encouraged a focus on the here and now rather than the long term, proved as problematic in the financial sector as elsewhere. The bankers of the nineties were essentially no different from corporate executives in other hot sectors of the economy. They learned how to drive up their own share prices, just as they helped others do so. The rise in share prices was supposed to create shareholder value in the long term. But in too many cases, the market focused only on the short run, today's bottom line. And with executives' pay depending on today's share price, they had more of an incentive to focus on today's profits and less of an incentive to focus on the firm's long-term reputation.

The same was true of analysts such as Mary Meeker at Morgan Stanley, Jack Grubman at Citibank's Salomon Smith Barney, and Henry Blodget, at Merrill Lynch, all of whom made millions as they pushed telecom and high-tech stocks. Each was accused of supplying the unwary customers who relied on them with analyses full of plenty of hype, but low on information about the true value of the firms.[4] The bonuses and other financial incentives they received encouraged short-term thinking. Getting a bonus for landing an investment banking deal became more important than providing good information which would help ensure that funds went where they would be most productive. Instead of blowing the whistle on companies that cooked the books or buried revealing numbers in layers of obfuscation, the banks helped them do it. Some Wall Street analysts truly didn't understand the companies they were touting; others, as we know from their derogatory e-mails, understood all too well. It hardly mattered.

New financial engineering techniques offered new ways not only for accountants to provide distorted information, as we saw in chapter 4, but for the banks to serve as accomplices. And so did deregulation. There were in fact a variety of new synergies between accountants and banks, which did not always serve the public well: The problems in accounting meant that the accountants did not check the power of the banks as they should have. The banks did less of what they had traditionally done, keeping an eye on the companies they lent money to. That was why problems in the banking sector had such large systemic consequences.

Deregulation enhanced the scope for conflicts of interest. It also had the advertised effect of increasing competition. Under normal circumstances, increased competition is a good thing. But in the nineties, the banks became so eager for short-term profit that there was a race to the bottom. Each bank knew that its competitors were engaging in similar practices, and if it didn't compete, it would be left behind; and each banking officer knew what that meant: smaller bonuses, perhaps even being fired.

The bubble—and the bad behavior—were reinforcing: the stronger the bubble, the stronger the incentives to take the actions to keep it going. The banks must surely have known that when the bubble burst, many of the loans they had made would fail. Thus, the banks' loan portfolios depended on keeping the stock market bubble going. If market participants had fully understood the incentives at play at the banks, brokerage houses, and among the analysts who worked for them, they might well have become skeptical of the information that they were given. This must have been understood by the many bankers who participated in the deceptions; they did not reveal the rewards they themselves were getting.

At the center of the Roaring Nineties, and the problems that finally emerged in the early days of the new century, was a symbiotic relationship between Wall Street and Silicon Valley. I was in an excellent position to see what was going on in Silicon Valley, which even before the nineties had established itself as the center of innovation, and on Wall Street. I straddled the two acutely different cultures—the innovative, high-tech culture of the West and the dealmaking culture of the East. From 1979 until I went to Washington in 1993, I divided my time between Stanford University, in the heart of Silicon Valley, and Princeton University, an hour's commute from Manhattan and Wall Street. On the West Coast, the preoccupation with computers, networks, and electronic commerce had reached a fever pitch: you could hardly go into a restaurant or café without hearing an excited burst of talk about the latest, wildest technology or business idea. On the East Coast, meanwhile, the conversation was all about finance, about initial public offerings, mergers, and acquisitions, and which company or sector was poised for takeoff.

Although New York and Silicon Valley differed in many ways, they were dependent on each other, and they knew it. New ideas require capital to be brought to fruition, and Silicon Valley had developed a new institution—the venture capital firm—to do just that. The venture capital firms could only finance new ventures if they could cash in on the successes of previous ventures. And while Wall Street could make plenty of money rearranging the pieces of the "old economy," it was in marketing the New Economy that the real riches lay. It mattered little that some on Wall Street knew scant about what they were selling: in the bubble economy, whatever they sold succeeded.

Everyone wanted a piece of the action. As new ventures got off the ground, the big investment houses would sell their securities to the public—to pension funds and other institutional investors, and to retail customers through a vast network of brokerages. In the nineties, America's ability to finance innovation was the envy of the world.

There were many similarities between what was happening on the two coasts. Both endeavors required creativity, but of a quite different kind. Money drove both, but in the West, it was moderated by science and often tempered by idealism, a concern for the environment or involvement in social action. On both coasts, *information* was the secret of success—computer code, in the Valley; financial data, on the Street. Silicon Valley and its venture capital firms thrived on information about technology, judgments about what would work, and knowledge about how to put together a start-up. The eastern investment banks leveraged knowledge about sources of funding, the trust that these sources had in them, the skills necessary for structuring complicated deals and the ability to pull them off. Both cultures exuded enormous confidence—confidence about what they knew and what they could do. And yet, in their attitudes, their manners, and, most noticeably, in their attire, there was a striking difference. Out west, every day was Casual Friday and then some; at Yahoo!, it was no surprise to find co-founder (and instant billionaire) David Filo in a tattered T-shirt and grungy bluejeans—and barefoot. It was a way of dress that underscored the commitment to substance over form. Many company managers and engineers defined their career choices in highly idealistic terms: Silicon Valley was a place where you could talk about the world-changing potential of something like an online pet food business, and not be laughed at. It was also a place where people seemed to have their minds laser-focused on the task at hand.

Those who made their money by following Wall Street's advice were willing to give the analysts and investment bankers full credit, just as most who benefited from the booming economy were willing to give credit to the men and women managing the economy in Washington. The bankers, no less than the policymakers, took the praise to heart.

Cashing in on the boom market

The changing economy had changed the role of banks, just as it had changed the role of firms. In the last chapter, we noted how the growth of large enterprises had led to the separation of ownership and control; those who managed the firms did so on behalf of millions of shareholders, whose interests they were supposed to advance. But in truth, they often advanced their own interests, at the expense of the average shareholder; and stock options and other devices that made it difficult for ordinary shareholders to see what was really going on only made matters worse.

With small shareholders unable to make sure that managers were doing the right thing, banks took on an increasingly important role. Managers wanted their firms to grow, and needed finance. But banks would only lend money if the firms had reasonable business plans, if there was a reasonable prospect of being repaid. Banks played an important role in *monitoring*.

From time to time firms needed still more money, and then they went to investment banks to issue bonds or shares. Investment banks also played an important informational role. In effect, they lent their reputation. They would only issue a firm's bonds if they thought it could repay; they would only issue a firm's shares if they thought they were fairly priced, in terms of what they were likely to earn. They stood behind these assessments, often committing themselves to buy whatever was not sold on the open market. But the investment banks had good connections with institutions and wealthy individuals that were saving and looking for somewhere to put their money. They were thus in a good position to place the stocks and bonds.

An investment bank that recommended shares or bonds that did not do well, would risk losing its business. It had its reputation to look after. The banks knew they could make money in the short run by promoting fly-by-night stocks; the firms would pay them for their endorsement. But the short-run gains of doing that would be more than offset by the long-run costs. The investment banks were highly profitable, and they didn't want to lose those profits.

The event which perhaps captured—some might say epitomized—the new mood of the banks was the decision of Goldman Sachs, one of the most prestigious of the investment banks (Robert Rubin had been its co-chair before heading Clinton's National Economic Council, Stephen Friedman too had been its co-chair before heading Bush's National Economic Council), to go public.[5] Most of the investment banks had been founded as partnerships. Now, one after another, they decided to cash in and become incorporated. Goldman Sachs took the plunge on May 4, 1999. Incorporation allowed Goldman to be listed on the New York Stock Exchange, and to participate in the bull market. But at the same time, it protected Goldman's executives against downside risk. As a partner, each had been liable for the mistakes, and the resulting financial losses, of the others. That made them strongly motivated to monitor each other's actions, which provided strong comfort to investors, but it was a task that was becoming increasingly difficult as the banks grew in size. Incorporation lifted that burden of responsibility from their shoulders, and offered the partners the opportunity to take advantage of soaring stock prices and make a short-term killing. Economic theory would predict that such moves by the banks would lead to greater risk taking, a greater focus on the short run, and this indeed seems to have been the case.

The analysts

As the scandals broke out, the one which generated the most outrage, because it touched the most people and was the easiest to understand, involved the analysts—those Wall Street experts who are supposed to look carefully at what each company is doing and tell investors which stocks to buy and which to sell. Millions of Americans rely upon analysts' reports, passed on to them by brokers, for advice in making decisions to buy and sell shares. As millions of Americans became small-time investors in the seventies, eighties, and nineties, they came to trust the brokers and the analysts upon whom they relied. They viewed them as professionals, not as hucksters simply trying to make an extra dollar of commission. In the nineties, America's investment banks broke that trust, as investors saw investment bank after investment bank touting shares that privately the analysts were disparaging. In some cases, analysts seemed to brag about their ability to dupe their unwary customers with the "crap" that they sold them. When it turned out that their "inside" view was far more accurate than their "public" view, the outrage was all the greater.

There had long been a potential for a conflict of interest. After all, investment banks make most of their money by doing deals, by issuing stocks and bonds. Companies come to them because they can "place" their new share issues, that is, sell their shares to others. The brokerage companies owned by the investment banks thus serve two masters—their retail customers and the banking headquarters. They balanced the two, perhaps not perfectly, by realizing that if they lost their retail customers' confidence, they would lose on both sides.

Things in fact began to change a little more than a quarter century ago. In 1975, fixed-minimum brokerage commissions were eliminated (competition in the industry had never been very robust), laying the groundwork for the rise of discount brokerages. But this eroded the profitability of the brokerage side of the business, putting all the weight on "making deals." Before 1975, analysts could be paid out of the trading margins. But with trading margins being competed away, this became more and more difficult. (Never mind that there was little evidence that the analysts were particularly good at forecasting which stocks would do well. The fact was customers wanted such forecasts, and the stories to back them.) And in the mentality of the nineties, everybody had to earn their keep. If analysts couldn't earn their keep directly from serving the interests of the retail clients, they could earn it by helping do deals. Investment houses became marketers. They did what it took to sell what they could sell. Financial analysts supposedly worked behind a "Chinese wall" in which they focused exclusively on the interests of their clients, and, of course, they had reputations to maintain—or so it was said. But economists have long been skeptical of Chinese walls—we shall see some other examples later where these walls proved much less impregnable than those in the industry claimed.

During my freshman year in college, I worked at a shoe store in Gary, Indiana. It was my first job—and a memorable lesson in balancing acts of this sort. If the shoe was too tight, we explained how leather breathed and would soon loosen up. And if it was too loose, we talked about the advantages of comfort, and how the shoe would soon take the shape of the foot. The object was to sell the shoe—to earn the commission. We never disclosed our commission, but I sensed that many of our customers knew that we were on commission by the way we treated them, and I was at least comforted by the idea that this made them cautious about believing what we told them. They really weren't relying that much on what we said.

But when it came to the IPO market, investors wanted to believe the stories they were told by the analysts even when they made no sense—when they pushed companies that had no reasonable business plans, or, even worse, had business plans that were almost guaranteed to fail. My nephew Alex, who lives in a New York City neighborhood dense with convenience stores, used to order a single can of Coke over the Internet from Kozmo.com and UrbanFetch.com (though they eventually instituted a required minimum order).[6] The Urban-Fetch.com driver who brought it to him wouldn't even take a tip. Pets.com was praised for selling dog food online—supposedly as a loss leader to bring in customers who would buy higher-margin items like expensive dog collars. The job of the analysts was to analyze: to see whether the projections of profits made sense. Could sales really increase as fast as projected—would people really buy that many diamond-studded dog collars—and if profits really were that high, what were the entry barriers that would stop other firms from competing them away? In some industries, like telecom, there was arguably a first mover advantage, based on the (fast disappearing) reluctance of telephone and cable subscribers to change service providers. But was there such loyalty in the purchase of dog collars?

The worse offenses were not those that arose from a lack of analysis, or even from a slightly rosy spin. They arose when an analyst came to a negative conclusion on a firm for which his or her investment bank wanted to do a deal. The CEOs of the firms issuing shares would play hardball, threatening to pull their business from the investment bank if the bank did not give a good rating to their company.

Wall Street's defenders do indeed say, "The investors should have known," and you can see how they might make such a claim: it doesn't take a lot of brains, after all, to figure out that an analyst might be under pressure to tout the stock of a company for which his investment bank employer is, at the same time, doing hugely profitable deals. With everybody making pots of money, it was no surprise that so few asked whether the numbers added up. But as an economist who has focused my professional life on imperfections of information, there are many puzzles: Could 70 percent of the class really be in the top half? Wall Street, like Silicon Valley—and Garrison Keillor's mythical Lake Wobegon—became a place where everyone was above average. If the analysts were to be believed, it seemed as if every stock could outperform the market. Why do investors fail to realize that money placed in a mutual fund that tries to pick "out-performing stocks" is unlikely to yield a better return than money invested in the S&P 500? If fund managers and investment advisers are so good at picking stocks, why are they risking your money rather than their own? Some of the policy implications are not likely to be favored by those in financial markets: Given the dismal track record of most fund managers and investment advisers, why not require them to disclose it? Why not make them point out just how badly they have performed, and how much money they have collected in fees along the way? Why not, at the very least, force brokerage firms to disclose which of the stocks they are touting are part of deals of the investment banks for which they work—and what the fees are on those deals?

In spite of the confidence that is so often expressed in how well markets work, there is a huge body of research suggesting that many investors are simply not rational, and if that is the case, then the prices that emerge in the market may not provide good "directions" for what to invest in. For almost a quarter century, beginning in the early seventies, the *rational expectations* school of economic thought dominated economic thinking. This portrayed the individual not only as a rational being, making consistent choices, but as someone capable of processing complex information and absorbing all the relevant knowledge. Its advocates focused on models in which everyone had the same information—there were no asymmetries. In fact, few people know enough math to process even the range of knowledge bearing on the simplest investment decision. (The rational expectations theorists conceded as much, yet asserted that, somehow, individuals acted *as if* they had processed it all.) Not content with upholding the rationality of individuals, they portrayed the economy itself as a rational mechanism—one in which, miraculously, prices reflect instantaneously everything that is known today, and prices today reflect a consistent set of expectations about what prices will be *infinitely far into the future*. The political agenda of this work often seemed barely beneath the surface: If the rational expectations school was right, markets were inherently efficient, and there would be little if any need, ever, for government intervention.

The heyday of the rational expectations movement has ended, I am pleased to report. Although such thinking still exerts enormous influence, it has been the subject of three broad attacks, each devastating in its own way. Earlier (chapter 1) I described the recent research focusing on the consequences of information asymmetries—the fact that different individuals know different things. The conclusions of the rational expectations theorists—most important, those relating to the efficiency of markets—fall apart if different people know or believe different things, as they plainly do. Markets are supposed to lead the economy to efficiency *as if by an invisible hand*. In the aftermath of the Roaring Nineties, it appears that the invisible hand wasn't working very well, and the theories of asymmetric information helped provide the explanation. Unfettered markets, rampant with conflicts of interest, can lead to inefficiency. We can never eliminate the problems; we can, however, mitigate them. In the nineties, we made them worse.

A second, related attack focused on the fact that different individuals have different beliefs about the world and how it works (for the conclusions of the rational expectations school to work, everybody not only had to have rational expectations, but they all had to believe that everybody else also had rational expectations). But—as the disagreements that we are airing now amply demonstrate—there is simply insufficient information on the basis of which everyone could agree about a single model of the world.[7] The third line of attack, noted briefly in chapter 3, spearheaded by psychologists Amos Tversky and Daniel Kahneman (the latter received the Nobel Prize in economics in 2002), zeroed in on the information-processing abilities of individuals and their rationality. Tversky and Kahneman found evidence of rampant irrationality; they even identified consistent patterns in the irrationalities of individuals—patterns clear enough to be studied by social scientists.

Business managers, unlike economists, have always been alert to the importance of irrationality. Marketing experts make their livings exploiting it. Insurance reps know they can sell coverage for low-probability events (rare forms of cancer, for instance) at premiums that far exceed the actuarial odds, because so many people are unable to resist a policy that costs but a few cents a day. Financial analysts, too, tend to be shrewd students of irrationality and herd mentality. As prices soared beyond all reason, some analysts clearly didn't enjoy the task of constructing rationales for continued stock purchases; but the market told them to set their qualms aside. The market, and the investment banks where they worked, egged them on. The banks gave clear signals—real monetary rewards—to those who treated investors as easy prey for stocks with little or no intrinsic merit. Your responsibility, the analysts were told, is to your company and yourselves. Let investors fend for themselves. (And to remove any lingering doubts, they could once again refer to Adam Smith—you advance the common good by making money for yourself!)

Now that the problems are well known, Wall Street firms have proposed remedying the damage by having independently funded analysts. That by itself will not do the trick. Far more information is required, for instance, about the track record of the analyst, the ratio of his buy and sell orders, and his incentive pay structure—is it based on sales or on the quality of his recommendations? And just in case the new "independence" turns out to be almost as much of a charade as the old Chinese walls, information about who is getting what fees for pushing which deals with each stock that is being touted should also be provided.

Fair disclosure

Although the gulf between what analysts told investors and what they believed came as a shock to many investors, Wall Street had been remarkably open about its hostility to the idea of treating small shareholders fairly—even as it preached the virtues of a new "people's capitalism" in which everyone had an equity stake. This point was brought home by Arthur Levitt's attempt, as chairman of the SEC, to insist on full public disclosure of the information that a corporate executive might feel inclined to pass on to a favored analyst. Levitt's proposal met fierce resistance, and for obvious reasons.

Analysts *were* listened to. One of the main reasons for the respect they commanded was the presumption that they enjoyed access to inside information. If everything they knew was publicly available, any investor willing to devote the time could come to his or her own judgment about a stock's merits. In the real world of highly asymmetric information, even the most confident investors knew they were at an informational disadvantage. They relied on insider analysts to turn *them* into insider investors.

When Levitt announced his fair disclosure plan, the Wall Street firms and their corporate clients raised a huge, self-serving ruckus. If forced to make information publicly and evenly available, they said, they would make no information available, and all investors would be worse off. It was an argument that, had anyone seriously believed it, would have called the whole market economy into question. On the face of it, though, it was an implausible claim: do good firms deliberately hide information that would lead investors to think well of them? Other specious arguments were also put forward: worried that they might be sued for providing misleading information, corporate executives protested that America's litigious society gave them an incentive for concealment. There was some grain of truth in this, but, of course, the same logic ought to have restrained the release of information to analysts—the presumed representatives of investors—and not just to investors in their own right.

Over tremendous opposition, Levitt finally got his fair disclosure proposal adopted on October 23, 2000. The dire consequences that so many had predicted failed to occur. The information flow did not dry up. At least on paper, the market looks a little bit fairer, a little bit more informed, than before. At least on paper, the small investor has more reason to regard the playing field as a level one, and to feel free *not* to pay an analyst or brokerage house for insights that, in the end, are likely to be unreliable, and, very probably, tainted.

The reason that the investment community resisted fair disclosure so strongly was that the preferential treatment of particular analysts was part of a web of "gift exchanges" which made the market work—that is, work for Wall Street, and for the firms trying to sell overpriced securities, generating huge profits, but not necessarily for the investor or the economy more broadly.[8] Earlier, we saw how analysts gave good reports on firms that they did business with, so that the firms would give the investment banks lucrative deals. Giving the analysts inside information gave the brokerage and investment houses with analysts an inside track over the discount brokers, who provided services to small traders at such low margins. An investment bank with a strong brokerage client base had an upper hand in doing the lucrative deals involving the issuance of securities, for it could more easily place the shares. Fair disclosure threatened to weaken the very foundations of these arrangements.

IPOs

Some of the gift exchanges were so hidden that, until the scandals broke out, few knew about them. Economists had long puzzled, for example, over why IPOs (initial public offerings, where shares of a company are first offered to the public) were typically offered at prices substantially below the "fair market" price, as demonstrated by the level to which they quickly ascended. It was investment bankers, responsible for bringing IPOs to market (and presumably well informed about a company's prospects), who set these artificially low prices. As a practical matter, they were giving away shareholders' money, which might reasonably have been construed as a form of corporate theft.[9] The IPO problem thus paralleled the executive stock option problem discussed in chapter 4. If a million shares worth $20 each are sold to new buyers at $10, the old shareholders are being deprived of $10 million that would otherwise be theirs. As the bubble grew, so, too, did the gap between what the shares were worth and what they were sold for.

Predictably, everyone wanted in on the game—who wouldn't, since the investment banks were effectively giving away money. The banks gave the money to favored clients, often in return for additional business or fatter-than-usual commissions. IPOs became an opportunity to reward the executives of institutions that traded through an investment bank's brokerage division. First dibs also went to executives of companies that placed their own IPOs with the bank. Some banks had a "friends and family" list of IPO beneficiaries. It was a cozy setup.

Although these understandings were, for the most part, implicit, in some cases the demand for kickbacks or extra commissions became almost explicit. The participants knew they were doing something that was, if not illegal, at least unseemly, so they were careful not to leave a paper trail, although here, too, private e-mails would eventually give investigators some damning evidence. The shadowy game of dishing out IPO shares to the privileged, like the equally shadowy game of linking analysts' ratings to underwriting business, proved to be a widespread pattern—seemingly standard practice at Citibank, Salomon Smith Barney, and Credit Suisse First Boston.

To a few in Wall Street, none of this posed a problem. Defenders of the IPO shenanigans compared them to giving a company a rebate. If the investment bank charged $100 million for doing a deal, what was wrong if it gave a $10 million discount to the executives responsible for placing that deal? Eliot Spitzer, the attorney general of New York State, has been vilified by some Wall Streeters for making a to-do about such practices. Spitzer has been described as a showboat populist, playing to the masses. But he was right to take these things seriously. If IPO shares were simply a discount, why not label them as such, and be open about it? Rather than charging $100 million, and giving $10 million back, why not just charge $90 million? Corruption thrives when things are hidden. Transparency and openness are fully as important in the private sector as they are in the public. But it wasn't just a discount: it is the company that pays the investment banking fees; it is the company *CEO and other top executives* who get the benefits, in the form of desirable IPO shares.[10]

Unsavory deals

It was the analysts scandal that brought the investment banks into the worst disrepute. But the banks were also involved in a lower-profile scandal that touched millions of investors. In these cases, they might more aptly be described as "aiding and abetting corporate theft," and they received handsome fees working as accomplices, helping to put together off-balance sheet partnerships and countless other arcane "deals," in the service of corporate managers who were trying to hide important information from shareholders. In chapter 5, I wrote about the accountants and how they helped corporations take advantage of tax loopholes. Sadly, some of the brightest minds in American banking also devoted themselves to loopholes and shelters, and they, too, were rewarded handsomely for their efforts. Having honed their skills in the effort to deceive Uncle Sam, they moved on to similar techniques—moving liabilities offshore to make a complex transaction even more complex, for example—that fooled investors and even, in some cases, the banks themselves. They made it harder for *anyone* to really figure out what was going on. Working with Enron and other clients, the banks created sham transactions, disguising loans as prepayments on energy contracts, for example. The banks made money from these deals, and the value of their stocks went up—just as Enron's did when investors were unable to decipher the true magnitude of its outstanding liabilities.

Of course, it was wrong for the banks to play this role, but with the bottom line driving everything, money triumphed over morals. They competed for fees that were, in many cases, remarkably small, in the belief that they were putting themselves in line to do far more lucrative deals for the same companies. True, the banks believed they would not have to bear any actual risk. They were just fronts, taking money in and paying it out. But that belief was predicated on a small and, as it turned out, dangerous assumption—that Enron would not go bankrupt. As sophisticated as they were, some of the nation's biggest banks were eventually horrified to learn that, in at least a few cases, they had the liability, without the income. It's a story that raises questions about the competence of bankers—and doubts about the systems of bank regulation being developed by the international community (the so-called Basel II Accord). Those rules tell commercial banks, among other things, how much capital they need. The formulas are based on the bank's own risk management systems—the same systems that gave us Enron and WorldCom.

Glass-Steagall

This chapter—in some ways this book—is a story of conflicts of interests gone out of control. The problems are endemic to the banking industry, and have long been recognized. Unfortunately, deregulation in the nineties exacerbated the problems.

For more than half a century, commercial banking, which takes deposits from households and firms and makes conventional loans, had been separated from investment banking, which helps firms issue new bonds and shares. The same company could not lend money and also sell securities, in other words. The Glass-Steagall Act, which barred this, was one of the reforms put in place by the administration of Franklin Roosevelt, in response to the wave of bank failures that had followed the Great Crash of 1929. But the ideas behind Glass-Steagall went back even further, to Teddy Roosevelt and his efforts to break up the big trusts, the large firms that wielded such economic power. TR and the Progressives of the early twentieth century were alarmed not only about the concentration of economic power but about its impact on the political process. When enterprises become too big, and interconnections too tight, there is a risk that the quality of economic decisions deteriorates, and the "too big to fail" problem rears its ugly head. Expecting to be bailed out of trouble, managers become emboldened to take risks that they might otherwise shun. In the Great Depression, when many banks were on the ropes, it was, in effect, the public that bore the risk, while the bank got the reward. When banks failed, the taxpayers paid the price through publicly funded bailouts.[11]

The Glass-Steagall Act of 1933 addressed a very real problem. Investment banks push stocks, and if a company whose stock they have pushed needs cash, it becomes very tempting to make a loan. The U.S. system worked in part because under Glass-Steagall the banks provided a source of *independent* judgments on the creditworthiness of businesses. When a "full-service" bank makes most of its money by selling equities and bonds or arranging "deals," issuing loans becomes almost ancillary—a sideline.

With Glass-Steagall, the United States rejected the course followed by other nations, such as Japan and Germany, that did not separate commercial and investment banking—I believe to our evident benefit. But American banks themselves saw Glass-Steagall as reducing their opportunities for making profits and not surprisingly began to insist that the rules separating commercial and investment banking had become passé. In an age of free-floating capital and giant multi-national companies, they argued, banks had to be integrated, to take advantage of what are called "economies of scope"—the benefits that businesses can reap by working in many different areas at once. Global competition was too intense for bank concentration to be a serious worry (though in fact, many borrowers, especially small and medium-sized firms, have access only to a few potential lenders), and Glass-Steagall supposedly put American banks at a disadvantage.

In the mid-nineties, the banks mounted a concerted campaign to have Glass-Steagall repealed. The conditions were favorable. Prosperity made the notion of bank failure seem very remote (though the S&L crisis of the eighties ought to have been a caution). Another significant positive factor fell into place with the appointment, in 1995, of Robert Rubin as secretary of the Treasury. Rubin was a banker himself—the former co-chair of Goldman Sachs—and he actively supported the repeal effort. While conceding the potential for conflict of interest, Treasury insisted that it could deal with the problem by requiring barriers—"Chinese walls," again—between one area of a bank's activity and another. As chairman of the Council of Economic Advisers, I worried about the conflicts of interest, about the effect on competition, but these worries were quickly shunted aside.

On the one hand, the banks were extolling the advantages of integration; on the other hand, they were vowing to keep their different operations separate. There was an obvious intellectual inconsistency in these claims: if the two parts were in fact kept separate, what were the benefits of integration? The banking industry and its Treasury Department champions also advanced another argument: scrapping the law, they said, was of no consequence, because the banks had learned how to circumvent it anyway. The logical response, of course, might have been an attempt to reverse or limit the circumvention that had occurred. But in the deregulatory fervor of the Roaring Nineties, neither the legislative nor the executive branch of government had any stomach for such an effort.

The consequences predicted by the critics of Glass-Steagall repeal only began to come to light as the corporate and banking scandals emerged. Most notable was Enron's banks continuing to provide it credit even as its prospects looked increasingly murky. Even if Enron was down, it was not out: so long as there were prospects for more big deals, issuing new securities, it made sense to continue to lend the company more money. And Enron's banks continued to lend to it even as its appalling problems began to surface.[12] In the succession of corporate and financial scandals that followed Enron, numerous other cases came to light in which banks continued to lend almost to the day of bankruptcy; they knew, or should have known, of the risk, but the lure of the mega-profits from new deals, should the firm weather the storm, made the lending attractive nevertheless. (In some cases, lending was motivated more by fear that bankruptcy would expose some of the banks' dubious deals and expose them to recriminations for touting the company's stock, so they hoped against hope that maybe, with the loan, the company would somehow manage to survive.)

Under the old regime, investors at least had some assurance that if a firm was in trouble, it would have trouble borrowing money. This provided an important check, which helped make the whole system work. There were reasons to keep investment and commercial banking separate, even if the commercial bank was on sufficiently strong footing that a government bailout was unlikely. In these cases, the banks—not the public at large—wound up paying the price. Ironically, the managers of the banks often avoided paying much of a price, as they found ways of sustaining their pay even when share prices fell. (And the public at large did pay, as many a firm claimed a tax rebate as its losses were exposed.) Next time, however, we may not be so lucky.

Mergers

The repeal of Glass-Steagall only expanded the already present opportunities for conflicts of interest. Some practices, like those associated with IPOs, had troubled economists for a while, but didn't become scandals until the nineties. It is perhaps remarkable that the conflicts of interests confronting analysts had not manifested themselves earlier. Mergers, on the other hand, had long been the staple of Wall Street, and had long been noted as a source of abuse.

Banks love mergers and acquisitions—in the first place, for the excitement of doing them; and in the second, for the huge fees they generate. From a banker's standpoint, there is no such thing as a bad merger: you make money when the deal is made, and you make more money when it gets unmade. Mergers come in and out of fashion, each wave attended by its own story of "synergies" and cost savings, which generally turn out to be less than envisaged. The eighties gave us the glamorous "Barbarians at the Gate"–type mergers. In the nineties, it seemed, any company involved in the media had to become multi-media.

The merger mania of the nineties, like that of earlier decades, rests on peculiar arithmetic: $2 + 2 = 5$. Add up two firms worth $2 billion each, and come away with a firm worth $5 billion—and enough money to pay the investment banker a nice $300 million fee, give the CEO a hefty bonus and ample stock options, hand a nice retirement package to the former CEO (after a brief stint as second fiddle, or an even briefer stint as co-head), and still give shareholders plenty to be happy about. This is called the conglomerate *premium*—the synergies from bringing disparate elements together. The problem is that, quite often, $2 + 2 = 3.5$: this is called the conglomerate *discount*. It usually appears a couple years after the merger, as those synergies just don't work out. While each company alone had a clear vision of its future together, the newly merged couple doesn't get along or know where it's going. As it strives to unravel the puzzle, profitable opportunities slip by.

Sometimes, 2 + 2 = 4 or 4.5, and with the cost of doing the deal being 0.75, shareholders are still left worse off—though both the banks and the CEOs still do well. The investment bankers are supposed to provide the information to ascertain whether there will be a conglomerate premium or a discount. In fact, their incentives were simply to do the deal. Once the conglomerate discount appears, of course, it is time to dismantle the conglomerate and sell off the pieces: the sum of the parts exceeds the whole.

To the usual forces that were at play, the Roaring Nineties added a few new ingredients. In the eighties, it was hubris that motivated many a CEO to acquire others: there was more status, and slightly higher pay, from being the head of a larger company—never mind about the profitability. The Roaring Nineties provided additional incentives and opportunities for mergers. CEOs, with compensation linked to the share price, of course, had a strong interest in seeing stock prices go as high as possible, by whatever means they could. Sometimes they had other incentives as well. Sprint, for example, had a provision in its contracts allowing executives to exercise options once shareholders *approved* a merger; the deal did not actually have to go through. The approval of the Sprint-WorldCom merger allowed some $1 billion in options to be exercised—$400 million by Sprint's chief executive, William Esrey, who responded to the outrage of his shareholders by not cashing in the options, for which act of public-spirited sacrifice his directors promptly rewarded him with fresh options on an additional 3 million shares.

But most important, the bubble economy provided those whose shares had soared with a form of play money with which to buy other firms, and those who were smart enough, like Steve Case at AOL, knew that it was best to turn it into something solid before it disappeared. Earlier, *Time* magazine had joined Warner Brothers, and since a multi-media company was clearly foolish to limit itself to content, Time-Warner joined CNN, the cable news network. Somehow, Time-Warner was persuaded that it made sense to be acquired by AOL, with its millions of Internet-access subscribers. Presumably, all the fun was in the New Economy, and they didn't want to be left behind. For the high-flying AOL, this was one merger that did make sense: at a time when many already suspected that its market value was vastly over inflated, the company and its shareholders exchanged their bubble stock for something a little more tangible and down to earth. Time-Warner shareholders lost out, and big. As the resulting synergies proved less than anticipated, AOL Time Warner quickly turned to the standard accounting tricks: a one-time write-off was in excess of $50 billion.

What was true for AOL was true for WorldCom and many other firms in the nineties; the bubble and its overinflated prices gave them the opportunity, and the means, to engage in mergers. Companies like Tyco International Ltd., AT&T Corp., and WorldCom Inc. went on a merging rampage, and became labeled, fittingly, "Serial Acquirers." It was the classic pyramid scheme, with each generation of investors supplying the money to reward the previous generation—until the whole edifice came crashing down.

WorldCom: A case study

As the bubble burst and the merger possibilities evaporated, companies had to find other ways to make money, and they moved to more and more "aggressive" accounting tricks. In some cases, they went from being barely within the law to being outside it. WorldCom CEO Bernie Ebbers, a former milkman and junior high school teacher from Alberta, Canada, had used his stock as collateral for enormous loans. In late 2000, Ebbers got hit with margin calls; forced to come up with a huge amount of money in a hurry, he (and other CEOs in the same boat) turned to his company for help. WorldCom obliged by granting him loans in 2000, 2001, and 2002, relieving him from the need to sell his stock, which would have further depressed the share price—no matter that, in cutting that deal, Ebbers placed shareholders at risk. Now his concern was not so much to get the share price up to make a killing as to prevent it from going down, so the market didn't kill him.

When WorldCom went bankrupt, on July 21, 2002, it was the country's second largest long-distance carrier and its largest mover of Internet traffic, with $32 billion in debt, and claimed assets worth $107 billion—but of that amount, more than $50 billion consisted of "goodwill," a mythical number that while it may be in accordance with standard accounting practices does not reflect any hard assets. Those amounted to less than $40 billion—and many of those were valued at the high prices that prevailed before the collapse of the telecommunications sector. Though it is still too soon to tell the full size of the write-down (bringing the assets down to a more realistic value), estimates have put the figure at $50 billion or more—an amount equal to the GDP of the Czech Republic or Hungary. WorldCom's problems came to light when the company revealed that it had improperly accounted for nearly $4 billion in expenses, an amount that would eventually be almost doubled, to $7 billion. One large category of deceit involved the classification of ordinary expenses as investments; as such, they did not have to be deducted from revenues, and profits accordingly looked that much bigger. Among its other shady practices, WorldCom billed one company, Cherry Communications, $225 million, which Cherry disputed; WorldCom nonetheless booked the amount as revenues, even *after* Cherry went bankrupt, without paying. In an earlier stage of duplicity, WorldCom had relied on more conventional methods of accounting deception (even being forced on one occasion to make a $3 billion correction).

As with Enron, WorldCom's bankruptcy exposed a nexus of unsavory deals between the company and its executives. Besides paying Ebbers an ample salary—more than $142 million in 1999—World-Com lent him some $408 million in all. The bankruptcy report spoke of "numerous failures, inadequacies and breakdowns in the multi-layered system designed to protect the integrity of the financial reporting system at WorldCom, including the board of directors, the audit committee, the company's system of internal controls and the independent auditors."[13] The problem, I would argue, was deeper, and touched not only WorldCom: the problem was with *incentives*—for the management, and for those who were supposedly watching over management.

At Ebbers's behest, WorldCom turned to Citibank when it needed to issue securities, and the CEO and the bank both profited, to the tune of millions of dollars. For Ebbers also relied on Citibank in his personal investment activities, eventually receiving a total of almost 1 million shares of IPOs, for a gain of $11 million. Another Citibank division, Travelers' Insurance, lent $134 million to Joshua Timber-lands, a private company controlled by Ebbers, taking a 2.5 percent equity stake in it (which it did not reveal). Eight months later, World-Com chose Salomon Smith Barney, another member of the Citigroup family, as lead underwriter of $5 billion in debt. Citigroup's private bank made yet another loan to Ebbers (of roughly $400 million, col-lateralized by WorldCom stock), giving rise to its own conflict of interest: such a loan gave Citigroup "a reason to want to prop up WorldCom stock," as Gretchen Morgenson of *The New York Times* pointed out.[14] And Citigroup had the means to do this, through its network of brokers and analysts. The brokers had counseled World-Com employees to exercise their options, and leave them unhedged—advice that cost them dearly, but buoyed the stock. Jack B. Grubman, Salomon's telecommunication analyst, had long been touting World-Com. The relationship between Grubman and Ebbers was close—he went to Ebbers's wedding (at Citibank's expense). He attended four WorldCom board meetings. He helped stage-manage conference calls in which the company gave analysts, including Grubman himself, information about its prospects and ability to meet market expectations; Grubman went so far as to propose a set of scripted questions and answers. And even as the problems at WorldCom came to light, he maintained his "buy" recommendation. In mid-1999, he elevated it to a "strong buy," anticipating an increase in the price from $75 to almost $130 a share. WorldCom was still a "buy," according to Grubman, as late as April 23, 2002, just three months before it filed for bankruptcy, and well after the accounting fraud avalanche had begun.

Grubman eventually resigned, and his resignation statement said much about the Roaring Nineties: "I did my work as an analyst within a widely understood framework consistent with industry practice that is now being extensively second guessed."[15] It was industry practice, and that is precisely the problem.

Lessons

A lot of things went wrong in the nineties, and the footprints of the banks can be found at the scene of one suspicious deed after another. Investment banks are supposed to provide information that leads to a better allocation of resources. Instead, all too often, they trafficked in distorted or inaccurate information, and participated in schemes that helped others distort the information they provided and enriched others at shareholders' expense.

The offenses of Enron and WorldCom—and of Citigroup and Merrill Lynch—put most acts of political crookedness to shame. The typical corrupt government official pockets a measly few thousand dollars—at most, a few million. The scale of theft achieved by the ransacking of Enron, WorldCom, and other corporations in the nineties was in the billions of dollars—greater than the GDP of some nations.

When individuals further their own interests, Adam Smith believed, they generally serve the interests of society as a whole.[16] It's a remarkably seductive hypothesis, and sometimes it holds up; yet all too often, it doesn't. Imperfect information presents some individuals with the opportunity to act in ways that allow them to benefit *at the expense of others, whom they are supposed to serve*. This is sometimes called the "principal agent problem": it arises when an individual is supposed to act for others, while circumstances give him or her the discretion not to do so. A central problem of modern economics is how to *align* interests—how to provide incentive structures that make the agent more likely to represent his or her rightful clients.[17]

Conflicts of interest will never be eliminated, in either the public or private sector. But in the nineties, with the push for deregulation, existing constraints were removed or lowered, leading to predictable results. What can we do to remedy such problems? We can, for one thing, make ourselves more sensitive to the potential for conflicts, and to the distorted incentives that they produce. And by imposing regulations that limit their scope and increase the amount of disclosure—including disclosures about the presence of these conflicts of interest—we can mitigate the consequences, both in the public and the private sectors.

Those who had long listened to the "financial experts" lecture America—and every other country—on how to run an economy, from deficit reduction to the design of tax policy, could not help but note the ironies. While pontificating on how government so often wastes money, these "experts" had presided over a market system which had wasted more money than most governments could have imagined in their wildest dreams. While talking about the importance of "value creation," they had contributed to the destruction of trillions of dollars of value with shortsighted, myopic policies that were hailed as doing just the opposite. While criticizing corruption and conflicts of interest in the public sector, and crony capitalism abroad, they not only allowed such conflicts to flourish and resisted attempts to curtail them but had themselves, in their political dealings with Washington, succumbed to them, unabashedly and without shame. While talking about the importance of good accounting, they had themselves engaged in bad accounting practices, been accomplices to others doing so, and resisted any efforts to change the rules in ways which would have improved the quality of information.

The financial experts bore only a part of the consequences of their bad behavior. They accepted fines of unprecedented levels—in excess of a billion dollars—but, in most cases, only after being assured that their CEOs would not do time. But the fines imposed did not rectify the damage, and in many cases it was not the CEOs but the companies that paid them; indeed, the fines imposed on corporations for such bad behavior represent a curious case where the victim is punished twice over. For ultimately, the shareholders—who have already been cheated by corporate management—bear the costs of such fines.[18]

The final irony is that just as the financial community was lecturing the government on fiscal rectitude, it was working even harder to find ways to help the Enrons and the other corporations avoid the taxes they should have been paying—worsening the fiscal position. And, as we shall see in the next chapter, it supported capital gains tax cuts, which, while they may have made the government's books look better in the short run, aggravated the long-run fiscal position, and even worse, helped feed the frenzy of the Roaring Nineties—which was perhaps what they were after, after all.

CHAPTER 7

Tax Cuts

FEEDING THE FRENZY

THE BUBBLE MADE MILLIONS of Americans rich beyond their wildest dreams. But that did not necessarily invigorate them with a sense of public duty. Just as the CEOs wanted to believe that it was their acumen that had led to the prices of their company shares soaring, they wanted to believe that it was their acumen and hard work, not luck, that had led to their portfolios doing so well. They were not in a mood to share their gains, or share any more than absolutely necessary. These perceptions—combined with the politics of the moment, bad accounting, and the focus on the deficit reduction mania—led to tax policies that made the bubble worse, and its aftermath more tumultuous.

Those who had done well financially in the nineties pushed to reduce the amount of taxes they would pay on their new wealth. Their objective was to reduce the taxation on the enormous gains they were reaping, including from the stock options with which senior executives were increasingly being rewarded. With capital gains taxed still lower than dividends and other forms of income, investors were encouraged to put more of their money into the high-tech firms—which offered not dividends (many had no profits with which to pay dividends) but capital gains.

Given the focus on balancing the budget, the tax cut, as desired as it was by the wealthy (and it was the wealthy who wanted it; few of the benefits went to lower- and middle-income Americans), would not have occurred were it not for the odd mixture of bad accounting and the politics of the moment.

In 1980, Ronald Reagan promised a tax cut that would lead to an increase in tax revenue, an endeavor that even his vice president George Bush had called "Voodoo economics." The theory was that with lower tax rates, workers would work that much harder, many more people would join the labor force, savings would increase by leaps and bounds, and these *supply-side* effects would generate so much more income that even at the lower tax rates, government revenue would increase. In fact, savings continued at a dismal level—even falling slightly; and there was little impact on labor supply. (Of course, some believed then, and continue to believe, that not even Reagan's advisers really swore by voodoo economics. They had another agenda: to create deficits that would force expenditure cuts, downsizing the role of the government. In short, their agenda was advanced whether the experiment in tax cuts worked as predicted or not.)

The declining revenues (relative to what they otherwise would have been), unmatched by expenditure cuts,[1] caused a decade-long fiscal crisis that Bill Clinton finally addressed in 1993.[2] But, according to the accountants who oversaw the government's books, there was one realm in which voodoo economics still worked, one realm in which one could increase tax revenues by cutting tax rates. A cut in capital gains taxes—the taxes on the increase in the value of shares and real estate—could actually increase revenues, particularly if it was temporary. The government, following the peculiar way that budget analyses are done by the public sector, looks at a ten-year budget window and asks, what are the revenue impacts in that ten-year period? This is, of course, a major improvement over looking at only one year at a time, or at two or three years into the future. But government policies last far longer than ten years and any limited window of accountability, even one as long as ten years, encourages all kinds of shenanigans. In 1996, we saw these forces in play.

I noted earlier how, after the 1994 election, in which Republicans seized control of Congress, Clinton's agenda was effectively killed. Clinton was an activist, but without the consent of Congress his hands were tied. Only when his agenda and that of the Republicans coincided could anything get done. This was how welfare "reform" and deregulation occurred. As we saw in chapter 4, the Republicans wanted to strip back the role of government in regulation, and that fit well with the New Democratic agenda. One of Clinton's own campaign platforms had focused on "ending welfare as we know it." And the Republicans too wanted to end welfare, period. On both issues, there was room for a deal, and deals were struck. Likewise, both sides wanted a tax cut, and yet both sides wanted to *seem* fiscally responsible. Because of peculiar accounting, a capital gains tax cut could, miraculously, make the budget look better.

In the narrow budget window used by government accountants, temporary cuts in the capital gains tax generate tax income in the short run, because they act like a tax "sale." One of the problems with capital gains taxes is that investors are "locked in." So long as they don't sell their assets, they pay no taxes. The tax is only paid on the realization of the capital gain. An individual who bought a stock at $100, if it is now worth $1,100, would have to pay tax on the $1,000 gain. If the individual faces state and federal taxes of 33 percent, he gets to keep only $867 to reinvest (the tax on the $1,000 capital gain is $333). If instead, he leaves it in his stock, he can continue to accumulate returns on the full $1,100. Even more important, if he is planning to pass the stock on to his children, the capital gain will completely escape taxes. The children will only have to pay capital gains taxes on any gains *after they inherit the stock*.[3] Of course, in spite of this locked-in effect, individuals do cash in on their shares, either because they need the money to live on today, or because they see another opportunity with so much greater expected return that it pays to pay the tax.

When the government announces a temporary lowering of the capital gains tax rate, many individuals who were previously "locked in" decide to grab the opportunity and cash in during the tax sale. That is why government revenue, in the short run, goes up. But in the longer run, it may actually go down. Some of the individuals who decide to realize their capital gains this year would have realized the capital gain in, say, eleven years' time, outside the budget window, when the rate is back to the normal level. Government revenue today is higher, but government revenue eleven years from now is lower—and the loss in the future is greater than the gain today. In effect, the government is borrowing against its future revenue. If the government is concerned with its *long-run* deficit position, as it should be, the lowering of the capital gains tax rate lowers long-term tax revenue and increases the long-run debt.

As chairman of the Council of Economic Advisers, I opposed Clinton's tax cut, for four reasons. First, I thought we should be concerned with the long-run fiscal position, and even if in the short run the capital gains tax cut made the books look better, it would only worsen matters in the long run. It is, of course, true that a few families might, even in the long run, wind up paying more taxes; some individuals who could otherwise totally escape taxation—by passing their assets along to their heirs—might opt to realize their capital gains during the "sale." But there is a right answer to that quandary. Make the tax system fairer, close the loophole, and force *everyone* to pay capital gains taxes.

Second, the distributional consequences were horrendous: almost all the benefits of this tax cut went to the upper 1 percent of the population. It was among the most regressive tax cuts imaginable—benefiting only those already better off. In this sense, it was completely inconsistent with what the Democratic Party traditionally stood for. Indeed, it was hard to reconcile Clinton's overall tax policy—the combined effect of the capital gains tax cut and the 1993 tax increase—with the values that he and the Democratic Party avowed to represent. He had raised taxes on upper-middle-income individuals who worked for a living, but he had lowered taxes on very rich individuals who made their money from speculation, and on CEOs who were making millions from stock options.

Third, the capital gain tax cut, like most tax cuts these days, was sold on the basis of "supply-side" economics—how it would spur innovation, encourage investment, promote savings. CEOs, who were getting so much of their income in the form of stock options, would be encouraged to work harder—evidently the so-called incentive pay didn't provide enough incentive for them to make the "hard decisions," such as firing unneeded workers to increase profits. But this supply-side argument made little sense, since most of the benefits would accrue to those who had already made their capital gains. As such, it would have no incentive effects. It was a pure gift to the rich. They had already made their investments, assuming that they would pay the higher capital gains tax rate. It would be, for them, a windfall gain. And a closer look at the numbers showed that a relatively small percentage of the gains at that point was related to new technology; much of the benefit would accrue to those who had speculated on real estate.

From the beginning of the administration, a central part of Clinton's tax strategy was to target tax cuts and make them more effective—more bang for the buck, a large stimulus for the economy for every dollar of increased expenditure or tax reduction. When we thought of how we could use tax policy to stimulate the economy, we focused on an investment tax credit: only those who actually invested in the economy would get a tax reduction (a marked contrast to the proposals eight years later by Bush). And to get even more bang for the buck, we suggested that the benefit only be given for *increases* in investment. This would provide high-powered incentives at the margin, but would minimize the "windfall" gains to firms who would have invested anyway, even without the tax benefit. Accordingly, as the demand for some kind of capital gains tax cut increased in 1996, the Council of Economic Advisers devised versions of the capital gains tax cut that were forward-looking, where at least there would be *some* incentive effects, perhaps some positive effect from increased savings or investment (though even here, economic theory and evidence does not suggest that the impact would likely be large). Unfortunately, the Treasury and Congress paid little attention.

There was a still fourth reason, in the circumstances every bit as important as the first three, to oppose the tax cut. The capital gains tax cut reinforced CEOs' proclivity to focus on short-run market value rather than long-run performance. When investors were "locked in" to their shares, they cared less about the market value of the shares today or even tomorrow. They wanted to know how a firm would fare in the long run. Cutting the capital gains tax helped focus investors' attention on the here and now. This in turn fed the frenzy, exacerbating the bubble, while at the same time setting in motion forces that would make the downturn greater, when the bubble burst.

In real estate bubbles, as prices soar, individuals are constantly "upgrading," selling their houses, leveraging the increased equity value to buy an even more expensive piece of property, and this process inflates the bubble. So, too, in the stock market. But the capital gains tax had acted as a dampener on the process. Because those who sold their shares had to pay a part of the increased value of their equity to the government, there was less money around to feed the frenzy. But now, with the capital gains tax cut, when those who worried that their particular stock might be overpriced, and therefore cashed in, it left them with far more money to reinvest into the stock market, thereby feeding the frenzy all the more.

Similarly, the tax cut made the incentives for giving stock options to CEOs all the greater and it made the (after-tax) return from providing distorted accounting information—the already all too strong incentives discussed in earlier chapters—all the more powerful.

The tax cut was enacted, and just as the supply-siders had predicted, there was an enormous increase in tax revenues. Was this the final vindication of supply-side economics? In part, yes: for it did inflate the bubble, and the bubble was the underlying cause of the soaring capital gains tax revenues. But critics of the capital gains tax cut had warned: the gains were likely to be only temporary. Even if there had been no bubble, some of the short-run gains were at the expense of (even greater) revenues that would otherwise have been realized. But there was a bubble, and when the bubble burst, capital gains became capital losses, and revenues plummeted.

Greed on the part of Wall Street and the real estate industry, wrong-headed accounting, a conservative political establishment perfectly willing to use this accounting for their long-run goal of downsizing the government, combined with more liberal politicians who wanted to put themselves in good graces with sources of campaign finance, all worked to pass the capital gains tax cut of 1997, one of the most regressive tax cuts in America's history (with strong competition to come four years later from Bush II). But there was one more ingredient: Not only did many of these forces succeed in convincing America that deregulation, however executed, would be of benefit to all Americans; they also convinced middle-class, and even poorer, Americans that they too would benefit from the capital gains tax cut.

The capital gains tax cut was politically popular. Everybody had their few shares (though most of their shares were held in accounts in which the accumulations were, in any case, tax-free). They would do everything they could to protect these little pieces of capitalism against the rapacious government. Ronald Reagan had had his ultimate victory. No matter that the capital gains tax cut saved the upper-income taxpayer $100 for every $5 that the middle-income taxpayer was spared. They were all in the same boat, all working to save themselves from those who would take—and supposedly waste—their money.

Every tax system is an expression of a country's basic values—and its politics. It translates into hard cash what might otherwise be simply high-flown rhetoric. There is a long tradition in the United States of small landholders (small farmers), dating back to Jefferson. Today, we are no longer a country of farmers, but we are still a country of property owners. We are a country in which almost 70 percent of Americans own their own houses, a larger percentage than almost any country in the world. And our tax system, with its large deductions for mortgages and real estate, encourages home ownership.

Through much of the Clinton administration—with the major exception of the capital gains tax cut—we tried to use tax policy to reflect our values at the same time that it enhanced the performance of the economy. Given the budgetary stringency, we had to face difficult choices, and we tried to target and shape the tax cuts, to do what was needed without losing too much revenue. We, for instance, increased tax deductions and credits for education, because we believed it was important that everyone receive a higher education. Early in the administration, we pushed for taxes that would encourage energy conservation and discourage polluting greenhouse gases.

In the beginning of the Clinton administration, in 1993, we also passed a provision concerning excess payments to CEOs, unrelated to performance. The intention was good: we recognized that corporate CEOs had the discretion to pay themselves salaries that seemed unjustified, and unjustifiable. We wanted to discourage excessive CEO compensation, but we did not, however, want to interfere unwarrantedly with the marketplace, with the provision of incentives. Yet, in acting as we did, we unwittingly provided one more impetus to the use of stock options. Just as the capital gains tax cut combined with other forces *directly* fed the bubble frenzy, the tax encouragement, combined with the defective accounting practices which so many had worked so hard to keep in place, encouraged these stock options to become the favored way of rewarding CEOs— with all the consequences we have described.[4]

We should have recognized, of course, that the so-called incentive pay of CEOs was, typically, not incentive pay. It went up when the stocks went up, whether it was attributable to the efforts of the CEO or not. And it went up when the stocks went down—for every CEO and the board which he had appointed recognized that were it not for the efforts of the CEO, share price would have gone down even more but for his valiant efforts.

As the Clinton years came to a close, I wondered: What message had we in the end sent through the changes that had been brought about in our taxes? What were we saying to the country, to our young people, when we lowered capital gains taxes and raised taxes on those who earned their living by working? That it is far better to make your living by speculation than by any other means. The New Economy—the innovations which continue to fuel the productivity growth and form the basis of this country's long-run strength— depend on advances in science, on researchers at universities and research labs, who work sixteen-hour days and more in the tireless search to try to understand the world in which we live. These are the people we should have been rewarding, and encouraging. Yet it was these people who were being more highly taxed, while those who speculated were taxed more gently. While we talked about incentives, most of the tax giveaway had no incentive effect at all. While we were teaching our young people something about our national values, we were also teaching our young people another lesson in political hypocrisy, or, some might say, in the ways of the world.

CHAPTER 8

Making Risk a Way of Life

IN THE ROARING NINETIES, fortunes were made, and both political and business leaders could, and did, claim credit. We were on a roll, and no one believed—or wanted to believe—that it would end. But end it did. And as it ended, what should have been easy to see before became all too painfully clear. Much as the lowering of a tide exposes the rough rocks beneath the surface, the lowering of the economic tide exposed the more unseemly aspects of the boom—the problems with accounting, CEOs, and banks, the nexus between markets and politics, and deregulation—which have been the subject of earlier chapters.

But there was another set of problems even more deeply hidden. Some of the changes in the economy that inflated the bubble also made the economy more vulnerable: when the bubble burst, they would make the downturn all the greater. We not only exposed the economy to more risk, we also undermined our ability to manage that risk. Changes in pension systems and employment policies meant that individuals were more exposed to the vicissitudes of the market: as the stock market went down, they saw their future pensions decrease; as the economy slowed, they saw a greater likelihood of being fired. At the same time, government policies too changed:

unemployment insurance did not keep pace with the changes in the economy, and welfare was cut back. In the past, these programs had injected funds into the economy as it slowed down, buffering those who might otherwise have suffered, but also helping to reinvigorate the economy and limit the extent of the downturn. Unintentionally, we had been creating a less stable economy.

Whatever Happened to the New Economy? The New Two-Edged Sword

The New Economy—meaning the marked changes in the economy during the nineties, with its emphasis on high technology and better communications—was supposed to bring the end of the business cycle. The new technologies were supposed to enable inventories to be better controlled—excess investment in inventories had been one of the primary causes of economic fluctuations in the post–World War II economy. Moreover, as the economy shifted from manufacturing to services (by the mid-nineties, less than 14.1 percent of U.S. employment was in manufacturing), the role of inventories in the economy was itself diminishing. But the New Economy did not bring about an end to the business cycle. Rather, it provided the basis for a boom and a bust that was, in fact, greater than the average of the postwar period.

However, while the New Economy may have been hyped, it was certainly real. The Internet was real. The innovations, advances in telecommunications, and new ways of doing business which followed were real. Just as the eighteenth and nineteenth centuries marked a change from an agricultural to an industrial economy, and the first three quarters of the twentieth century marked a movement from a manufacturing to a service economy, the end of the twentieth century marked a movement to the weightless economy, the knowledge economy. A revolution in the production of ideas, this movement was as important as earlier changes had been in the production of goods. There was an increase in the pace of innovation, reflected in the increased rate of increase in productivity; and while measurement and accounting problems may have led us to overestimate the magnitude of that increase, it too was real.

Indeed, even as the economy has slipped into recession, these increases in productivity have continued, making the problem of job creation all the more difficult. This is the double-edged sword of productivity increases. When the economy is using its resources fully, productivity increases allow for an increase in GDP, higher wages, and improved living standards. When the economy goes into a recession—when what limits output is not supply but demand—everything is turned on its head. If, because of limited demand, output only increases by 1 percent this year, but each worker can produce 3 percent more output, it means that fewer workers are required; unemployment will increase. In the short run, it is even possible that higher rates of productivity growth can actually lead to lower levels of output. The higher unemployment rate depresses wages, and the increasingly uncertain job situation depresses consumption, or at least its rate of growth. But with large excess capacity, neither higher profits from the lower wages nor even lower interest rates may lead to increases in investment. With consumption growth slowed, and nothing taking its place, overall output will be dampened.

Increased sensitivity in the labor market

In short, with the increased pace of productivity, we had to run just to stand still! As the economy went into a downturn in early 2001, even fewer workers were needed. In the past, firms had kept on workers in recessions, even when they weren't really needed. Economists referred to this as "labor hoarding." Firms knew that *in the long run* it made sense to treat your workers well, to keep them on even when they might not be immediately needed; it enabled the firm to attract and retain the best workers, and the loyalty made workers work harder on behalf of their employer.

During the nineties a new culture had developed, one in which firms focused on the bottom line—today's profits, not long-run profits—and took quick and decisive actions when they faced problems. Firms that kept on workers when they were no longer needed were viewed as softhearted and softheaded. "Chain-saw Al" Dunlap, Sunbeam's CEO, who got a reputation for axing workers and cutting costs with a new ruthlessness, may have been an extreme case, but he was emblematic of the new culture. Fire workers as soon as it is clear that you don't need them. You can always hire them back again later. Firm loyalty—either of workers to their firm or the firm to its workers—were values of a bygone era. This meant that employment fell far more quickly as the economy went into the downturn.

Increasing worker anxiety

With company loyalty to workers lowered, and productivity increasing in ways that made it more profitable to fire workers, it is no wonder that worker anxiety increased. Blue-collar workers had always worried about job security, but over the years since the Great Depression, unions had worked hard to provide some protection. Yet unions had become increasingly weak, and job insecurity spread from blue-collar workers to white-collar workers. More and more workers were facing being "downsized." Unfortunately, the safety net did not keep pace: unemployment insurance replaced a smaller fraction of earnings, and more workers were left uncovered. Older workers especially often found it difficult to find a new job. Yet without special congressional action, unemployment insurance only lasted for twenty-six weeks. After that workers had to fend for themselves, or go on welfare.

The results became especially apparent as the 2001 recession continued; the number of *long-term* unemployed, those for whom benefits expired, soared—more than doubling. Eventually, unemployment benefits were extended for another thirteen weeks, but only until the end of 2002. By then, the extended benefits of almost a million Americans had already run out, and three quarters of a million more faced a cutoff of benefits, after Congress failed to renew the extension. It was not just that the Bush administration and the Republican Congress had seemingly given these almost 2 million workers a Christmas present of heightened anxiety—where would their next meals come from?—but that in doing so, it further undermined the strength of the economy. Not surprisingly, the Christmas shopping season of 2002 was a weak one.

While some conservatives worried that unemployment benefits reduced the incentive of workers to look for a job, clearly the problem was that there simply were not jobs to be had. Those who looked could not find them.

Even earlier in the decade, within the Clinton administration, we had recognized that with the increased pace of innovation, there would be large changes in the labor market. We knew that the idea of a lifetime job was a thing of the past. We talked about "lifetime employability," not lifetime jobs; and of "lifetime learning," to enable individuals to move more easily from job to job. The data showed that those who were more educated moved more easily, and suffered smaller income reductions when they lost a job and got a new one. With job mobility, one needed to have more portable pensions, and with health insurance usually provided through the employer, that too had to be more portable. In addition, something had to be done about insurance coverage while individuals were unemployed. Unfortunately, with the Republican-controlled Congress, little of what was needed to be done was actually accomplished. As a result, as the economy slowed down, worker anxiety increased. It was a testimony to the overall optimism of Americans—combined with the favorable terms for refinancing mortgages—that consumption remained as robust as it did as the economy slid into recession.

How pension "reform" increased economic vulnerability

The changes in the economy of the nineties forced workers to bear more risk, not just on the job but in retirement, and this too contributed to the vulnerability of the economy. Individuals have come to rely on private pension programs for an increasing share of their retirement income. There are two forms of retirement programs: defined benefits, in which the company guarantees a certain benefit, related to the worker's income and length of service; and defined contributions, in which the company contributes a fixed amount into an Individual Retirement Account (IRA). Changes in both during the nineties presented problems for the economy in the new millennium.

Many firms switched to defined contribution schemes, and many individuals, lulled by the seemingly high returns in the stock market, chose to put most of their money into equities. This was an important part of creating a "people's" capitalism, but it meant that when the market went down, they felt the full brunt of the stock market downturn. With defined benefit pension schemes, the employer insulated the worker from the effect of the stock market fall. In their quarterly statements, households saw what they had set aside for their retirement go down and down and down. At first, they lost what they never believed they had; they never really believed in the gains—many suspected a bubble, and they were right. But eventually, the declines in the stock market were so large as to compromise standards of living in retirement, and when that happened, households would feel the need to set aside more for their retirement—to consume less.

But the defined benefit programs presented perhaps even more problems for the stability of the economy. During the nineties, firms that had kept their defined benefit programs had *seemingly* over-funded their pension programs.[1] The government had long been concerned that firms put aside enough money to fulfill the promises they make to workers. Many firms had not done so—had effectively cheated their workers—and when they had gone bankrupt, the retired workers were left to fend for themselves, often condemned to an old age of poverty. The government, responding to this obvious "market failure," had provided insurance, and in return, had set standards for how much firms had to set aside to be sure they could fulfill their commitments. When too much was set aside, firms could take money out of their pension funds, adding it to profits; when too little was set aside, firms had to add to the funds, reducing profits. The numbers that the government allowed firms to use for calculating how much to set aside represented rosy scenarios—returns of 9 percent, far above that which had historically been achieved. (Since workers may retire twenty, thirty, even forty years after working, what matters is not returns this year, but returns over the long run. With returns of 9 percent a year, money doubles every eight years; to have $100 at the age of sixty-five, you have to set aside only $6 at age twenty-five. Employers could promise large benefits in the future, without taking much out of today's profits.) During the nineties, firms could get away with these astronomical numbers because the actual returns were even more astronomical. With the stock market boom, they had—under their overly optimistic assumptions—more than enough money to meet their obligations. Under the rules, they could take the excess money out of the pensions and add it to profits. By one estimate, 12 percent of the earnings growth of 2000 came from pension income. The stock market bubble thus made profits look even bigger—reinforcing the bubble itself. But it was a mirage.

With the stock market bust, all of a sudden their pension programs were vastly underfunded. They had counted on returns of 9 percent. The stocks were yielding a negative return—sometimes a very negative return. And it became increasingly clear that the 9 percent number, which was looking more and more like pure fiction or wishful thinking, would have to be revised downward. But at a lower number, even a number that was rosy by historical standards, even firms that had invested more conservatively, or just been lucky and not lost a large fraction of their portfolio, would have to set aside more money. With a more realistic 4.5 percent return, it takes sixteen years to double one's money, so that to have $100 at the age of sixty-five, one has to set aside two and a half times as much at age twenty-five as one did with an assumed 9.0 percent return. During the boom, firms took an enormous amount of money out of the pension funds and added it to profits. During the bust, firms would have to take money out of profits and put it into pension funds, making profits look smaller, leaving the firms with less money to invest, and leaving investors even more pessimistic about the performance of their formerly high-flying firms. It was clearly important to insist that the pensions be better funded, and that the mythical numbers that had been used for projecting returns be revised. But bringing those numbers down to reality helped bring the stock market back to reality.

The magnitude of the underfunding was astronomical. One study of just the 348 companies in the S&P 500 with defined benefit pension programs concluded that this underfunding amounted to between $184 and $323 *billion* (if non-pension benefits, such as health benefits, are included, the deficit is in the range of $458 to $638 billion). A Merrill Lynch study showed that companies with off-balance-sheet pension liabilities that exceed their total equity value include Campbell Soup, Maytag, Lucent, General Motors, Ford, Goodyear, Boeing, U.S. Steel, and Colgate Palmolive. While the accounting standards may have disguised the true size of the pension liabilities, they were in fact real liabilities, obligations of the corporations to their workers. They represented a potential source of bankruptcy for many of America's most important companies.

To put these numbers in perspective, the government insurance program for pensions, Pension Benefit Guarantee Corporation, created under the Employee Retirement Income Security Act (ERISA) of 1974, has reserves of approximately $7 billion. Although in the nineties the Pension Benefit Guarantee Corporation had been running a surplus, once the bubble burst, it started to run deficits, and at present it looks increasingly as if a bailout will be necessary. Ironically, just as the evidence of the mismanagement of private pensions mounts, the Bush administration has begun a campaign to partially privatize Social Security—the one part of the retirement system that today is working remarkably well.

Helping Individuals Manage Their Retirement Risk

Even as financial firms talked about risk management, they were not managing their own risks well, and the advice they gave to corporations actually exposed the economy, and workers, to increasing risk. Within the Clinton administration, we took seriously the task of risk management—providing enhanced retirement security in an increasingly insecure world. There were two initiatives in particular that were of some importance.

Pension portability and costs

The first change reflected our analysis of the changing labor market. At the Council of Economic Advisers, we saw our economy evolving in new ways. Individuals were no longer working for a single employer over their lifetime, but rather were moving from job to job. The fast pace of change meant firms would rise and fall and jobs would be restructured quickly. We needed to move from thinking about traditional forms of job security to *lifetime employability*. Of course, workers—particularly unskilled workers—will be at a disadvantageous position relative to their employers, and the role of government is to ensure that employers do not take advantage of these asymmetries in "power."

Lifetime employability meant, for example, we had to have an education system oriented to teaching people how to learn—learning to learn—accompanied by lifelong training. With long-term employment relationships, firms would have an incentive to undertake some of this effort. But the fact that workers now moved from one job to another meant that this would no longer be the case. Similarly, if a worker worked for a single employer, it made sense for him to look to that employer for his pension. But if workers moved from employer to employer, it was important that the pension program be *portable*, and one of our initiatives was intended to do exactly that.

With small firms growing more important in the economy, it was also important to make sure that the costs of running a pension program were not too high. Over the years, America had developed a highly complicated legal structure regulating pensions. The underlying motives were good: one wanted to encourage "fair treatment," meaning that the executives of the company were not just taking advantage of the preferential tax treatment of pensions to give themselves large benefits but were providing commensurate benefits for ordinary workers, for whom the pension was, in some ways, even more important. But the consequence of these regulations was that the cost of a pension program for a small firm was enormous, the legal fees and other transactions costs exceeding hundreds of dollars per worker, in order to set up the programs and accounts, and then maintain them and ensure that they complied with the regulations.

At the Council of Economic Advisers, we had a triple objective: making the economy more efficient by reducing wasteful transactions costs; increasing economic security for the aged by encouraging more firms to provide pensions; and increasing national savings by encouraging them to set aside money for their workers' retirement. We saw an opportunity for a win-win policy. Working with the Department of Labor (which was particularly concerned that workers have coverage) and the Department of Treasury (which was particularly concerned about abuses of the tax exemption of pensions), we crafted some simplified pension programs, which succeeded in getting the transactions costs down to negligible levels. With the passage of the Small Business Job Protection Act in 1996, many firms that previously had not provided pensions to the workers now found it attractive to do so.

Indexed bonds

In the previous instance, we worked closely with Treasury; in other reforms, the financial perspectives of Treasury and the economic analysis at the Council were distinctly different, providing new opportunities for seeing special interests at work.

When we arrived in Washington in 1993, there was no way that individuals could insure themselves against the risks of inflation; and though these risks had abated, no one could be sure if they might return.[2] Social Security is indexed against inflation, that is, benefits rise as the cost of living increases. This is an important feature of the program, because it ensures that individuals are at least partially protected. But over the years, individuals had come to rely increasingly on private pensions, and on the private side, there was little they could do to protect themselves against the possibility that inflation would reduce the value of their pension.

Still, this was a problem that the government could remedy easily because the government was in a position to issue inflation-indexed bonds. With inflation-indexed bonds, an individual who saves $100 is guaranteed to get back his $100 *in real terms*—that is, an amount of money that allows him to purchase the same bundle of goods he could have purchased with the original $100, with interest also guaranteed in real terms. (Presumably, the private sector could have done the same, though there is some worry about what kinds of reserves a private insurance system would need to set aside in order to make sure that it could fulfill its promise; in any case, the private sector did not provide annuities or other long-term financial instruments that were indexed against inflation.)

There was a further compelling argument for the government's action at this time: our almost single-minded focus on the budget. The government was paying higher interest rates on long-term bonds because investors feared inflation; so if the government insured people against this risk, borrowing costs would come down. It was a wonderful idea: we could improve the security of the aged at the same time we improved the fiscal position of the government.

But Treasury bureaucrats viewed the plan with skepticism—hostility might be a better word. It took me a long time to figure out why; after all, they should have liked something that would strengthen the budget; for that, above all else, was what financial markets seemed to focus on. Part of the explanation was innate conservatism. Financial engineering might be something for which we praised the private sector, but the government bureaucrats were living up to their stodgy reputation.

There was another reason: bond traders in the United Kingdom, where such indexed bonds had long been issued, complained that people just bought these bonds and kept them for their retirement. And bond traders make money from people buying and selling bonds, over and over again. The idea of individuals putting aside money for their retirement, knowing that they could get a safe, real return, should have been viewed as positive; to the bond traders, it was a disaster.[3]

The argument put forward by Treasury bureaucrats was somewhat different. They claimed their worry was that "there would be a party that no one would come to." On the face of it, this position contradicted ordinary economic analysis: people want to buy insurance against the risks they face, so much so that they are willing to pay a "premium" for the insurance, and inflation risk in the past has been an important risk. Why wouldn't they come to the party, especially if the bonds were well explained? We decided to test the market. The Council of Economic Advisers directly approached the largest pension fund and the largest provider of mutual funds, people whose job it was to provide income security for the aged and who were in touch with their client base. They expressed enormous support for the idea.

When Treasury found out what we had done, they were furious. We had trodden on their turf, and in a way that was highly dangerous. After all, Treasury claimed to speak for the investor community, to articulate its concerns. It would simply not do to have someone else with such "inside" information. But to its credit, Treasury put aside its petty concerns (though not until after we had heard some stern lectures), and Deputy Secretary Larry Summers did yeoman's work in persuading the Treasury Department to support this initiative that made such common sense. The indexed bonds were finally issued in January 1997. Ironically, by then, inflation had remained so moderate for so long that many if not most investors were paying less attention to it. The lower interest rates on the bonds meant that the government did save some money, but by then too the deficit had been brought under control, so that saving seemed less crucial than it had a short while earlier. Still, it was an innovation, the importance of which will, no doubt, be felt more strongly sometime in the future, as budget deficits once again begin to loom and the threat of inflation appears more strongly than it does today.[4]

Reforming Social Security

The big debate about retirement security did not, however, involve private pensions or government-indexed bonds, but rather Social Security, the government retirement program that had been established in 1935 and today covers almost all American workers.

The United States has an extremely successful Social Security system. It has virtually eliminated poverty among the aged by providing income security to millions of Americans. It has insulated individuals against the risks of inflation—a kind of insurance that, as I have noted, simply cannot be bought directly, or even indirectly, in the market—as well as the risks of the ups and downs of the stock market, which have been so evident in recent years. The program has low transactions costs—a fraction of the costs of private insurance, especially annuities. It is highly responsive to its "clients," the millions of Americans who depend on it for their retirement income.[5] It managed one of the few examples of a successful large-scale computerization by the government. In addition, it engages in a modicum of redistribution, ensuring that the poorest have a basic level of subsistence.

In spite of these successes, there have been repeated calls not just for reform but for privatization, and these calls became louder during the nineties. One might well ask, why? The answer, simply put, encompasses the same set of ingredients we have encountered before: ideology, interests, and greed.

As some individuals saw stock market prices soar, they forgot about the advantages of the Social Security system—the fact that it actually did provide security. Instead, they thought, if instead of putting away money into the Social Security system, I could only put my money into the stock market, I too would be rich beyond my wildest dreams! They believed, or they wanted to believe, that the booming market would last forever. Wall Street encouraged this by contrasting the low returns on Social Security with the high returns on the stock market. Wall Street had, of course, very strong incentives to push privatization. Assume, for instance, that even a fraction of the money that went to Social Security went to its brokerage accounts, and it continued to earn the kinds of fees that it currently earns—0.5 to 1.0 percent (or sometimes even more)—of the amounts managed. This was the true gold lodestone: hundreds of billions of dollars in extra revenues. The United Kingdom had partially privatized its old-age pension system, which had a substantial effect on benefit and transaction costs—money that went from workers to the financial firms that managed their funds.[6] Private companies charge fees—that's how they stay in business—fees for buying into their funds, fees for selling, fees for managing, fees when they buy shares of a stock, fees when they sell. Each fee may seem small, but when added together, the amount adds up—often to a substantial fraction of the gross returns.

Granted, there are some *fiscal* problems with America's Social Security system, for example, a long-run gap between revenues and payouts.[7] But these problems are small and arise from past mistakes. Early recipients of Social Security received more than they contributed, and subsequent generations have had to make up the difference. But they will have to make up the difference whether Social Security is privatized or not. Under the current arrangements, Social Security returns are lowered slightly, in order to pay for these earlier "debts." With privatization, or even partial privatization, some other way would have to be found.

Critics do not complain about the inefficiency of the Social Security system; they simply cannot. The fact is that the public Social Security system is almost surely more efficient, in the key dimension of transactions costs, than any private system is likely to be. Of course, transactions costs to some (the beneficiaries who view it as bad) are income to others (those in Wall Street who would manage the privatized accounts). Wall Street likes transactions costs—the higher the better. Free market ideologues say that competition drives down fees to the minimum level or effectively to zero. Virtually nowhere has it succeeded in doing so. Even in the United States, perhaps the best functioning and most competitive of all capital markets, the persistence of high fees in so many funds, unrelated to performance, shows that reality is far different; the hope that competition would drive down fees has not been realized. (Some would say the persistence of enormous underwriting fees in investment banking provides an even more compelling example.) And the economics of information provides a part of the rationale. This is an area in which imperfections of information are particularly important: surveys show that most Americans do not even know the difference between bonds and stocks; how are they then supposed to make well-informed decisions about which stocks to buy, or even which brokers to choose?

Some have tried to argue that the returns of the Social Security trust fund (which are invested exclusively in Treasury bills) are low, and that far higher returns could be had if the money was invested in equities. But clearly investing in equities brings with it greater risk. The ideologues tend to believe that markets work well. If that is the case, of course, the increased return of investing in equity *only* reflects the increased risk. If individuals want more risk, they can leverage up their risk in the remainder of their portfolio. The fact that Social Security is conservatively invested does not impose any real constraint on an individual's overall investment strategy. And the poor, those who cannot afford to save beyond Social Security, should invest conservatively—their well-being in retirement depends on it. In short, if capital markets work well, the low returns provide no argument for the privatization of Social Security.

But in practice, capital markets often do not work well—the return on equities, for instance, almost surely exceeds that which could be justified by the risk.[8] Part of the problem, of course, is that many investors are not well informed, and there are often marked irrationalities in their approach to risk.[9]

It is at this point that the conservatives are faced with a dilemma. If they say that markets work well, then they cannot complain about the low returns on the Social Security trust fund. The returns are low simply because the risk is low, not because there is any inefficiency in the way the government manages the fund; and if markets worked well, there would be a variety of ways by which individuals who wanted to expose themselves to greater risks (with commensurately higher incomes) could do so. Many conservatives, however, really believe that the returns on the stock markets exceed those on Treasury bills, even accounting for the greater risk. In effect, they believe that government is mismanaging your money. But they are loath to admit that markets do not work well. For if they do not work well, the question is why, and this in turns leads to the next natural question, is there anything the government can do to improve markets? Do we really want to leave individuals' retirement security to ill-informed, irrational investors, investing in capital markets which work imperfectly?

There is yet another approach, equally loathsome to the conservatives, and that is to have the government itself invest in securities. The government could, for instance, purchase an indexed fund of stocks, a broad range of securities. It could invest a fraction of its portfolio— increasing the returns, though at the same time increasing the risk. But while individuals *in their own accounts* may have a difficult time managing the risk (for example, what happens if the market goes down precisely in the years that the individual goes into retirement?), the government is in a far better position to do so. The government could, moreover, purchase these shares at lower transactions cost; it could get a more diversified portfolio; and it need not interfere with the operation of the firms themselves. It would simply be a "silent partner," much as it is now currently through the tax system. Such a system would allow individuals to remain protected against social risks like inflation and the vagaries of the stock market, and at the same time, almost surely, put the Social Security trust fund on firm financial ground, given that equities have such higher returns than bonds.

Unfortunately, government investment in securities has one fatal flaw: it does not generate income ("transactions costs") for the financial market. No wonder then that both the Treasury and the Fed opposed it, with arguments that I found unconvincing. One objection was that the government might vote its shares and thus influence firm behavior. Clearly, it would be easy to pass a proscription against that. And even if it did vote its shares, it would be in a minority. Would it be that bad having a vote against the kind of corporate greed we saw in earlier chapters? Limiting the outlandish salaries for CEOs? Or in an earlier period, not doing business in South Africa during apartheid? The government's voice would be only one voice among many, but perhaps it is a voice that should be heard.

Those in Treasury put forward another argument, even more specious—without as much demand for their Treasury bills, they might be forced to pay higher interest rates on Treasury debt. But, even if this were true, privatization would have the same effect.

The stock market crash of 2000 highlights perhaps the greatest weakness of privatization of Social Security: it leaves individuals vulnerable to the irrational pessimism of the stock market, just as earlier it allowed them to benefit from its irrational optimism. When the stock market was booming, a good many people thought, if only I had put my money in tech stocks rather than been forced to pay Social Security contributions, I would be wealthy by now. At this juncture, they should realize the folly of their ways. Had they put their money into the typical tech stock, they would be looking forward to a bleak retirement. Social Security was designed to provide just that—*security*, not a gamble.

Private, individual Social Security accounts would actually exacerbate the fluctuations of the economy: they make bubbles bigger, and busts worse. Today, at least within Social Security, as the market goes down, individuals are partially insulated from the vagaries of the stock market. If all of an individual's money were in a stock market, as the stock market goes down, individuals would eventually come to worry about their retirement; they would have to save more and consume less. And as they consumed less, the economic downturn would worsen.

With the continued weakness in the stock market, talk of privatization has faded away. But the stock market will recover in time. And as it recovers, so too will the greed that has motivated demands for privatization. There will be those who see new opportunities for profit, who will try, and may even succeed in finding a principled approach to private greed.

Productivity is now up, the economy will eventually recover from the downturn that began in early 2001; and this is good news for the long-term fiscal strength of Social Security. But even if there remains some fiscal problem, it can be handled by minimal changes in Social Security taxes, such as changes in the retirement age. There is no good rationale for privatization, even partial privatization. But there are many good reasons to oppose it.

Managing Risk

Economic systems can be highly unstable—they all have their ups and downs. Over the past seventy years, we have learned a great deal about what causes these movements, and how to intervene actively in the economy to make it more stable. By and large, the Keynesian medicine has worked: downturns are shorter and shallower, upturns are longer. We have also learned, however, that there are limits to activist intervention. It takes time for policies to have an effect—as I noted earlier, monetary policies typically take six months to more than a year to have their full effect. It is often difficult to be sure an economy is going into a recession, and too big a stimulus could ignite inflation. There are some ways of making the economy more stable—ways of administering medicine when the patient needs it, and in the right dose, which is important, because there is never certainty in economic policy; good policies recognize this. Such methods are known as automatic stabilizers. For instance, unemployment benefits work this way: the government spends money if and only if there is an economic downturn, reflected in increased unemployment. Unfortunately, over the years, these automatic stabilizers have been weakened. In the nineties, we missed the opportunity to strengthen them—and even when the need became increasingly apparent, as the economy went into a recession, Bush turned the other way.

In early 2001, no one was sure whether the downturn that was just beginning would be short and shallow, or long and deep. I was on the pessimistic side. But that is why automatic stabilizers are so attractive: they kick in if and only if the economy needs the additional spending. There are two obvious ways to install them: increased unemployment benefits for people who need it and assistance to individual states. In an economic downturn, most states face a shortfall in revenues, and almost all have to work under the constraints of a balanced budget, that is, their expenditures are limited to their revenues; when the economy goes into a recession, the country's revenues decrease rapidly, and states have to cut back expenditures and increase taxes. (By the end of 2002, the contractionary effects of this situation were beginning to be felt. California alone faced a deficit of more than $30 billion. Some estimates put the total contractionary effect of state and local cutbacks at as much as 1–2 percent of GDP. The cutbacks in expenditure were likely to be felt most strongly on education and health, something that the country could ill afford; and the increased property taxes that many communities were forced to enact to offset declining income tax revenues risked pricking the real estate bubble.)

Lessons

Managing risk is always difficult—our financial institutions, which are supposed to have special competencies in doing so, showed just how hard it evidently is. To anticipate any downturn, and to take oversetting actions, is not an easy matter. Since World War II, we have managed the economy far better than we had done previously. But we have not ended the business cycle and downturns remain very costly. That is why it is important to design economic systems and policies that enhance economic stability. Even before the nineties, changes were in place that were making the economy less stable. One of the important built-in stabilizers was being weakened, as the unemployment insurance system—always weak in comparison with those of other advanced industrial countries—did not keep pace with rising income and the changing structure of the U.S. economy, so that more and more workers were left uncovered.

In the nineties, we eroded the built-in stabilizers further, through cutbacks in welfare, payments for which naturally rise as the economy weakens. Yet there were even more fundamental changes in the economy. For all the talk of the New Economy ending the business cycle, the changes of the Roaring Nineties actually may have increased our economic vulnerability, by making the economy more sensitive, more responsive to shocks. Practices such as loyalty between firms and their workers, which insulated workers from some of the vagaries of the marketplace, and defined pension programs, which insulated workers from some of the vagaries of the stock market, not only resulted in a kindlier, gentler capitalism but helped stabilize the economy. New discipline, driven by myopic bottom-line financial markets, combined with the new "flexibility" of the market meant that this gentler form of capitalism was to be a thing of the past. It also meant that as the bubble burst, the consequences not only for individuals but the economy as a whole would be even greater—in spite of all the bravado about learning how to manage risk better.

It is too soon for a full appraisal of the changes in the nineties. We do know that the first downturn of the new millennium is lasting longer than many of the other recessions of the post–World War II era. The true test will come over time: Will the economy and especially unemployment prove more or less stable? Will fluctuations be more or less frequent? Will they be shallower or deeper? There are high costs to economic downturns and large benefits to reducing risk and increasing stability.

CHAPTER 9

Globalization

EARLY FORAYS

I F ECONOMIC RECOVERY and deficit reduction were the first victories of the Clinton administration, management of foreign economic policy appeared to be its second. The administration pushed through two landmark trade agreements, and circumvented Congress to finance a bailout of the Mexican economy. One of the trade agreements created the North American Free Trade Area (NAFTA), joining the United States with Mexico and Canada in the largest free trade area of the world, with 420 million people and a combined GDP of $11.8 trillion. The second, marking the completion in 1994 of the Uruguay Round of trade negotiations that had begun in 1986, created the World Trade Organization, an international organization designed to enforce the rules of the game in international trade, just as the International Monetary Fund created at the end of World War II managed the global financial system. The idea of such an international organization had been a dream for half a century. The agreement reduced further trade barriers on goods, and greatly expanded the trade liberalization agenda to services, intellectual property, and investment. Later, there were other seeming achievements, a regularization of economic relations with China, and the laying of the groundwork for a free trade area embracing all of the Americas and another embracing the Pacific Rim. The fact that so many of these achievements were so hard fought—Ross Perot's campaign against NAFTA criticized the supposed (but in fact nonexistent) "giant sucking sound" that would happen as NAFTA took jobs away from Americans—made the sense of accomplishment all the greater.

Looking back, our management of foreign economic policy appears to be less of a triumph. Just as at home our bubble economy had sowed the seeds of its own destruction, so too did our policies abroad pave the way for a number of problems overseas. By the second half of the nineties, failures in development policies gave rise to criticism of the ideology we had urged on developing countries, especially through the IMF. Around the world there was a heightened sense of economic insecurity as one crisis was followed by another. These complaints were coupled with a sense that the United States had been unfair in its trade negotiations. This feeling grew throughout the nineties and reached new heights as the political unilateralism of the Bush II administration caused a whole new set of resentments and anti-American feeling abroad.[1] The issue is not whether globalization can be a force for good which benefits the poor of the world; of course it can be. But it needs to be managed in the right way and too often it has not been.

While others may have suffered from the mismanagement of globalization, and while in the long run this mismanagement will be costly for the United States—especially as all of the problems of the Clinton administration became multiplied and magnified by the succeeding Bush administration—in the short run America benefited, showing once again that what is good for the United States may not be good for the rest of the world, but even further, that what is bad for the rest of the world may not be bad for the United States. The policies which the United States had pushed contributed in no small measure to the global financial crisis of 1997–98,[2] which led in turn to lower commodity prices. Lower inflationary pressures, combined with the need to prevent a global meltdown, led to lower interest rates; and as the rest of the world weakened, America increasingly appeared as the bastion of strength, though this changed as we slid into recession in the late nineties.

Some of the same forces that had contributed to the problems in the United States underlay the failures abroad. America pushed the ideology of the free market and tried hard to get access for U.S. companies overseas. In doing so, we in the Clinton administration too often put aside the kinds of principles for which we should have stood. We did not think about the impact of our policies on the poor in the developing countries, but on job creation in America. We believed in liberalizing capital markets but didn't think about how it might lead to greater global instability. We thought more about what America might gain in the short run from hard bargaining—and how that in turn might enhance the administration's standing—than we did about how perceptions of unfairness and hypocrisy might in the long run set back America's interests. While we talked about democracy, we did everything we could to maintain our control of the global economic system, and to make sure that it worked for our interests, or more accurately, for the financial and corporate interests that dominated this part of our political life. At home, Wall Street's interest in having Social Security privatized (discussed in the last chapter) was checked by a broader realization that privatization could hurt old-age security; abroad, it was only Wall Street's voice that was heard—after all, the aged abroad neither voted in the United States nor made campaign contributions.

And just as at home we became a victim of our own success, so too abroad. In the United States, our policies *seemed* to be working—we were, after all, experiencing an unprecedented boom. With short-sighted financial markets in control, we did not want to look into the future, to ask whether they were sustainable. So too abroad. Countries that followed our advice seemed to prosper, as we did, so why shouldn't we tout those policies?

Since the Seattle riots of December 1999, with the discrediting of globalization and the view of triumphant American capitalism that underlay it, it is sometimes difficult to remember the heights to which optimism about globalization had soared. I arrived at the World Bank as its chief economist just at the peak. I remember speeches where I spoke with pride about the sixfold increase in flows from the developed countries to emerging markets, necessitating rethinking the role of "official" (bilateral and multilateral) assistance. We were to focus on the poorest countries, and on health and education, areas into which private money still was not flowing. This changed quickly. With the global financial crisis, the flows diminished enormously, and in some parts of the world the money went the other way—from the poor countries to the rich. In Latin America, the boom that the inflow of money had brought about was more than offset by the bust that followed.

The same could be said for each of the areas of globalization. In the mid-nineties, we put forward a vision of the world in which trade liberalization would bring unprecedented prosperity to all, in both the developed and less developed countries. By the end of the nineties, the treaties that we had hailed so proudly were seen as unbalanced, trade liberalization as a new way in which the rich and powerful could exploit the weak and the poor. Just as the market economy had not delivered what it had promised to the countries of the former Soviet Union—it brought unprecedented poverty, not unprecedented prosperity—trade liberalization often did not deliver what it had promised. Export-led growth had been the hallmark of the most successful region in the world, East Asia, but the policies its nations had pursued were a far cry from the trade liberalization policies that had been pushed on Latin America. Latin American policies focused on opening up their markets to imports, rather than promoting exports, and too often jobs were destroyed rather than created.

Unfair trade treaties

Our moment of greatest pride—the completion of the Uruguay Round of trade negotiations—turned out to be one of our greatest failures. Since World War II, there had been a series of rounds of negotiations to lower the barriers to trade among countries. In each round, countries would offer to open up their markets more, if others reciprocated. The Uruguay Round was, in some ways, the most dramatic of these rounds, for it opened up whole new areas of trade liberalization: as manufacturing was shrinking in importance and services were expanding, it was important to bring these sectors of the economy into the ambit of trade liberalization.

But even as we opened up these new areas, we did so in an unbalanced way. The United States pushed other countries to open up their markets to areas of our strength, such as financial services, but resisted, successfully so, efforts to make us reciprocate. Construction and maritime services, the areas of advantage of many developing countries, were not included in the new agreement. Worse still, financial service liberalization was arguably even harmful to some developing countries: as large international banks squelched local competitors, the funds they garnered would be channeled to the international firms with which they felt comfortable, not the small and medium-sized local firms. It was these concerns which had motivated the United States at home to impose restrictions on national banking (until they were largely removed in the Clinton administration); the Midwest and rural areas worried that the New York banks would siphon off funds to the money centers. As foreign banks took over the banking systems of developing countries like Argentina and Mexico, worries about small and medium-sized firms within these developing countries being starved of funds have been repeatedly voiced.[3] Whether these concerns are valid or not, whether they are exaggerated or not, is not the issue: the issue is that countries should have the right to make these decisions for themselves, as the United States did in its own country during its formative days; but under the new international rules that America had pushed, countries were being deprived of that right.

Agriculture was another example of the double standard inherent in the trade liberalization agenda we pushed. Although we insisted that other countries reduce their barriers to our products, and eliminate the subsidies for those products that competed against ours, the United States kept barriers for the goods produced by the developing countries—and the United States continued massive subsidies. Agricultural subsidies encourage American farmers to produce more, forcing down global prices for the crops that poor developing countries produce and depend upon. For instance, subsidies for one crop alone, cotton, that went to 25,000 mostly very well off U.S. farmers, exceeded in value the cotton that was produced, lowering the global price of cotton enormously.[4] American farmers, who account for a third of total global output, despite the fact that U.S. production costs are *twice* the international price of 42 cents per pound, gained at the expense of the 10 million African farmers who depended on cotton for their meager livings. Several African countries lost between 1–2 percent of their entire income, an amount greater than what these particular countries received in foreign aid from the United States. Mali, for instance, received $37 million in aid but lost $43 million from depressed prices.

Mickey Kantor, the U.S. Trade Representative responsible for negotiating trade agreements in the early days of the Clinton administration, exemplified both the short-run success and the long-term problems which lay behind those initial successes. Kantor had been Clinton's campaign manager, and I found him to be devoted, energetic, and engaging. By background, he was a lawyer, and although he was not an expert on international economic policy, he knew how to get a trade agreement that American companies liked. He struck a hard bargain to get the best deal for the United States. But whereas such aggressiveness may do well in American courts, it serves our country's long-term interests less well in the court of global opinion.

One of the new areas over which he bargained hard was intellectual property rights, such as patents and copyrights. Like services, these were an increasingly important source of income to U.S. firms. In the Uruguay Round he insisted, at the behest of American drug companies, that there be the strongest intellectual property protections possible. The Office of Science and Technology Policy and the Council of Economic Advisers opposed this stance. Intellectual property rights need to balance the concern of users of knowledge with those of producers. Too tight an intellectual property regime can actually harm the pace of innovation; after all, knowledge is the most important input into the production of knowledge. We knew that the argument that without intellectual property rights, research would be stifled was just wrong; in fact, basic research, the production of ideas that underlay so many of the advances in technology, from transistors to lasers, from computers to the internet, was *not* protected by intellectual property rights, yet America remained the leading producer in these areas as well.

Patents often represent privatization of a public resource, of ideas that are largely based on publicly funded research. They create monopoly power and interfere with short-run efficiency. Market economies only lead to efficient outcomes when there is competition, and intellectual property rights undermine the very basis of competition. In some instances, the benefits from the additional induced research might be worth the cost; but what is required is a careful balancing of benefits and costs, comparing the benefits of any additional research that stronger property rights might induce with the costs of monopoly power and less well functioning markets. The drug companies which were pushing for stronger intellectual property rights were not interested in this kind of careful balancing; they believed that the stronger the intellectual property rights, the higher their profits. The Council of Economic Advisers and the Office of Science and Technology Policy worried—rightly so, as the agreement finally emerged—that in the trade negotiations in Geneva, the U.S. Trade Representative was not doing the careful balancing that was required, but was simply reflecting the pressures he was under from the drug companies.

The Council of Economic Advisers worried too that these new protections could lead to high drug prices in developing countries, depriving the poor and the sick of medicines they badly needed. We worried that when the Uruguay Round treaty was signed, we were simultaneously signing the death warrant for thousands of those in the developing countries who would be deprived of life-saving drugs.[5] Our worries turned out to be real, and the public outcry was one of the factors undermining confidence in the way globalization was being managed.

Some leading academic supporters of trade liberalization, such as Columbia University's Jagdish Bhagwati, had questioned the whole idea of bringing intellectual property rights within the ambit of the WTO. For unlike trade liberalization, which, at least under some idealized (and somewhat unrealistic) conditions can make everyone better off, stronger intellectual property rights typically make some better off (the drug companies) and many worse off (those who otherwise might have been able to purchase the drugs). There was little doubt that American firms would be better off; there was more doubt about whether the developing countries would be. Indeed, many noted the irony that during America's rapid growth in the nineteenth century, we were widely accused of stealing Europe's intellectual property rights. In an address to Congress in 1790, George Washington pointed out that the objective of patent legislation was to give "effectual encouragement, as well to the introduction of new and useful inventions from abroad, as to the exertions of skill and genius in producing them at home." Non-U.S. citizens were not granted patent protection until 1836. Having succeeded, were we now pulling up the ladder behind us?[6]

Although we had anticipated these problems, the Council had not fully anticipated a raft of others: the charges of bio-piracy, of American firms patenting traditional medicines and foods, charging developing countries for what they had always thought to be theirs. The most notorious case entailed a Texas-based company, RiceTec, Inc. (a subsidiary of RiceTec AG of Liechtenstein), receiving a patent (no. 5,663,484) on basmati rice lines and grain, which had been grown for centuries by farmers in the Punjab region of India and Pakistan. In this case, the international outcry, including pressure from the Indian government, eventually led the company to withdraw most of its claims (though it did get a patent on three crossbreeds). But it is expensive to fight these battles, and that automatically puts the developing countries at a disadvantage.[7]

That we bargained hard was understandable, and that the combination of hard bargaining and our economic strength would lead to a trade agreement that was "unfair"—that gave us more benefits than it gave others—was predictable. But it was *so* unfair, so unbalanced, that some of our gains were at the expense of others—the poorest region in the world, sub-Saharan Africa, was actually worse off.

In the aftermath of these agreements, America was increasingly seen as hypocritical, because of the large gap between our free trade rhetoric and our actual practice. (Of course Europe was, in some ways, equally guilty; its farm subsidies were even larger than ours, with the average European cow receiving $2 a day in subsidies, a striking number, since half the world's population lives on less than $2 a day. But Europe did less free market preaching, and America was trying to claim "leadership.") After the agreement bringing free trade between America and Mexico was signed, America looked for new ways to keep out those goods that were successfully competing with the United States. It tried to keep out Mexican avocadoes, for example, claiming they would bring with them fruit flies that would destroy our California crops. When the Mexicans responded by allowing U.S. Department of Agriculture inspectors into their country, and they could not find evidence of fruit flies, the Americans said, "But of course, they are small and hard to see." Then the Mexicans offered to sell the avocadoes only to the Northeast in the middle of winter—the cold air would be instant death to any fruit fly—and America still balked. (I eventually found out why: peak consumption is Super Bowl Sunday in January, as guacamole dip has become part of the ritual.) Only when Mexico threatened to retaliate by throwing up barriers to American corn did America come to its senses.

We tried to keep out Mexican tomatoes and Mexican trucks, Chinese honey and Ukraine women's coats. Whenever an American industry was threatened, the United States swung into action, using the so-called fair trade laws, which had been largely blessed by the Uruguay Round.

At the Council of Economic Advisers, we asked, why should there be a double standard beween what is "fair trade" for goods produced by American producers and those produced by foreign firms? Dumping—selling goods at below cost—is unfair, and can be used to establish a monopoly position, which, in the long run, will harm consumers. But American anti-trust laws have well-defined standards for ascertaining such predatory behavior. Why should foreign firms be subjected to different standards—standards under which a large fraction of U.S. firms would be judged to be engaged in predation? When

Kodak charged Japan with anti-competitive behavior in sales of Kodak film in Japan, the Council asked, how would their charges fare in an American anti-trust court, and our conclusion was—not very well. With Kodak film having only a one-third market share in Japan, to the U.S. Trade Representative it was obvious that it was because Fuji was somehow engaged in some anti-competitive practice. The fact that Fuji had only a one-third share in the United States was not taken as evidence that Kodak might be engaged in anti-competitive practices here, but as further demonstrating the superiority of Kodak products, reinforcing the conclusion of some nefarious activity on the part of Japan. There was an obvious interpretation: there does seem to be an advantage for the home player, but that doesn't mean that there is something scurrilous going on. Nonetheless, the U.S. Trade Representative pressed charges of anti-competitive behavior—and eventually lost.[8]

The most amusing of our attempts to keep out foreign goods was the broom-corn broom episode, where we imposed "safeguard" measures to protect America from an onslaught of imports of brooms made with the tassles of a special corn (called, not surprisingly, "broom-corn"). Safeguard measures are intended to give countries time to adapt to a rush of imports, especially when such imports might have broader, systemic consequences. Here was America, with unemployment dropping to 3.8 percent, saying that it needed safeguards. One might well ask: how many jobs were on the line? We never got a clear answer, but it was somewhere between one hundred and three hundred! If America couldn't absorb this kind of shock, what did it say about poorer countries, with much higher levels of unemployment, and with no unemployment insurance or welfare system? Surely, they would always need to resort to safeguards.

To be fair to ourselves, the Clinton administration resisted many claims—for instance, those of the steel industry. Later, George W. Bush was to put politics above principle, enacting safeguards hurting those in America's steel-using industries as well as steel producers in the developing world. Whether he was entitled to do so under WTO rules remains to be seen (in March 2003, the WTO ruled against the U.S. steel tariffs; however, the United States declared its intention to appeal the decision). But that is not the point: combined with the almost simultaneous increase in agricultural subsidies, America's free trade credentials, already tarnished, became badly bruised. Countries asked: what good is a free trade agreement which eliminates tariffs, if America then uses a whole variety of non-tariff protectionist measures to keep out competitive goods?

Although such hypocrisy works against America's long-run *economic* interests, our narrow pursuit of economic interests sometimes worked against our broader political interests as well. When competition from Russia lowered aluminum prices, the Clinton administration helped create a global cartel, setting back reforms in Russia: a commitment to the market economy and economic reforms only went so far—everything was fine so long as our own economic interests were not adversely affected. For a while, the dumping laws were even used to prevent the importation of nuclear material from the warheads of Russian missiles. Clearly, leaving the material in Russia, with its poorly paid government officials and lax security, presented a serious risk of nuclear proliferation.[9] Yet in this instance, commercial interests were put ahead of national security interests.

Similarly, the efforts to defend offshore bank secrecy described in this chapter not only reinforced views of our hypocrisy, but in the aftermath of September 11 looked particularly destructive of our own interests, since it became apparent that the terrorists were partially funded through these secret bank accounts.

In trade negotiations for the admission of China to the World Trade Organization, Kantor had argued that China should be treated as a developed country, quickly lowering its tariffs (developing countries were given longer periods to lower their tariffs after being admitted to the WTO). The fact that China was a poor developing country, and thus by WTO rules should have been allowed longer times to bring its tariffs down to the levels agreed under the WTO, meant little to him. He unilaterally declared that China was not a less developed country—much to amusement elsewhere. But then, in 1999, as negotiations were moving along, and China's premier, Zhu Rong Zhi, came to the United States to seal the deal, the U.S. Treasury insisted on a rapid opening up of China's financial markets, allowing, for instance, short-term speculative capital to flow in and American banks to sell their risky derivatives. China was loath to do this, having seen the devastation wrought by the 1997 East Asian crisis, which brought major recessions and depressions to Thailand, Korea, Indonesia, and Malaysia. China had been spared, because while it had opened up its doors to foreign direct investments, to those who were willing to building factories and create jobs, it had not welcomed this "hot money" since it knew that it brought with it enormous instability, but not higher growth. Even the U.S. Trade Representative understood that this was asking too much from China, but even if it made little economic sense, insisting on the opening of financial markets served America's short-run financial interests. When Zhu was forced to return to China empty-handed—he was not willing to jeopardize his country's stability and refused to agree to Treasury demands—it was a major setback for those in China pushing for reform and closer integration into the world. America's broader interests had been compromised. In this case, the story has a happy ending: the reformers recovered, China eventually did join the WTO. While we dragged our feet about letting the Chinese in, they had used the time well to prepare the economy for the new trade regime; in effect, they got the extra time they had asked for and the United States had refused.

Promoting Global Instability

The Clinton administration willingly took on the task of changing the global trading system—to make it work better for America. But the problems posed by the global financial system were thrust upon us, first by the 1994–95 Mexican crisis, then by the East Asian crises, then by the Russian crisis, then by the Latin American crises.

The Mexican crisis

In the early 1990s, Mexico had been one of the great success stories of market-based "reform." It had liberalized, reducing trade barriers and other government restrictions, and privatized, selling off government banks, even its roads. But its growth was based as much on heavy borrowing abroad, and suddenly, in December 1994, financial markets became worried: had they lent Mexico too much money? Would it be able to pay back what it had borrowed? Such sudden changes in sentiment can set off a crisis; as the price of bonds plummets, lenders refuse to roll over loans, those within the country panic and try to take their money out, and the exchange rate falls precipitously. The Mexican crisis was handled boldly, an exercise of presidential leadership, a massive bailout of those who had invested in Mexican bonds. The U.S. Treasury—and many others—viewed it as a major success: exchange rates stabilized; although there was a worry that the crisis would spread, like a disease, to other countries in Latin America, there was no serious contagion, American investors got their money back (which was part of the reason for the bailout), and America got repaid with interest.

But it is more questionable whether the bailout *caused* Mexico's recovery. A closer look at the data shows that the recovery had more to do with trade with the United States, based on the strong growth there and the newly signed NAFTA, than with anything done by the

IMF.[10] As the country went into crisis, its exchange rate fell, making exports more attractive, imports less so, and this stimulated the economy. To the extent that money mattered, it was not so much the IMF influence but trade credit from America: interest rates in America were low, and its exporters could get trade credit from the U.S. firms with whom they dealt.

As time went on, whether the bailout in itself was a success or not became even more questionable. Every crisis eventually comes to an end, with exchange rates stabilizing and growth resuming. The question was, did the intervention result in the crisis being much shallower and shorter than it otherwise would have been? I doubt it. Mexico did not restructure its banking sector in an effective way, even though this was supposed to be a central part of the World Bank–IMF program. The result was that those parts of the economy not producing for exports (which did not accordingly have easy access to credit in the United States) languished. Real wage growth was held back for years, unable to reach pre-crisis levels until years later. And then, as America slipped into its slowdown and recession, so too did Mexico.

Because we cannot run a controlled experiment, we cannot be sure of the role of the big bailout in the recovery. But the seeming success of the Mexican "experiment" induced us to try the same recipe again, and again, and again, first in Thailand, then in Indonesia, then in Korea, Russia, Brazil, and Argentina, with results ranging from mere failure to disaster. In each of the succeeding bailouts tens of billions were spent, to no avail: the money did not even arrest the decline in exchange rates, and the policy package, consisting of high interest rates and drastic expenditure cutbacks, only made the downturns worse (as standard economic theory predicted it would). The deepening recession did mean that imports were quickly reduced, and the surplus of exports over imports meant the countries quickly had a pile of dollars to use to pay back their creditors. If that was their objective—and not the maintenance of the strength of the economies—then again, the programs might be declared a victory.

The East Asian crises

The worst disaster was in Indonesia, which faced a crisis in October 1997. The IMF, at the direction of the U.S. Treasury, responded with its usual recipe of fiscal and monetary austerity. In December 1997, at a meeting in Kuala Lumpur, before the assembled finance ministers and Central Bank governors of major industrial countries and Asia, I represented the World Bank. I warned that, given the history of ethnic fractionation, if the IMF's contractionary policies were maintained, within six months there would be political and social turmoil. Even if one did not care about the resulting deaths and social consequences, it was bad economics: the policies were supposedly meant to induce capital to flow in, but instead, there would be massive outflows and further economic havoc. The head of the IMF, citing the "success" of Mexico, simply reaffirmed its position: Indonesia would have to stay the course, feel the pain. The final event precipitating the riots occurred in May 1998, with the announcement of cutbacks in food and fuel subsidies to the very poor. Evidently the IMF was willing to supply billions to bailout Western banks, but when it came to much more miserly sums to provide assistance to the poor, the money had run out. The day after these cutbacks were announced, riots broke out: the disaster we had forecast came about. The country has yet to recover fully.

Indeed, many of the countries that did the best during and after the Asian crisis were those that did not follow the standard IMF/Treasury prescriptions. China avoided a downturn by pursuing expansionary monetary and fiscal policies—precisely the opposite of what Treasury and IMF had imposed elsewhere in the region. Malaysia, the country with the shortest and shallowest downturn, not only had no IMF program but imposed capital controls, for which it was sharply criticized by the U.S. Treasury, the IMF, and others. By following its own course, Malaysia was left with a legacy of debt far smaller than those who had listened to the Treasury/IMF advice. With capital controls, it was able to avoid raising interest rates to the usurious levels imposed elsewhere. With lower interest rates, there were far fewer bankruptcies, leaving Malaysian banks to face far fewer troubles. In Korea, by contrast, 50 percent of the firms were forced into distress, and in Indonesia, some 75 percent. Thailand, the country that followed IMF/Treasury advice most closely, is only just now returning to the levels of GDP that it had half a decade before the crisis.

Korea's reasonably rapid recovery was cited by both sides of the debate as evidence that they were right. But there are several reasons why I believe that Korea's recovery happened, if anything, in spite of the IMF program, not because of it. Indeed, the program, when it was put into place, did not even stop the slide of the currency. If the problems were as deep-seated as the IMF's accusations suggested, they could never have been resolved in such short order. The Koreans were judicious in deciding when, and when not, to do what the IMF told them. Korea had seen the miserable failure of the IMF/Treasury strategy for restructuring the financial institutions in Indonesia. There the IMF shut down sixteen banks and announced more (which were not named) and that depositors would have only very limited insurance. To no one's surprise—other than the IMF's—there was a run on Indonesia's banking system, which converted what would have been in any case a serious recession into a full-scale depression. Korea, by contrast, effectively nationalized its banking system, keeping at least a mild flow of finance. The Koreans also recognized that underlying their economic downturn was a normal cyclical downturn in the demand for computer chips. They refused to follow IMF advice to get rid of the excess capacity. Consequently, when the computer chip market recovered, they were ready to take advantage of it, and this was critical to Korea's recovery.

The IMF (and by implication the U.S. Treasury, which was very involved in forming IMF policy, especially during this period) eventually admitted that its Indonesian financial restructuring strategy was a failure, that it had underestimated the extent of the downturn, and that it had pursued excessively contractionary fiscal policies. But it was not a lesson well learned: when Argentina faced a crisis, fiscal stringency was again the order of the day, with again the predictable outcome—increasing unemployment, decreasing GDP, and eventually political and social turmoil. What was remarkable was not that there eventually were riots; what was remarkable was the patience of the Argentinean people and the failure of the IMF to anticipate the riots.

The Latin American crises

To Latin America—and indeed, to much of the developing world elsewhere—the Argentine experience was particularly telling, for Argentina had been the poster child of the kind of reform that the IMF and U.S. Treasury (on a bipartisan basis) had urged on developing countries. (Because these reforms represented the "consensus" of policymakers between 15th Street, where Treasury was located, and 19th Street, at the headquarters of the IMF, in Washington—but not the consensus of policymakers in developing countries—the particular set of reforms were called the "Washington Consensus" reforms.)[11] If this is what happens to those that followed those policies, countries said, they wanted none of it

Sowing the seeds

The bailouts were not only of questionable value in dealing with financial crises, the early bailouts arguably contributed to the problems that followed. For lenders, knowing that they would likely be bailed out, took less care, less due diligence, in lending; and borrowers, knowing that if enough of them did not buy insurance against exchange rate declines, they too would be bailed out by the IMF, left themselves exposed to these risks.[12] Some economists went further: the bailout money helped feed the speculative sharks. Speculation—betting that a currency will crash—is a zero-sum game. The speculators win, at someone else's expense. Sometimes, it is gamblers on the other side, those who think that the currency will not crash. But on average the gains of the winners equal the losses of the losers—minus transactions costs—so speculation is a losing proposition, except for one thing: the money that comes from the IMF and governments, spent in a valiant but ineffective attempt to prop the currency up. The more money supplied in the bailouts, the more profitable the speculation business.

THIS IS JUST one of the ways that the crises of the late nineties took seed in the U.S. Treasury. Earlier, Treasury (and the IMF) had pushed for rapid financial and capital market liberalization—the opening of these countries' markets to the onslaught of speculative money that can flow in and out overnight, leaving economic havoc in its wake, and deregulating the banking system. Some joked that the United States had experienced the devastating effects of deregulation, culminating in the huge S&L bailout. Not wanting to be selfish, it wanted all the countries to share in this experience. But while the United States was rich enough to bear the costs, others were not so fortunate. Capital market liberalization was a two-edged sword, but with one edge far sharper than the other. When markets were optimistic, when there was excessive exuberance, capital flowed in, and even though only a fraction went into productive investments, growth was enhanced. But earlier chapters of this book have shown how in the United States, irrational exuberance was followed by irrational pessimism, so too abroad, only more so. And this is a pattern that has been repeated time and time again. Although the United States is able to bear these market vicissitudes reasonably well, the consequences for developing countries are far more serious. The result was that countries lost far more as capital flowed out than they gained as capital flowed in.

In 1993, the Council of Economic Advisers opposed Treasury's efforts to force Korea to liberalize rapidly. Korea had laid out a plan of gradual liberalization. The almost one hundred crises that had marked the previous quarter century, while devastating for the developing world, had provided ample data with which to ascertain factors causing crises, and of these, rapid financial and capital market liberalization stood out. Why push Korea to move faster? What would America gain by having Korea liberalize a few years earlier than it otherwise would have done? American workers would gain nothing, but Wall Street firms were worried: gradual liberalization might allow others to enter as well, or even enable Korean firms to compete on an even footing. In chapter 4, we saw that the deregulation of the telecom industry led to a race—the first to get established would dominate the market and make monopoly profits (or so it was believed). The same reasoning applied here, and many Americans believed that our firms were in a clear position to win the race, if it began now. Who knew what the situation would be in five years' time? Unfortunately, as typically happens when matters of central concern to the financial markets are in dispute, Treasury's position prevailed. Korea was pushed to open up its capital markets rapidly. Four years later the Council's worries were, regrettably, realized. The U.S. Treasury had won the debate, but Korea had lost, and with the ensuing global financial crisis, so too had much of the rest of the world.

The Asian financial crisis of 1997, the global financial crisis that followed the year after, with crises in Russia and Brazil, made it clear that *something* was wrong.[13] It was, or should have been, clear that there were systemic problems. When there is a bend in the road and a single car has an accident, one can blame the driver. But when, day after day, crashes occur at the same spot, one suspects there is something wrong with the road. As the leader of the free world, it was incumbent on the United States to do something. Global discussions began, under the rubric of "reforming the global financial architecture." One should have been suspicious: the grander the title, the less the substance. The discussion, largely conducted among the same parties, the same finance ministries and central bankers that had failed so miserably in managing the crises, amounted to little more than a discussion of changing the shape of the table and rearranging the chairs. If wars, as Clemençeau famously said, are too important to be left to generals, economic development and global economic stability are too important to be left to the finance ministers and central bankers of the advanced industrial countries, and the international institutions they oversee, the World Bank and IMF. Certainly that is the case if we want to create a more democratic and stable global system.

Little of substance has been done. With the continuing, ever-mounting crashes in international finance, there is now a growing awareness that something is wrong with the system—and one of the greatest failures of the Clinton administration was that it did little to fix it.

The reason was perhaps obvious: while the system was not working well for the emerging markets, America, and particularly U.S. financial firms, were well served. I noted earlier how America actually benefited from the global slowdown. Just as at home, investment banks made money putting mega-mergers together, and then when they failed, made money taking them apart, America's financial firms made money as the capital flowed in, and then made more money advising the governments on how to manage the capital inflows; when countries went into crises, as they so often did whether they followed the advice or not, the financial firms then made still more money advising on restructuring. When urged on by the U.S. Treasury and the IMF, countries like Thailand had fire sales, Western financial firms bought up corporations in the crisis countries on the cheap; sometimes they did little else but to hold on to them until the recovery set in, and then resell them back to the Thais—sometimes to the original owners. No matter which way things went, the investment banks made money.

We should have begun by looking at some of the longstanding, almost obvious problems with the current system, besides the recurrent crises.[14] What would seem to be basic, and even obvious, principles were often contradicted. Money *should* flow from the rich countries to the poor. Yet year after year, exactly the opposite occurs—America, the richest country in the world, is seemingly unable to live within its means, borrowing more than a billion dollars a day. One would have thought that the rich, being far more able to bear the risks of volatility in interest rates and exchange rates, would bear those risks, especially when they lend money to the poor. Wall Street prides itself on its sophistication, its ability to shift risk, presumably from those less able to those more able to bear it. Yet time after time the poor nations are left to bear the burden. When the U.S. Fed raised American interest rates to unheard-of levels, our S&Ls were pushed into bankruptcy; but as we saw in chapter 2, they were bailed out. By contrast, Latin America faced bankruptcy and a lost decade of growth. When Russia devalued in 1998, Moldova, which had been one of the better off parts of the Soviet Union but had seen its income plummet 70 percent in the mismanaged transition from communism to the market economy, had to devalue as well; but its debts were denominated in dollars and other hard currencies, and a difficult-to-manage debt became unbearable: by 2002, 75 percent of the government's budget was going to service the foreign debt. Of course, no one expected the world to be fair; but at least, according to conventional economic wisdom, it was efficient. Yet these and other similar phenomena suggest that it is neither.

One of the root causes of the problem was the international reserve system. Every year, countries around the world set aside reserves as insurance against a variety of contingencies, such as an abrupt downturn in foreign lenders' sentiment or a sudden collapse of export prices. Poor countries are forced to hold substantial sums, typically in low-interest-paying U.S. government (or sometimes euro) bonds. The return they get on these funds is far lower than they could get were they to use the money for badly needed investments in education, health, infrastructure, or factories. Again, America benefits from the low-interest loan from the developing country; but this comes at the expense of the poor. The amounts held in reserves are substantial—now over $2 trillion worldwide—and a significant fraction of this is held by developing countries.

As developing countries, under pressure from the United States and the IMF, have stripped away their restrictions on borrowing from abroad, America benefits even more, but in ways which may even stifle growth in the poor nations. Consider a poor country in which a firm borrows short-term U.S.$100 million from an American bank. The country knows that the American bank may at any time demand to have its dollars back, refusing to roll over its loans. (Often rather than simply letting the firm default, pressure will be put on the government to do something.) Financial markets look at whether the country has set aside enough dollar reserves to meet the short-term dollar obligations, not just of the government but of the firms within the country. When there is a shortfall of reserves, there is a good chance that financial markets will panic. Governments, knowing this, have adopted prudential standards of putting aside more reserves even when private firms borrow more in dollars. In our example, this means the government will have to set aside $100 million in reserves. Net, the country *as a whole* receives nothing. But it pays the United States, say, $18 million in interest, and receives back, on its reserves, less than $2 million. This may be good for growth in the United

States, good for America's fiscal position, but it has to be bad for the developing country.

Moreover, there is in these international arrangements a built-in deflationary bias, depressing global income. Because reserves need to grow in tandem with growth in imports and foreign liabilities, and need to be increased as risk increases, every year billions more are set aside—between $100 and $200 billion a year. This is income that is not spent, but simply put into these reserves.

In addition, the system has a built-in instability: the IMF (and others) constantly warn countries about trade deficits. But the sum of the world's trade deficits must equal the sum of the surpluses; if some country imports more than it exports, some other country must be exporting more than it imports. If a few countries, like Japan and China, insist on having a surplus, in total, the rest of the world must have a deficit. If some country reduces its deficit (as Korea did after the 1997 crisis), the deficit must simply show up somewhere else in the system. The deficits are like hot potatoes. And as a country finds itself with a large deficit, it faces a crisis. In this way, the deficits are as much a fault of the surplus countries as they are of the debtor countries.

The only thing that keeps the system working at all is that the United States, the richest country in the world, has become the "deficit of last resort." As other countries strive to eliminate their deficits, as Japan and China continue to run huge surpluses, America is willing and able to run the huge deficits that make the global arithmetic add up. This is the ultimate irony. The financial system allows the United States to live year after year far beyond its means, even as the U.S. Treasury, year after year, lectures others on why they should not. And the total value of the benefits that the United States gets out of the current system surely exceeds, by a considerable amount, the total foreign aid the United States provides. What a peculiar world, in which the poor countries are in effect subsidizing the richest, which happens, at the same time, to be among the stingiest in giving assistance in the world—giving but a fraction of what Europe and Japan provide as a percentage of their incomes.

With these failings in the global reserve system, with symptoms that something was wrong, very wrong, with the global financial system becoming increasingly apparent, it should have been clear that some major changes were needed; tinkering at the edges would not suffice. But, regrettably, no fundamental reforms were undertaken. Indeed, there were few discussions of any of the underlying problems, including those of the global reserve system, or the inadequacies in how the private market handled risk. Remarkably, little was done even about the problems that were being directly manifested. It was evident that capital market liberalization was the immediate cause of many of the countries' problems, and yet, not surprisingly, discussions of this were taboo.

Reform in the international arena is typically a slow process. While even if the Clinton administration had tried pushing for meaningful reform, it might not have succeeded in accomplishing that goal in the short span of eight years, at least it could have started the process. For instance, underlying several of the crises was the fact that countries and firms had borrowed from abroad more than they could repay. When that happens inside the United States or any other advanced industrial country, there are bankruptcy proceedings. In the nineteenth century, debtors were thrown into prison—this didn't do much to enable them to repay what was owed, but provided a strong incentive not to over-borrow. When developing nations borrowed too much, America or the European powers simply sent in their troops to force the country to repay. France invaded Mexico in the middle of the nineteen century; a coalition of European powers bombarded Caracas as recently as 1902; and America took actions in the Caribbean even more recently.

We don't do this any more, but it's clear that there needs to be a change in the way debt defaults are handled so as to avoid the economic chaos and widespread misery that countries such as Argentina have suffered. Ever since the debt crisis of the eighties, it has been clear that some sort of international bankruptcy code such as we have in the United States was needed, and it became even more apparent in the crises of the nineties. But Treasury was distinctly uninterested. Only after the departure of the Clinton administration did serious international discussions begin.

Another major reform that Clinton's Treasury at first recognized but then dropped was increased transparency. When, not long after the discussions of reforming the global financial architecture began in late 1997, it was suggested that the transparency the United States was pushing in developing countries be extended to offshore banking centers and hedge funds, the United States Treasury suddenly seemed to change its views. At one of the meetings in Washington discussing global financial reforms, the U.S. deputy secretary went so far as to explain why some secrecy, some lack of transparency, was a good thing. It provided greater incentives to gather information, thus enhancing what is called the "price discovery function" of markets. Matters became even worse under the Bush administration. The "club" of the advanced industrial countries—the Organization of Economic Cooperation and Development—finally undertook an initiative in 2000 to limit bank secrecy. But shortly before September 11, 2001, Paul O'Neill made it clear that the United States would veto even that limited initiative. After September 11, it became clear that this bank secrecy was key in financing Al Qaeda.[15]

The Clinton administration's Treasury not only failed to address the fundamental problems of the global financial system; when others made suggestions, even those with considerable merit, they were quick to veto them, with little discussion, especially when they threatened to undermine U.S. hegemony. Early in the Asian crisis, Japan suggested the creation of an Asia Monetary Fund, and made a generous offer of $100 billion to help underwrite it. Japan was highly (but quietly) critical of the way the IMF and the U.S. Treasury were managing the crisis. Just as the United States stood to lose the most by a meltdown in Mexico, its neighbor, Japan felt the same way about its neighbors. But the United States evidenced little understanding of the special features of the Asian economies, and, at least initially, remarkably little sympathy for their problems. (At one point, as Thailand, which had stood strongly by the United States throughout the Vietnam War, went into crisis, the United States resisted providing significant aid, suggesting that its downturn would be but a blip in the soaring global economy.) America had become a strong advocate of regional trade agreements, especially those, like NAFTA, in which we would play a dominant role. But the Asia Monetary Fund, with the ample resources supplied by Japan, would limit America's ability to dictate policy in the region. The U.S. Treasury knew that, and was willing to risk the region's downturn becoming worse without the aid. Many in Japan, Malaysia, and the crisis countries are still bitter about how the United States handled those events.

The Triumph and Defeat of the Washington Consensus

What I found most troublesome as I went from being chairman of the President's Council of Economic Advisers to being chief economist at the World Bank was that the IMF and the U.S. Treasury so often appeared to be pushing abroad positions that were precisely the opposite of what we had fought for at home. We fought against privatization of Social Security at home, while we pushed it abroad. At home, we fought against the balanced-budget amendment, which would have constrained our ability to use expansionary fiscal policy in the event of a downturn; but abroad, we imposed contractionary fiscal policies on countries going into recessions. At home, we fought for a bankruptcy law to protect debtors and give them a fresh start; abroad, we treated bankruptcy as if it were an abrogation of the credit contract. At home, we fought against changing the charter of the Fed to focus exclusively on inflation—we worried in fact that the Fed was placing too little emphasis on job creation. Abroad, we demanded that Central Banks focus exclusively on inflation.

At home, we recognized the limitations of markets and argued that there was an important (but limited) role for government. But while we did not believe in market fundamentalism, the view that markets by themselves would solve the economy's (and society's) problems, we pushed market fundamentalism on the rest of the world, both directly and through the IMF. I could have understood Ronald Reagan or Margaret Thatcher doing this. But I could not understand Bill Clinton doing this. Indeed, Clinton appointed as president of the World Bank Jim Wolfensohn,[16] someone who was much more in tune with Clinton's own philosophy and concerns, and there were dramatic reforms at the World Bank during his administration—often over the objections of the U.S. Treasury. And that is the point: Treasury's views did not coincide with those of Clinton. Treasury had its own perspectives, its own ideology, its own agenda, and it was largely, though not completely, able to follow that agenda internationally through its domination of the IMF.

These market fundamentalist ideas were reflected in the basic strategy for development (and for managing crises and the transition from communism to the market) advocated, beginning in the 1980s, by the IMF, the World Bank, and the U.S. Treasury, a strategy various referred to as "neo-liberalism" or, because the major players planning it were all in Washington, the "Washington Consensus." It involved minimizing the role of government, through privatizing state-owned enterprises and eliminating government regulations and interventions in the economy. Government had a responsibility for macrostability, but that meant getting the inflation rate down, not getting the unemployment rate down.

The most successful countries, those in East Asia, had not followed this strategy; government had played an active role, not just in promoting education and savings and redistributing income but also in advancing technology. Latin America became the best student of the Washington Consensus, with Argentina and Chile the star pupils. We have already noted what became of Argentina. Chile has remained a success, though the 7 percent growth rates of the early nineties have moderated greatly, to half that level. But the question is, is that country's success because it followed the Washington Consensus policies, or because it was *selective*, and at critical junctures rejected the Washington Consensus? For instance, it did not fully liberalize capital markets, imposing a tax on capital inflows until the global downturn meant that such a tax was irrelevant. It did not fully privatize—a significant fraction of exports still arises from government-owned copper mines, which are just as efficient as the private ones, but deliver far more revenue to the government rather than shipping profits abroad. Most important, as the president of the country, Ricardo Lagos, has emphasized, Chile's leaders stressed education and health, social issues that were not at the center of the Washington Consensus. Yes, they did engage in extensive trade liberalization, which made good sense for a small economy (though the United States did not fully reciprocate), and they did maintain a strong budgetary position—most of their debt today is left over from their failed and costly experiment with financial sector deregulation under the military dictator Pinochet, who flirted with free market ideas with sometimes disastrous consequences.

Today, all over Latin America, there is disillusionment with the policies that the United States and the IMF had pushed. Growth under liberalization is just over half of what it was under the old pre-reform regime (although still better than during the lost decade of the eighties). Unemployment is up 3 percentage points; poverty (measured at a low-income level of only $2 a day) is up *even as a percentage of the population.*[17] Where growth has occurred, the benefits have accrued to those at the upper part of the income distribution. All over Latin America people are asking, has reform failed us, or has globalization failed us? Voting patterns have reflected this disillusionment: the election of a so-called leftist, Luis Inacio Lula da Silva, in Brazil, with overwhelming popular support, reflects a demand for a changed economic policy. But whatever their answer, the prospect for progress is bleak—and even confidence in democracy has been undermined. This too is part of the heritage of the nineties.

What was and what might have been

The disappointment in how we managed globalization was all the greater because of *what might have been*. The end of the Cold War meant that the United States was the sole superpower—it was the dominant military *and* economic power. The world was looking to America for leadership. In my judgment, leadership means that one cannot try to shape the world simply to advance one's own interests, and democratic leadership means that one advances one's viewpoints by persuasion, not by bullying, by using threats of military or economic power. We had no vision of what kind of globalized world we wanted, and we weren't sensitive enough about how what we wanted would be viewed by the rest of the world.

Further, we weren't responsive to the historical sensitivities of many of the countries we dealt with. France and the United Kingdom fought the Opium Wars in China in the middle of the nineteenth century, but at the end America joined with Russia and the European powers in the 1858 Treaty of Tientsin to force China to open its doors to opium, so that their citizens would become addicted to it and Western countries would have something to exchange for goods from China, such as its porcelain and jade. The story may not be well known among American schoolchildren, but it is amongst the Chinese. Similarly, the Japanese remember Admiral Perry's "opening" of Japan in a far different light than Americans do and view the trade agreements that followed as unfair. Such historical memories naturally affect others' perceptions of U.S. motivations at the bargaining table, a perception reinforced by America's tendency to use muscle to get what it wants. America threatened to scuttle the entire financial services liberalization negotiations unless Malaysia caved in to the demands of a single American insurance company, AIG, that had long been doing business there. America repeatedly threatened trade sanctions, imposing special duties, against China, Japan, Korea, India, and a host of other countries when they didn't quickly agree to its demands; often, we were the prosecutor, judge, and jury, not even going through the channels of the World Trade Organization.

When we needed rhetoric to justify what we wanted, we talked about free markets, but when free markets seemed to put America's firms at a disadvantage, we talked variously about "managed trade" or "fair trade." We had a rationale—others were not committed to free trade, so that we had to manage the trade to get it free. Japan would not willingly open up its doors to our goods, so we had to establish targets, how much it should import from us in various categories. When they did not buy enough automobiles or chips from us, we put pressure on them to buy more.

There was a most peculiar "logic" behind this policy. We believed that trade was good, but imports were bad. Exports were good because they created jobs; which perforce meant that imports, which had the opposite effect, could not be good. We believed that America was more efficient, produced better products than any other country. It followed that any country which could outcompete America on its home ground was engaging in unfair trade practices—it was dumping goods at below cost—and, in this logic, any country that did not buy our goods had to be engaging in some form of restrictive trade practice. Of course, from the perspective of economics, these sentiments were nonsense. Each country has a *comparative* advantage, goods that it has a *relative* advantage in producing. It is those goods which it exports; and it imports the goods which it produces at a relative disadvantage.

In general, countries will export approximately what they import—there is a balance of trade. Sometimes, this general principle gets obfuscated because of exchange rates. If the exchange rate is high, that is, the dollar is worth many euros or yen, then foreigners will find it expensive to buy American goods, and Americans will find it cheap to buy foreign goods. The result is that there will not be trade balance—imports will exceed exports. There will be a trade deficit. The Clinton administration—like those before and after—believed that the trade deficit was caused by unfair trade policies. It was not. It was caused by the high exchange rate, what the U.S. Treasury hailed as the "strong dollar." The continuing trade deficit, especially the deficit with Japan, was blamed on others; the fault lay at home. This misunderstanding had serious consequences, as America blamed others for its own problems.

Macroeconomics, the relationship between savings and investment, in turn explained the high exchange rate. For a quarter century, America had continually saved little; to finance its investment, accordingly, it had to borrow from abroad. The influx of money bid up the dollar's exchange rate. In the Reagan and Bush years, much of this foreign borrowing went to finance a consumption binge in which the government was at the center. This was called the "twin-deficit problem." After the Reagan tax cut of 1981, the government spent more than it received year after year, and was forced to borrow, and much of the money came from abroad. The good news of the Clinton administration was that it put the government in a strong fiscal position: it eventually eliminated the deficit that it had inherited.

There was a spirited recovery of investment. This was good for the long-run prospects of the economy. But, unfortunately, America's households did not do their part; they did not save. Once again, the country had to borrow massively from abroad, this time to finance the investment—some of which, it eventually turned out, was *misinvestment*—spurred by the stock market bubble. The deficits of the Reagan-Bush years portended ill for the country's future. It was like a family borrowing year after to year to finance the family vacation. The deficits of the Clinton years at least went to investment. In the long run, if the return to the investment financed by borrowing yielded a return in excess of what America had to pay in interest, the country was actually better off. Again, it was little different than a firm borrowing to finance a new factory; the borrowing makes sense, so long as the investment pays off. But by the same logic, if the money that was supposed to be spent on investment is spent on consumption, or if the investments are poor investments yielding low returns—an Edsel car that never gets produced, or ten or twenty times the amount of fiber optics than the country needs—then the country is worse off. It is more indebted, and has nothing to show for it. This is where the problems discussed in early chapters—the bubble economy—and globalization link up.

It is not, then, Japan or China who are to blame for the persistent imbalance in America's trade, but America's consumers and its government. During the Clinton years, America's consumers simply didn't increase their savings enough to finance the burst of investment. In the Reagan and George W. Bush years, the U.S. government, because of the insatiable desire for tax cuts, unmatched by an equal appetite for expenditure reductions, forced the country to borrow massively abroad.

When I was at the Council of Economic Advisers, we tried to lay down a set of principles for guiding U.S. foreign economic policy, to ascertain when we would intervene, to exert pressure on other countries. We were sensitive to the criticisms that had been leveled against Bush I and his coddling of special interest groups in his trade policy. We joked that the big victory in his efforts to open Japan's retail sector to foreign competition was that he succeeded in forcing Japan to allow Toy "R" Us to open a store—so that it could sell inexpensive Chinese toys to Japanese children. China's workers were better off, Japan's children were better off—but what did it do for America? In a sense, the joke was unfair. Legal structures that impede entry of foreign retail stores are an impediment to trade, and in the long run, if we are to have a world with true free trade, such impediments to trade have to be removed. But in another sense, our joking was on the mark: America's foreign economic policy had long been driven by lobbying of particular firms that saw opportunities for their products. Although the business sector may use free market rhetoric, when they see an opportunity for the government to help them, they seldom let ideology stand in the way.

The Council of Economic Advisers tried to formulate a set of priorities for U.S. foreign economic policy based not so much on a global vision as on something we thought would be more broadly and easily acceptable: what would be best for the American economy, both in the short and long run, and especially for what had been agreed to be the focus of the Clinton administration at that juncture, the creation of jobs. The officials at the Treasury moved quickly to squelch the idea, arguing that we didn't need to prioritize, that it would only confuse matters! And they worked hard, and successfully, to make sure the president didn't get a chance even to hear the arguments. The reason for their strong reaction was obvious: forcing, for instance, other countries to open up their markets to destabilizing and non-transparent derivatives was unlikely to appear high in the set of priorities, for, despite the profits it might generate for Wall Street, it would not create many jobs.

America's international economic policy was driven by a whole variety of special interests which saw the opportunity to use its increasing global dominance to force other countries to open up their markets to its goods on its terms. America's government was seizing the opportunities afforded by the new post–Cold War world, but in a narrow way, benefiting particular financial and corporate interests. America needed a vision of where the global economy was going and how it might shape it, and there were those inside the administration, like Bo Cutter, number two at the National Economic Council, who worked hard to develop such a vision. I would have liked us to try to work toward a vision of how a world without economic borders—a world with true free trade, consonant with our rhetoric—might have looked. It would have meant that we would have had to eliminate our agricultural subsidies, or at least redesign them in ways that did not encourage our farmers to produce more, thereby lowering global prices and hurting producers elsewhere in the world. It would have meant that we would have had to open up our markets to labor-intensive services, such as construction and maritime. It would have led, too, to an elimination of a whole variety of other protectionist measures; it would have meant that we would have looked at "unfair" trade practices by foreign firms through the same lens that we do firms at home.

A global vision would have meant that we would have encouraged countries abroad to worry about some of the same things we worry about at home, such as jobs and retirement and health security. Nothing better illustrates how much we lost that vision than our actions in the area of health. One of the major initiatives of Clinton's first two years was to ensure that Americans had better access to health care. Yet the unbalanced intellectual property regime that we "successfully" pushed for in the Uruguay Round in 1994, at the behest of American drug companies, did just the opposite abroad.

We needed not just a vision of what a world without economic borders would look like, but a world in which there was more global social justice, in which our sense of caring also went beyond our borders. When I argued that we should do more for the developing countries, when I cited statistics showing that we were the stingiest of the developed countries in giving aid (at the time our aid amounted to less than 0.1 percent of our GDP, in contrast, say, to the Scandinavian countries, which give ten times as much, close to 1.0 percent of their GDP), I was told that such comparisons were irrelevant. We did not see ourselves as having a moral obligation, we did not see the despair in these countries as spilling out of their boundaries, making a global world that was less safe for us all; the only arguments that were admissible related to our immediate *economic* advantage: a kind of mercantilist philosophy which saw growth in the developing countries as positive merely because it opened up more markets for American goods.

We were focusing on helping the United States—even if it made the poor poorer, as it did so often. We were more concerned about the ability of Western countries to take resources out of Africa than about contributing to the long-term well-being of Africa. When British Petroleum unilaterally declared that it would publish what it was sending to the Angolan government in oil royalties, other oil firms did not follow suit.[18] The Angolan government did not want this information to be public—and for obvious reasons. And the American government made no effort to put pressure on American firms. America should have taken the lead earlier, but it did not. The exploitation was perhaps not as bad as it had been in the days of the Cold War, when we supported people like Mobutu, giving them money and arms, because the West was afraid of Soviet domination in Africa. Money was lent to Congo knowing full well that it would wind up in Mobutu's Swiss bank accounts; but the people of Congo have been left with the debt, and America has been slow to provide debt forgiveness even for these otiose debts. The U.S. Congress did manage to pass the African Growth and Opportunity Act on May 18,

2000—after five years of wrangling. But in return for a limited open-ing up of the American market, African countries had to agree to stringent conditions—variants of the infamous structural adjustment conditions of the IMF that too often stifle growth, create unemploy-ment, and worsen social conditions.[19]

SOMETIMES, THE CONSEQUENCES of mistaken policies are not realized for years. It took a decade before the full implications of financial sector deregulation in the eighties was felt in the United States. In the case of the mistakes in globalization, time was not so kind. The day of reckoning for the mistaken policy of pushing capi-tal market liberalization was to be short—for Korea, only four years, with the crisis of 1997. The day of reckoning for the broader mis-takes in managing globalization was only two years after that: it took place on our own shores, as we pushed for a new round of trade negotiations in Seattle in December 1999, with civil demonstrations of a magnitude that had not been seen in more than a quarter cen-tury, during the Vietnam War. The international outrage over how the previous round of trade negotiations had made drugs for AIDS and other illnesses inaccessible in many developing countries forced the drug companies to roll back their prices in those countries. So intense was the backlash against globalization that international discussions for a new round of trade negotiations had to be held where demon-strations could easily be prevented—in Doha, Qatar.

The contrast between the mismanagement of *economic* globaliza-tion and the successes in other areas perhaps made U.S. failure in that area particularly glaring. The end of the Cold War meant a renewed commitment to democracy—no longer did we take the view that democracy was fine so long as it produced the results that we wanted, no longer were we supporting (at least in most of the world) dictators like Pinochet in Chile or Mobuto in Congo. There was a strong commitment to multilateralism, to global democracy—an understanding that democracy means that you cannot always get your way, and that you must persuade others of the rightness of your views, not just bully them. We signed agreements to improve the global environment, at Rio and Kyoto and elsewhere; to strengthen the rule of law, through the International Criminal Court; and, perhaps most important, we lived up to our financial commitments to the United Nations, eliminating the arrears that should have been an embarrassment to the country for years.

Some of the mistakes that were made in the area of economic globalization are in the process of being rectified. There emerged at Doha an agreement for new talks, to be called the Development Round, in recognition of the fact that previous trade negotiations had been unbalanced, to the disadvantage of the developing countries. Even at the IMF, there is now recognition that short-term speculative capital flows represent risk without reward for most developing countries. With the failure of the last big bailout, in Argentina, the weaknesses of the strategy that was at the center of the Clinton administration's approach to crisis have become universally recognized, and the search is on for alternatives. More attention is now being paid to poverty, and the Bush administration has increased the level of assistance, though we remain the stingiest of the major advanced industrial countries.

Still, those in the developing world—and even those in the developed world with concerns about the environment or social justice—have been left with a bitter taste from these early "successes" of globalization.

For America, September 11 brought home that we can be affected by what happens abroad—and not just through the goods we sell abroad. While poverty does not cause terrorism, poverty and the despair to which it gives rise provide fertile feeding grounds for it. More broadly, as interdependence has grown, America will have more and more occasion to draw upon others for their support and cooperation. This will be forthcoming if and only if they see America as exercising its leadership not solely in its own parochial interests or the interests of America's corporate and financial establishments.

CHAPTER 10

Enron

ENRON, THE ENERGY company that went from almost nothing to an enterprise with annual *reported* revenues of $101 billion to collapse in bankruptcy, all within a few short years, has become emblematic of all that went wrong in the Roaring Nineties—corporate greed, accounting scandals, public influence mongering, banking scandals, deregulation, and the free market mantra, all wrapped together.[1] Its overseas activities too are an example of the darker side of U.S. globalization, crony capitalism, and the misuse of U.S. corporate power abroad.

To most of America in the late nineties, Enron seemed the model of the new American enterprise: deregulation had opened up new opportunities, and it had seized those opportunities. It showed why deregulation was good; how innovative American firms could help shape a more productive economy, if only they were given the chance. Enron was a role model in more than one way: it took an active role in public policy, pushing energy and deregulation policies that would strengthen America, even if it also strengthened Enron's balance sheets. Ken Lay, its CEO, served as a trustee of non-profit organizations, such as Resources for the Future, perhaps America's most important research institution promoting market-based conservation of natural resources, as well as on a public commission set up by Arthur Levitt concerned with the problems of valuation in the New Economy. Later, Lay was to serve as a key energy adviser to President George W. Bush.

The demise of Enron

I begin this story at the end, with the demise of Enron, which was full of drama, with desperate last-minute attempts to save the firm that ultimately failed. Enron pulled down with it one of the most venerable accounting firms, Arthur Andersen, and it sullied the name of its bankers, J. P. Morgan Chase, Citibank, and Merrill Lynch. Like any good drama, there were good guys and bad: the former were few, and include the whistle-blower, Sherron Watkins, who informed CEO Ken Lay about many of the key problems and almost lost her job as a result; the latter include Andersen's lead Enron accountant, David Duncan, who was responsible not only for the bad accounting but for shredding important documents; its law firm, Vinson & Elkins, supposedly the most prestigious in Texas, which thought it was guiding Enron on how to avoid violating the law; and Enron's chief financial officer, Andrew Fastow, who has been indicted for fraud, money-laundering, and conspiracy, and for enriching himself at the expense of Enron; even by Wall Street's standards, what he received—some $45 million—appeared outlandish. There was outrage, too, as it was revealed that top executives were cashing in on their holdings at the same time they were urging their employees to keep their shares. Ken Lay sold 1.8 million shares, for more than $100 million; another top executive sold shares worth more than $350 million; and the total for the top executives was $1.1 billion. But Enron's employees saw their futures jeopardized with more than $1 billion of employee pensions that had been invested in Enron shares disappearing with Enron's bankruptcy.

Though dramatic, the end was remarkably simple: as the accounting tricks with which it had hidden liabilities and exaggerated its income suddenly came to light, it became clear that Enron was not what it seemed. Almost every firm requires loans from banks to operate, and banks won't give the loans if they don't have confidence in the company. There was a confluence of events, any one of which might have spelled trouble for Enron: The resolution of the energy crisis in California deprived Enron of some of the profits it had been making by market manipulation. The falling stock market touched all firms, Enron included, but naturally that made banks and rating agencies more wary. Enron had transformed itself from a gas pipeline company into a dot-com, an online energy and commodities trading corporation; that was part of its pride during the late nineties, and part of its downfall. Enron had provided guarantees to some of the off-balance-sheet "partnerships" and shell corporations, backed by stock, and as the share price fell, Enron was left increasingly exposed. As attention began to focus on the company, both the market and regulators sensed that something was wrong, and the regulators began closing in. (The deceptions would eventually turn out to be far worse than anyone had thought.) The Glass-Steagall Act's repeal meant that bankers held on longer than they otherwise would have— they still hoped to make money from Enron's multiple deals—but eventually, as the stock continued to plunge, they could not continue to lend. With the failure of desperate moves to prevent a bankruptcy, to get an injection of funds from elsewhere—the deceptions that helped Enron in the boom made it even more difficult to raise funds in the bust—bankruptcy became inevitable.

Underlying Enron's demise was deception: deception which enabled it to make profits by manipulating the deregulated California energy market, enriching Enron's shareholders at the expense of California's consumers, producers, and taxpayers, and deception in which its executives effectively stole money from Enron shareholders to enrich themselves. There was not one single event, but a rich panoply of practices. Enron and its accountants sometimes stepped over the line, but much of what Enron did was legal. Though several people lower down in the pecking order have been indicted, as this book goes to press, its chief executive officer has not: he has denied direct involvement or knowledge of the illegal activities, and much of his gains were through perfectly legal generous stock options.

Enron used many accounting tricks that were increasingly becoming standard. It appears that its chief financial officer made the same discovery that so many other corporate executives made during the nineties: the same accounting tricks that could be used to distort information to boost stock market prices could also be used to enrich themselves at the expense of other shareholders. In developing these forms of deception, Enron had a slight edge over its competitors. Enron's niche in the market was innovation—financial innovation, new ways of buying and selling electricity (or other commodities), using sophisticated financial products, such as derivatives, which entail splitting off different pieces of an income stream, sharing risks among different investors in quite complicated ways. We described in earlier chapters how corporations had long learned how to use then fancy financial techniques for moving income around, in ways to reduce their tax liabilities, and then applied these techniques with equal vigor and vim to make the cash flow and balance sheets look better. During the nineties, they did so to boost stock prices—which because of their stock options so enriched them; with the economic slowdown, it became even more imperative to provide distorted information, to prevent balance sheets from looking as bad as they really were. Enron, at the forefront of financial engineering, was also at the forefront of using these techniques. And just as elsewhere American banks worked hand-in-hand with corporations and accountants to enhance these activities, so too in the case of Enron's deceptions.

The problem in writing about Enron's escapades is that they were deliberately made complicated, so that it would not be easy to see through them. But behind the complicated financial structures accompanied by fancy legal footwork, there were a few key deceptions. The first involves recording *today* sales for gas or electricity for delivery some time in the future. Enron was in many businesses—it began largely as a gas pipeline company—but with deregulation it had taken up becoming a trading company, buying and selling electricity and gas. It saw itself as creating a market. Yet the market it created was not just buying and selling gas and electricity today, but selling it today for delivery next week, or next month.

Enron's accounting trick was to record the value of the sale today of, say, gas, for delivery next year as *revenue* today, but not what it would have to spend to buy the gas. Revenues without costs generate huge profits! Of course, eventually Enron would have to record a cost for the purchase of the electricity. One can in fact continually blow up one's income this way, so long as one is growing; for each year, sales exceed purchases. It is a classic Ponzi scheme, like the chain letters of the past.[2] Such schemes still occasionally occur: people who make money by selling franchises to others, who sell it on to others, and on and on. But all such Ponzi schemes eventually come to an end. Particularly when growth stops—as it does as the economy slows down—such schemes collapse.

A second category of deception is only slightly more complicated. Enron realized that it didn't actually have to sell gas to anyone to take advantage of this "trick." It could create a fictitious company, a shell corporation, as they are sometimes called—call it Raptor—and sell gas to it. Of course, the fictitious company didn't want the gas, but Enron could solve that problem, too: it would buy the gas back. When it made a commitment to buy back the gas, it created a liability, but it didn't record that liability, just as it didn't record the expenses that it would eventually have to incur to buy the gas.

With Enron selling today gas for delivery to this fictitious company, Raptor, and meanwhile, Enron agreeing to buy gas from Rap-

tor next year, what, one might ask, is Raptor doing, buying and selling gas, receiving gas from Enron at the same moment that it is delivering it back to Enron? Smells fishy. It was. If Enron "books" the sale
today, it makes its income today look higher, even though—if
accounting systems did what they were supposed to do, which is provide accurate information concerning the position of the firm—it
should also report a corresponding "liability," the promise of a delivery with the associated costs. Alternatively, since Enron controlled
Raptor, one could argue that one should "consolidate" the two
together, treating them as a single entity, in which case the buying and
selling would be nothing more than internal bookkeeping systems.
There is no *real* sale, and therefore no *real* income.

With a little help from the banks, the deal could be made even
sweeter. Assume now that Enron needs to borrow some money, but
everyone—both Enron's executives and the banks—realizes that it
would look bad for Enron's books to have a hefty increase in debt.
The bank can lend the money to Raptor. Raptor can use the money
to pay up front for the gas which it has bought for delivery next year.
The bank can feel secure, since it knows that Enron has a contract to
buy the gas back from Raptor. And if the buy-back deal involves a
high enough price, Raptor can easily pay the interest due. In effect,
the "forward sale" is nothing but a loan, but it is a loan which does
not show up on Enron's balance sheet. And by paying Raptor a still
higher price, Enron can make Raptor highly profitable. If Raptor,
which is nothing more than a shell corporation, is owned by some of
Enron's top executives, it becomes a way of transferring money out
of the corporation into the pockets of these executives. They might
even feel justified in their perfidy: after all, by hiding the loan, they
are making the company's balance sheet look better, contributing to
the growth of the stock market price. And, after all, wasn't that their
major responsibility?

The dot-com bubble provided other ways of easily booking

income. Assume you start a dot-com—one that is going to buy and sell deregulated electricity over the Internet. Your stock price soars— the combined euphoria of the Internet and deregulation proved irre- sistible in this era of irrational exuberance. But Enron was not like the other bubble stocks, which were all based on the *hopes* of future profits but the reality of current loses. Enron was showing large prof- its. It knew that the foolish markets would pump up their stock price even higher, if it could only pump up its revenues and profits still higher, and with so much of their compensation depending on stock options, the executives had an especial incentive to do this. If Enron could start such a company, and then sell the pumped-up shares for a large capital gain, it could record a huge profit. To help things along, it could create an off-balance-sheet partnership, lend it its stock, with which it could collateralize a loan from a bank—and with the repeal of Glass-Steagall, the close relationship between retail banking and investment banking meant that Enron's banks were more than willing to participate in such trickery. If the bank wanted more assurance, it could provide a guarantee; if still more money was needed to buy the overpriced stock, it could lend the money itself. It was almost as if Enron was selling its own company to itself to book a profit. But from the perspective of Enron shareholders, it was a heads-you-win-tails-I-lose proposition. If the stock price stayed high, all the gain went to Enron executives and their friends. If the stock price plummeted—what actually happened—Enron and its share- holders were left with the responsibility of repaying the banks.

Had the bubble continued, Enron might have continued, and the deceptions never come to light. Enron executives would have crowed how they brought wealth to their shareholders. So what if they had enriched themselves? It was their just desserts for having done so well for their shareholders. They could have gone to church holding their heads high. It was the crash of the bubble, and the bad behavior that it brought on and out, which has led to the criticism. But to my mind, the Enron story helps bring out the fundamental nature of what is wrong: shareholders didn't have the information with which to judge what was going on, and there were incentives not to provide that information, but to provide distorted information. The market system had provided incentives in which by doing well for themselves, they did not benefit others, but rather their gains were at the expense of those they were supposed to be working for, and they had exposed them to risks which they could not even imagine.

Electricity deregulation

Enron was a product of deregulation, in every sense of the term. Its early money was made in natural gas, as that market deregulated. It benefited from the perverse incentives provided by banking deregulation. It sold itself as the company that was making deregulation work. But it was in energy deregulation that it really made its name—and in which it most exposed the weaknesses of the deregulation movement. Enron claimed to show the creative spirit that deregulation—especially energy deregulation—could unleash; it succeeded in showing how difficult it was to deregulate well, and the consequences of badly designed deregulation

From the New Deal of the 1930s until the Reagan years of the 1980s, key parts of the energy industry had been highly regulated—consumers purchased their electricity from a regulated monopoly, which owned both the generators and the wires over which electricity was transmitted. Gas also was highly regulated, particularly the transmission of gas through pipelines from where it was produced (such as in Texas) to where it was used. There was a clear economic rationale for such regulation. Gas transmission and electricity were viewed as *natural* monopolies, industries in which it was difficult to have more than one firm. The costs of two firms providing electricity wires to each neighborhood, or to each home, would almost double the cost of delivery; and even with two firms, they might have simply conspired to charge a monopoly price—it would not have provided assurances that consumers were well treated. Similarly, one big gas pipeline from Texas to California was more efficient than say four competing small ones.

Economists had long debated the best way to handle such natural monopolies. Some countries chose to have the government manage these monopolies in the public interest; and some chose to have unregulated private markets; some chose to have the private sector produce, but to regulate these private firms. Europe, for the most part, chose the first course, America the third. (Almost none chose the second, unregulated private markets.) Many argued, however, that governments could not do a good job managing economic enterprises, and in many cases they were right, but in some cases they were wrong. France's state-run electricity system is more efficient than that of the United States; the professionalism of its managers has long been noted, as has the quality of its engineers. In spite of these successes, free market ideology has had a powerful influence, so that in the last quarter century, there was a movement throughout the world toward the third approach, one which has private production with limited regulation. Increasingly, the view was that even regulation should be limited in scope. It was argued that we could benefit from competition in electricity generation and competition in marketing. The only natural monopoly was in transmission, in the grid. The challenge was thus to split what had been integrated firms that generated, transmitted, and sold electricity into different parts, attract entry into the parts where competition was possible—generation and marketing—and regulate the grid in ways which ensured that the whole system worked seamlessly. California led the way in deregulation, which began in early 1998.

There was so much confidence that deregulation would work, that consumer prices would fall precipitously, that discussions, both inside the government (such as at the Council of Economic Advisers) and out, focused on how to deal with the consequences of *low* prices. At the new low prices, the old electricity firms that had invested in generating capacity would not be able to recoup their investments. The question was, how and how much they should be compensated for the changes in the rules of the game—investments that had been made under the assumption that they could get a fair, regulated rate of return? The technical term was "stranded costs," investments stranded by the new regime.

California's energy deregulation did not work out the way that its advocates claimed. Deregulation had been sold under the usual free market mantra—reducing regulation gives free rein to market forces, markets forces lead to greater efficiency, competition ensures that the benefits of those market forces are passed on down to consumers.[3] Instead, just two years after deregulation, prices rose dramatically and supplies were constricted. Prices which had averaged $30 per megawatt hour from April 1998 to April 2000 reached triple, then quadruple, that level in June 2000, and by the first part of 2001 had increased eightfold. For the first time, there were supply interruptions of a kind that one expected in poor developing countries, but not in the hi-tech center of the world. California's major electricity companies were forced into bankruptcy; they had long-term commitments to supply electricity at fixed prices, but had to purchase electricity at far higher prices. In a short span of time, they lost billions.[4] The experiment with deregulation was a debacle. California had led the experiment in electricity deregulation. America, and California, had to pay the price.

Governor Gray Davis of California eventually intervened to save his state. The power shortages were not only leading to sky-high prices but also hurting California's high-tech businesses; a power interruption could do untold damage to the high-tech sector. California was at risk of losing its reputation as a great place to do business. It cost the state more than $45 billion to put matters back on an even keel.[5] After the Federal Energy Regulatory Commission finally imposed price caps in June 2001, prices came down from the $234 per megawatt hour they had averaged earlier in the year to just $59 per megawatt hour for July and August.

The question is, why the failures, and what lessons are to be drawn from them? The advocates of deregulation say that it was not done perfectly—but nothing in this world is ever done perfectly. They would have us compare an imperfect regulated economy with an idealized free market, rather than the imperfect regulated economy with the even more imperfect unregulated one. But even those who were profiting from deregulation were willing to admit its imperfections. Enron's CEO would claim, "An imperfect market is better than a perfect regulator."[6]

By the time the crisis broke out, there was a new president, even more committed to free market ideology, and strongly under the influence of those who would profit from deregulation. President George W. Bush was particularly close to Enron's CEO, Ken Lay; he had received substantial sums from Lay in his election campaign, and he turned to Lay for advice on energy policy. Bush joined Enron in arguing for letting the "market" prevail. If this entailed bankrupting firms that seemed to have been efficient under the old regime, so be it; if it meant hardship on low-income individuals who could no longer afford the skyrocketing utility bills, so be it. It was a new form of social Darwinism—let the fittest survive. The greatest sin was interfering with market processes.

But to those who understood market processes, the episode was a mystery. If deregulation and competition were supposed to lower prices, why were prices rising? The Northwest had experienced low rainfall, and this had led to less hydroelectric power entering the grid, but the shortfall on this account was not enough to explain the soaring prices. There were some hints at the underlying problem. Why was it that suddenly, as shortages developed, so much generating power was off line, needing to be repaired? Would it not have made more sense to wait to make all but the most urgent repairs? Why was it that the price of natural gas on the West Coast seemed so high, when there seemed to be unused capacity in the gas pipeline? Economists had a natural suspicion of manipulation, and these concerns were raised early on by *New York Times* columnist and Princeton economist Paul Krugman. The reply from the free market crowd: "Nonsense."[7]

At the time, there was no smoking gun, no way of proving market manipulation. The free marketeers had their day, and Enron had its day, as prices continued at their extraordinary levels, and Enron continued making extraordinary profits. In just the three-month period July to September 2000, its commodity sales and service business recorded an increase in income of $232 million over the previous year.

At this juncture, defenders of deregulation had to look elsewhere for the fault, and they had an easy answer: the problem was not too little regulation but too much regulation. Environmental deregulation had prevented the construction of new energy-generating plants, and in the process of deregulating electricity, California had retained some regulations, and these too were at the crux of California's difficulties. One regulation imposed price caps on what consumers could be charged, though at the same time the price for purchasing electricity by the electricity companies was left flexible. The price cap on consumers was a way of reassuring those who were skeptical about deregulation: after all, the ardent advocates of deregulation so believed it would lower prices that there was essentially no risk in putting that provision in. Had they been unwilling to do so, it would have demonstrated a lack of conviction—and with such a damning admission, deregulation might not have proceeded at all.

A second regulation restricted utilities from signing long-term contracts purchasing electricity, but again, there was an understandable

rationale for this regulation. Before, the electricity companies produced, transmitted, and sold electricity. With deregulation, the power
companies were in the retailing business. They bought electricity
from other producers and sold it on to their customers. Given the
long-term obligations (at fixed, or at least maximum prices for the
electricity they sold), it would have made sense for them to engage in
long-term contracts to buy electricity. But if much of the market was
provided by such long-term contracts, the spot market (the market
today for trading *today's* electricity) might have been very thin.
(Because of changes in weather, with so much electricity in California
used in air conditioning, there are in fact large variations in the
demand for electricity, not only during the day but from day to day.)
With most electricity bought and sold in long-term contracts, there
would have been relatively little supply left over.

The danger in such situations is apparent: by withholding a relatively small amount of electricity from the market, suppliers can drive
up prices and profits. Thin markets, with such limited supply, are
especially vulnerable to manipulation. The prohibition against long-
term contracts was an attempt to ensure *thick* and competitive markets. There was another reason, less public-spirited: those who traded
in electricity liked there to be more trade—that is how they made
money. But there was a downside risk from relying on spot transactions. Spot markets can be highly variable. Changes in demand and
supply can cause large changes in price, even when markets are relatively thick. Poor households and small businesses are particularly
vulnerable to such price variability. They need price certainty in order
to plan their budgets. It is a risk against which they cannot buy insurance—and a risk which they did not have to face in the old regime.
Price caps limited this risk, but shifted the risk onto the retailers,
those who marketed the electricity. In the deregulation process, concerns about risk were shunted aside, in the enthusiasm that deregulation would bring lower prices. If the price today is 5 cents a kilowatt,

who could complain if there was price variability—if the price some-times was 4 cents, sometimes 2 cents? Whatever the outcome, con-sumers and businesses would be better off. Few—except economists well versed in the dangers of market manipulation—would have dreamed that California, under the urging of firms like Enron, had bought into the worst of all possible worlds: a world of heightened risk and subject to market manipulation.

In response to the criticism that it was market manipulation that was contributing, if not causing, the problems, the Bush administra-tion took the offensive: it seized on the high prices as an excuse for expanding drilling in environmentally sensitive areas, like the Arctic, and rolling back environmental regulations. California's energy shortage was, they claimed, not due to manipulation but to environ-mental restrictions limiting the expansion of capacity. At the time, the argument did not seem very persuasive. After all, at the time that deregulation occurred, it seemed that there was no shortage of capac-ity; there was worry about excess capacity. The energy companies were not clamoring to build new plants. There were other oddities about the seeming supply shortage. There also seemed to be a natu-ral gas shortage, and yet a fifth of the pipeline capacity was not being used.

But in retrospect, the argument that environmental restrictions caused a supply shortage appears even less persuasive: with the restoration of regulation, the energy shortage has again disappeared. Indeed, not long after, analysts began downgrading energy companies because of a worry about *excess capacity*—not shortages. There had been shortages, but evidently, they were all the result of market manipulation, including by those who wanted to see environmental regulations stripped away. Environmental costs are *real* costs: air pol-lution leads to shorter and less healthy lives; greenhouse gases lead to global warming. America's cities are cleaner, and our lives healthier, because of environmental regulations (some of the most important of which were passed under Bush I). Making electricity companies pay for these real costs is simply good economics.

Whether the crisis was caused by manipulation, or by a temporary shortage, there were far better ways of handling it than that chosen by the Bush II administration.[8] (I hesitate to call this "free market" policy, because of the large role in its formulation by Enron and possibly others who were in fact manipulating it; it was not really a free, competitive market.) Brazil faced an electricity crisis at roughly the same time, but fortunately, it had a government where the perpetrators of the manipulation had less influence, a government that was at the same time less ideological and more committed to protecting its people and businesses from economic hardship. Brazil's leaders did what most economists would have recommended—look for a way that one could get the right incentives in place and at the same time minimize the distributive consequences. There was an easy, and standard, solution. So long as consumers buy an amount less than the amount they purchased last year, they pay a fixed price (the same or slightly higher than last year's). But there is a free market for *increases* in consumption. Such two-part (or multi-tiered) pricing of electricity has long been commonplace. This system allows free play to market forces *at the margin*, but avoids the huge redistributions—with their associated high social and economic costs, including bankruptcies—that soaring electricity prices can otherwise entail. Brazil managed its way through its electricity crisis far better than did the United States.

Whether it was free market ideology, Enron lobbying, or just an absence of thoughtful and creative economists that prevented the Bush administration from taking the kind of approach that Brazil took may never be clear. But as the problems mounted, government action eventually became irresistible, even to the free market regulators that Bush had appointed at the Federal Energy Regulatory Commission. The smoking gun(s) might never have been discovered had it not been that Enron's greed eventually led to its own bankruptcy, and the resulting court processes eventually uncovered the documents showing how the market manipulation processes worked—for instance, by shipping electricity out of the state to exacerbate the scarcity, driving the prices still higher. It turned out the Enron was not alone; other electricity traders, whose job it was to make the market work better, took advantage of the opportunity to manipulate the market, to enhance their profits at the expense of the state of California and its citizens. They worked together with a variety of strategies with nicknames like "Death Star" and "Get Shorty." Recorded conversations show the immense power of the manipulators. (They even seemed to have a slight degree of compassion; at one moment, one manipulator was recorded as saying, "I don't want to crush the market too bad.")[9]

The trail of market manipulation led from electricity to gas. The pipeline company El Paso had deliberately restricted the flow of gas through the pipeline. The gas pipeline had, like electricity, been considered a natural monopoly, and as deregulation proceeded, there was worry about how it might abuse its monopoly power. One concern was, however, given insufficient attention. El Paso owned the pipeline, but it was also a major producer of gas. Even if it did not overcharge other firms using the pipeline, its control of the pipeline might enable it to restrict the entire flow of gas, to allow the market price to soar. Under regulation, with the price of gas fixed, the company had no incentive to do so. Now it did. It did what it had an incentive to do. What it lost in revenues from shipping gas it more than made up for in the higher price of the gas it sold. Though eventually it made a settlement with California worth nearly $2 billion, even with those penalties manipulation had proved profitable, with El Paso's consumers having paid over $3 billion more than they would have without the manipulation. (Market manipulation also affected Washington, Nevada, and Oregon, all of which also received money from the settlement.)

It would take two years of sifting through the complicated and hidden records for the Federal Energy Regulatory Commission finally to reach a verdict on what had happened: their conclusion was that efforts to manipulate electricity and natural gas had been "epidemic." Enron was accused of manipulating not only the electricity market but also the natural gas market. Previously, it had been thought that the market was too big for a single firm to manipulate. Enron had shown otherwise. Ironically, as this book goes to press, some of those who have benefited from the market manipulation, as it led to distorted high prices, continue to argue that the longer-term contracts signed at those higher prices should still be enforced.

Foreign ventures

In America, during the Roaring Nineties, Enron was touted as one of the models of the New Economy, an innovative firm, taking advantage of the new opportunities afforded by deregulation, to make markets work better. Better markets meant a better life, presumably for all Americans and for the rest of the world.

We saw in chapter 9 how America, in the nineties, embraced globalization. Enron too stood for globalization, American style. It preached deregulation abroad, just as it did at home. It worked with governments—abroad and at home—to help create the conditions that were conducive to investment. It brought to its ventures abroad the same kind of hard-nosed modern business practices and acumen that had served it so well at home and it invested billions of dollars abroad.

But just as many in the developing world looked upon globalization and how America was managing it in quite a different light than it was viewed in America, so did those in the developing world look upon Enron quite differently. Long before Enron's reputation became tarnished at home, it was looked at askance abroad. Enron's power project in India was one of the largest foreign direct investments in that country's history, and in India and elsewhere, Enron became the symbol of everything that had gone wrong with globalization. Nothing tells the story better than its investment in an electric power plant, the Dabhol II plant in the state of Maharashtra, India. While the whole transaction was tainted by unsavory political influence, it is the economics of the deal that concerns me here. The World Bank, though it was hardly Enron-unfriendly, having provided over \$700 million to various Enron projects, strongly criticized the project as costing too much, concluding that it was not economically viable. There was one way that it could be made economically viable—for Enron, but not for India—which was to guarantee Enron high electricity prices. Of course, high electricity prices would mean that India, struggling to compete on global markets, would be put at an even greater disadvantage.

Enron received a so-called take or pay contract, that left Enron taking the profits and India paying the price and bearing the risk. It was the kind of private/public partnership that the private sector finds so profitable throughout the developing world. Under these contracts, the government in effect guarantees that Enron will sell the agreed-upon quantity of electricity at the agreed-upon price, no matter what the economic conditions, no matter what the global price of electricity. It removed from the private sector all commercial risk concerning demand. The investor had only one responsibility: to be able to deliver a plant at a cost that enabled it to provide the electricity at a profit. But the price was set so high that there was a virtually no risk to Enron. One might have thought that the essence of a market economy is that those who make the investment bear the risk—not government. One might have thought too that if Enron was so convinced that it was a good project, then it would have been willing to bear the risk. (Indeed, Enron's 2000 revenues were more than a fifth the total GDP of India!) But in the drive to push privatization, or at least the profits of America's private companies, these principles were put aside.

One might also have thought that given that so much of the risk was being borne by India, the return would be relatively low, but not so: the contract provisions were designed to yield Enron a before-tax return of 25 percent. The prices that were set in the contract stunned outside observers. Before Enron was forced to back down in 1995, it proposed a tariff of 7–14 cents per kilowatt hour for the electricity produced at the Dabhol II plant. Even afterwards, when the price was reduced by some 25 percent—and Enron was still able to earn a return that exceeded the normal levels allowed by Indian law—the price of electricity from the project was much higher than that available from domestic producers, more than twice as much by some estimates. With the take or pay provisions underwritten by the Indian government—commitments in excess of $30 billion over the life of the contract (a single contract equal to 7 percent of that country's GDP) and those commitments largely underwritten by guarantees of the U.S. government through an agency that insures against such risks—and with further U.S. government subsidies provided by America's Export-Import Bank, the numbers didn't add up. Why had the Indian government signed the contract when it could get electricity at better terms elsewhere? Part of the answer was: the United States put on political pressure. Enron officials joined a cabinet trip to India, and direct pressure was put on India by the American ambassador. Though Enron continued to maintain that it abided by the Foreign Corrupt Practices Act, which prevents bribes to government officials, those in India remain unconvinced. And these suspicions of heavy-handed techniques, combined with the obvious

adverse economics—to pay what the Indian government had promised, there would have to be cutbacks in other investments and social
expenditures—generated vocal opposition.

When riots broke out, the police acted abusively, according to later
reports by Human Rights Watch. Whether justified or not, Enron
was blamed, further intensifying the antagonism. When India threatened to cancel or alter the deal, the full pressure of the U.S. administration was brought to bear, both during the Bush and the Clinton
eras. During the Bush administration, the phone calls allegedly came
from the vice president; during the Clinton, only somewhat short of
that level. The administration had put themselves in a position where
they thought they could legitimately bring pressure on behalf of a
particular American corporation (which happened to be a big bipartisan campaign contributor): since the United States had partially
guaranteed the loans, American taxpayer money was at risk. But the
problem goes back further: why did the U.S. government guarantee a
project which even the World Bank had rejected as not economically
viable, a project which would make India less able to compete in the
global marketplace, while it earned Enron huge returns not commensurate with the risks it was bearing? What was the role of political
influence?

Enron and crony capitalism, American style

Enron's behavior, and the related political interventions, naturally
raised such questions. Unfortunately, the Dabhol story was not an
isolated event. Problems were encountered in Enron projects in
Argentina, Mozambique, and Indonesia. Although it was a company
that seemed to be based on deregulation—getting government out of
the way—it was a company that thrived by getting government to do
its bidding.

In the United States, Enron had invested heavily in developing relations with government officials—both before they went into office,

while they were there, through party donations, and after they left. The money was spread reasonably evenly—about three fifths to the Republicans, two fifths to the Democrats. This in itself should have raised suspicions. One can understand giving money to support candidates that are in favor of one's position, and by and large, the Republicans were far more in support of deregulation. But Enron, it would appear, approached the money issue far more tactically. For a relatively small contribution, it seemed some congresspeople would be more inclined to support at least some of Enron's positions. But there was a defensive element as well: If you give enough money to both parties, you can maintain influence, regardless of the party in power, and you can also protect your benefactors. When the Enron scandal broke, the close association between the Republicans and Enron, and especially between Bush and Ken Lay, its chief executive (so close, that at one point he was the inside favorite to be a member of the cabinet, probably as secretary of energy), led many to suspect that the Democrats would make political hay. But they did not, or at least much less than they surely would have, had they not themselves benefited from Enron's well-placed "political investments."

Within both the Bush and the Clinton administrations, the list of those who had done work for or received money from Enron (either allegedly for work or as campaign contributions) was long. They included, for instance, Robert Zoellick, Bush's U.S. Trade Representative, and Lawrence Lindsey, head of the National Economic Council, both of whom received some $50,000 in consulting contracts. Attorney General John Ashcroft received a campaign contribution of $574,999 in 2000. The ties continued after some left office: the American ambassador to India was appointed to the Enron board; Robert Rubin became chairman of the Executive Committee of Citibank Group, one of the banks that was engaged in Enron's many nefarious activities. A senior Bush administration official, Thomas White, the secretary of the army, had been Enron's vice president.

So there was a nexus of connections. Given the large returns that Enron earned on so many of its investments, one would have thought that these investments in political connections surely must have paid off. And there is ample evidence that they did. Much, perhaps all of it, was within the law, although sometimes the law was changed, sometimes barely skirted. (There used to be a five-year restriction on a government official lobbying his or her former agency; in the final months of the Clinton administration, this was greatly reduced. Had it not been, some of the lobbying of a former U.S. Treasury official might have been against the law.) But the question is not whether it was within or outside the law: America was supposed be setting a model for the market economy that should work. The lesson it taught was one of "crony capitalism." There was more than a little irony on the side of both Ken Lay and the U.S. government: Enron, the seeming champion of free market economics, and Ken Lay, a severe critic of government, were so willing to receive government assistance—billions of dollars of loans and guarantees—that Lay made use of his friends in high places to push his firm, and then did all that he could to avoid taxes (with remarkable success). And America, especially U.S. Treasury officials, was lecturing East Asia on crony capitalism, and then apparently practicing it themselves.

While Enron used the influence it seemingly bought to get help and financial assistance from the government—it received more than $3.6 billion in risk insurance and public financing—company officials realized that it could make even more money by helping shape laws that provided the right environment—so that, for instance, it could profit, whether legitimately or illegitimately, from deregulation—and to prevent actions that might harm it. The company wanted to be able to manipulate the energy market, and it wanted to be able to continue to use accounting tricks to exaggerate its profits and increase its market value. And Enron, through its influence, while it did not get everything it wanted, did get a great deal. Enron, and its leaders, had enormous standing in both the private and public spheres of influence. It was no surprise then that when SEC chairman Arthur Levitt set up a commission to look at valuation in the New Economy in 2000, Ken Lay would be one of its members. (I was another of the members.)

By the end of the nineties, there were increasing worries about a bubble, and Levitt (among others) was concerned that the accounting techniques and procedures that had been developed to value, say, a steel company would not work in the New Economy. In the "old economy," firms had assets like buildings and equipment; these assets had a normal lifetime, and we knew how to depreciate their value over time. The accounting rules were imperfect—they did not reflect perfectly the decrease in the market value of an asset as it aged. But the rules provided good rules of thumb, and when there were biases—for instance, when accounting rules assumed a shorter life for a building than was really the case, or valued land at its purchase price not taking into account the appreciation in value—analysts knew how to adjust their assessments of the firm's market value.

In the New Economy, many firms had few hard assets; they rented offices and cars, sometimes even computers and telephones. Their assets were computer software—often in the process of development; or subscriber lists. Among their *true* assets were their key employees, but even these assets were hard to value—they could leave the firm and set up a rival enterprise. And even in old economy firms, "good-will"—an appraisal of the firm's ability to earn profits not embedded in other physical assets—often represented a substantial part of the value of the enterprise. When one firm bought another at a price substantially in excess of the value of its physical assets, it was buying something, an asset, and somehow, one had to name it ("goodwill") and value it.

The importance of good accounting standards should by now be clear: the information provided the basis for valuing the firm, and therefore was critical in decisions concerning how much capital to allocate to it. Bad accounting implied bad information, which in turn implied bad resource allocations. That, of course, was an economists' perspective. The market perspective was somewhat different: high profit numbers meant high market values, and high incomes for the executives of the companies.

As we noted in chapter 5, Arthur Levitt was aware both of the distorted incentives facing the accounting industry *and* the executives of the companies for whom they worked, and he was aware too of the wide latitude of discretion given by the accounting rules for the New Economy firms to misrepresent their true situation. As the SEC Commission met in 2000, however, the conflicts of perspective readily became apparent. The economists on the Commission were clearly more worried than the members from Silicon Valley, the entrepreneurs of the New Economy. Those from Silicon Valley had every confidence in the market, and why shouldn't they? After all, the market, in its wisdom, had recognized their enormous abilities and contributions, and rewarded them well. The deregulation mentality made the suggestion of increased government regulation—or even the SEC's modest fair disclosure proposal (discussed in chapter 5)—an anathema. What worried many were shareholder suits, which they viewed as simply reflecting the rapacious greed of lawyers, not part of a system of checks and balances against the rapacious greed of corporate executives.

There were strong divisions within the Commission. Given these divisions, the final report could do little more than draw attention to the problems of valuation in the New Economy—that in itself was an important service—noting the differences in views about how they might be addressed. I was in the minority, who thought that stronger regulatory actions should be taken, such as disclosing stock options. Ken Lay was among the majority who liked the status quo and resisted even the mild changes that the SEC was proposing. Their motto was: Trust in the market; the market will take care of the problem. In a sense, Ken Lay was right, but not exactly in the way that he and the other members of the Commission anticipated. And as the market "took care" of the Enron overvaluation—forcing it into bankruptcy—deeper problems were exposed, such as market manipulation, as we have seen.

The problems with America's energy policy, however, go beyond deregulation and accounting. When the Bush administration decided that America needed a new energy policy, they formed a circle of advisers who were mostly involved in the production of oil and gas, and so naturally liked to see increased opportunities for production. The Bush administration had hoped to keep the members of this advisory group secret, but as so often happens, the information gets out, one way or another. Being producers, the advisory group was more concerned with increasing production—for instance, by opening up the Arctic to more development—which would presumably increase its profit, than with conservation. It was a policy which put America's security at risk because it means more money goes to the Middle Eastern oil countries that fund terrorism, and because higher oil prices weaken the U.S. economy while benefiting the oil companies. Conservation would have been a better idea, as it would have driven down the demand and price of oil and strengthened the U.S. economy. The irony, of course, is that Bush tried to sell his policy as enhancing America's energy security, by making us less dependent on foreign oil. But it was a shortsighted policy. The vast majority of the world's oil reserves lie in the Middle East; the United States, with just 7 percent of the world's supply, cannot in the long run be energy-self-sufficient—unless we greatly reduce our consumption. Bush and his team were advocating a "Drain America first" policy—use up our reserves now, meaning that in the future, we will be even more dependent on the Middle East.

There were broader social reasons to pursue the conservation-based strategy: the world was beginning to see the effects of global warming, based on the accumulation of greenhouse gases in the atmosphere, which were appearing even faster than had been expected fifteen years ago. I had been on the international panel of scientists which looked at and weighed the scientific evidence and found it overwhelming. Yet, Bush at first suggested that the matter was still in dispute. It was only when the National Academy of Science reaffirmed what the scientific community had already said—that there were significant increases in atmospheric concentrations of greenhouse gases, and that these were likely to cause significant climate changes—that Bush backed down on the *science*, but not on the policy. (Interestingly, Ken Lay supported restrictions on greenhouse gases, so long as they were accompanied by trading; Enron had created a trading company—they knew how to trade electricity, and they could make money trading carbon emissions just as well. This is an idea which most economists would have supported; Bush, however, rejected it.)

The similarity between Bush's energy proposals and what Enron wanted was obvious, leading the senior Democrat on the House Committee on Government Reform, Henry A. Waxman of California, to comment in a letter to Dick Cheney: "The policies in the White House energy plan do not benefit Enron exclusively. And some may have independent merit. Nonetheless, it seems clear that there is no company in the country that stood to gain as much from the White House plan as Enron."[10]

THE INTERTWINING BETWEEN the public and private spheres that Enron had refined to such a high level could be looked at in two ways: Enron was a public servant, helping the government to understand the complexities of the market economy, so that what the government did would lead to a more efficient economy. Or Enron was a master of corporate greed, trying to use the government in every way that it could to enrich itself. There was a little grain of truth in the first view—just enough to make those public officials who were doing Enron's bidding feel some comfort that in doing well by Enron perhaps they were doing well by the country.

That same argument of public-spirited justification was used to try to help Enron as it approached bankruptcy. A former Treasury high official, Robert Rubin—by then a top executive at Citigroup—called the undersecretary of Treasury, Peter Fisher, about the impending downgrading of Enron's debt. In doing so, he could feel that he was not just helping out Enron; after all, who knows what consequences might befall the entire American economy if Enron were to collapse? (At the time, many did not know the extent to which Citibank was exposed, how much it had helped Enron engage in its duplicitous practices, and how much it had loaned to Enron, money which likely would not be fully repaid if Enron went bankrupt.) It was the same excuse that had been used earlier as the New York Federal Reserve helped orchestrate the bailout of the largest hedge fund, Long Term Capital Management. It was the thinking that had repeatedly been used for the IMF bailouts. If Western banks and investors were not bailed out, who knows what the consequences might be. And it was the same kind of argument that had been used to stifle public debate of monetary policy: such talk might roil the markets. Just as those who advocated free markets more strongly seemed more than willing to use government help and subsidies, so too they seemed to exhibit so little confidence in markets, worried that they would be so easily disturbed.

Enron was, at the time, the largest bankruptcy ever. That by itself would have made it of considerable interest. The duplicity that quickly emerged—senior executives encouraging their workers to buy shares even as they were selling their own; the hardships imposed on workers who lost their jobs and their pensions, and the contrast to senior executives who seem so well protected; the close connection between Enron and its CEO and the Bush administration—all ensured that the Enron story would become a media sensation. But it has only become clear gradually, as the months unfolded, the extent to which the story of Enron was the story of the nineties—the excesses of deregulation, accounting chicanery, corporate greed, bank complicity. So too, as globalization embraced the world, Enron embraced globalization, and Enron showed the world the darker side of globalization. Its demise, and the problems that were uncovered with that demise, have strengthened the criticism of globalization. Events since have shown that, if Enron's problems were extreme, they were not isolated; indeed, in some ways, they were pervasive.

CHAPTER 11

Debunking
the Myths

S OME OF THE INVESTMENTS of the nineties were essential
to creating the New Economy. But the race to be first, the excessive exuberance over the New Economy, led to overinvestment.
Resources were wasted, on a massive scale. That much is clear.

We are still so well off that we may not suffer immediately from
this diminution in our wealth, but some of the consequences are
already becoming known: a loss of confidence not only in markets,
and especially the stock market, but in government. If we don't learn
from our mistakes, for which the private sector and the government
both bear responsibility, we may not be so lucky next time.

In explaining our success in the nineties to ourselves and the
world, we have largely drawn on a set of myths that desperately need
debunking: that deficit reduction by itself led to the economic recovery during that decade; that the brilliance of our economic leaders
created our newfound prosperity; that deregulation and self-
regulated markets are the key to sustaining that prosperity, and
should thus be exported to the rest of the world; that the key to success is subjecting oneself to the discipline of financial markets; and
that American-style globalization will inevitably lead to global prosperity, benefiting financial markets in America and also the poor in
the developing world.

These myths arguably served a purpose. The deficit reduction myth, for instance, rallied the country behind the politically hard measures (which passed the House by a single vote in 1993) that were required to restore fiscal responsibility after twelve years of soaring deficits. The globalization myth helped us move toward overcoming protectionist sentiments. But no matter how useful these myths were in the short term, ultimately they are harmful.

The myths have been so powerful in shaping, or misshaping, our economic policies that it is worth summarizing them, even at the risk of repeating what has been said in earlier chapters.

The deficit reduction myth

The deficit reduction myth suggests that if, say, Argentina or Japan is in a recession and has large deficits, cutting those deficits will bring back prosperity. But almost all economists recommend instead an expansionary fiscal policy, fueled if necessary by larger deficits.

If we, or others, come to believe the deficit reduction myth, it will make economic downturns worse. It reinforces the ideology of fiscal conservatism. I believe strongly in the importance of investment, especially in new technology, for long-term growth; and especially in an economy such as the United States, where it is difficult to induce high levels of *private savings*, it is important for the government to maintain a balanced budget, or even a surplus, over the long run. But in the short run, deficits may be absolutely essential for the recovery from a recession, and the economic and social costs of prolonging a recession are enormous, far greater than the costs associated with the increase in the deficit.

The myth that wars are good for the economy

Even among those who hold that deficit spending is bad for the economy in the short run, some are still of the mind-set that war will be good for the economy. Their memories stretch back to World War II, which involved total mobilization, when the war helped the economy get out of the Great Depression. But modern warfare, which does not require full mobilization, is far different: the Gulf War certainly did not get us out of the recession of 1990–91, and may well have exacerbated it. Any stimulus from increased war expenditures is more than offset by the depressing effect of war uncertainty, including the uncertainty over the impact on the price of oil, and the crowding out of other expenditures. War may be necessary to maintain the country's security, but war is not good for the economy either in the short run or the long.

The hero myth

The myth that prosperity was the work of our economic heroes is dangerous too: it shifts attention away from where it should be—on policies. And it increases the vulnerability of the economy: economic vicissitudes inevitably cast doubt on our heroes' ability to perform miracles, and a loss of confidence in these heroes will bring a corresponding loss of confidence in the economy.

Moreover, often the economy changes so slowly that cause and effect are not always clear. We had invested heavily in computers and high technology for decades, but the investments mysteriously kept failing to be reflected in data on the nation's productivity. In the 1990s, the payoff finally came—and much of the credit went to the short-term policies of Rubin and Greenspan, too much in my judgment, as I hope should be clear from the discussion in chapters 2 and 3.

From today's vantage point, our heroes of yesteryear surely appear more mortal than was once thought. But as the puff pieces that glorified these supposed heroes have disappeared from the media, even more troublesome questions are beginning to be raised. Were they partially asleep during their watch? If they were so powerful as to have helped create the boom, if they were so willing to accept credit for what happened then, surely they must be given some blame for what is happening now?

There are two views of the world, both then and now, which are at war. One sees history as determined by underlying forces, our heroes as but today's actors on the stage, the personification of these underlying forces. If they were not there, someone very much like them would be on the scene, doing much that they would have done, with much the same outcomes. Others see leaders playing a more pivotal role. Most economists and social scientists more generally belong to the first camp, and, not surprisingly, I agree. We give our leaders both more credit, and more blame, than they deserve.

Economies are like large ships: with few exceptions, they cannot be turned around quickly. The seeds of today's successes and failures were almost surely sowed in earlier years.

How we interpret our history matters. If our success then was due to good leaders, then it follows that our fortunes are in their hands, and our task is simply to choose those leaders. If our success then, and our failures today, are due to policies, whether the management of deficits or the deregulation of the economy, then there is the possibility of restoring prosperity by reversing policies.

I believe that leadership matters, but mostly because leadership does have an impact on the policies that get adopted, and because leadership is required for a vision of where the economy, where our society, is going. It is not obvious that without Clinton's leadership, there would have been deficit reduction, or that without Reagan and Bush, there would not have been huge deficits that had to be reduced.

The myth of the invisible hand

No idea has had more power than that of Adam Smith's invisible hand, that unfettered markets lead, as if by an invisible hand, to efficient outcomes; that each individual, in pursuing his or her own interests, advances the general interests. The nineties and their aftermath showed that the CEOs, in pursuing their own interests, did not strengthen the American economy—and even as they benefited themselves, others paid the price.

Those earlier decades had shown that CEOs did not necessarily work to enhance total share value. They also showed the role of investment banks in aiding and abetting: they made money as the deals were put together, and they made money as the conglomerates were broken up. But there was an even deeper problem. When they did achieve an increase in share market value, it was sometimes at the expense of others. Firms often issue debt to acquire other firms. When they issue a great deal of debt, they increase the likelihood of the firm going bankrupt. The new bonds may be so risky as to be junk bonds: the market recognizes that there is a significant likelihood of default. One of the tricks perfected by Michael Milken and Co. during the 1980s was how to disguise these nascent problems. If you borrow more than you need, you can use some of the extra funds to service the debt for the first two years or so, and the intervening time between the deal and the collapse left plenty of room for events upon which one could blame the downfall. But typically, at the time the firm issues the new debt, it has existing creditors and claimants— those who had lent it money, retirees who depended on the ongoing firm for their pensions. The junk bonds eroded the expected value of these claimants. In the case of other bondholders, the effect was immediate and apparent, as the price of these bonds fell. In the case of the workers, it would only be evident if and when the firm went bankrupt. But some of the gains of the shareholders were at the expense of these other claimants. Hidden theft had evidently been part of capitalism for a long time. The innovations of the Roaring Nineties perfected these skills—rewarding their CEOs with riches beyond the dreams of all but the cleverest of the manipulators of the seventies and early eighties.[1]

Just as the captains of industry were trumpeting the virtues of shareholder value maximization, but designing compensation systems to ensure that they won, no matter what, economists were explaining why shareholder maximization, especially when focused on the short run, might not lead to overall efficiency, and further, why standard interpretations of Smith, which emphasized the ruthless pursuit of self-interest, were wrong. Smithian logic seemed to suggest that there was no role for morals, for virtues like loyalty and trust. Smith, aware of the limitations of markets, knew this was not so. And modern economics explained why economic systems in which such virtues are prevalent actually work better than those in which they are absent.

The older theories had simply assumed that it was costless to write and enforce contracts, so that every time anybody did anything for anybody else, there was a contract that was rigorously adhered to. This is a far cry from the real world, in which contracts are often ambiguous, contract disputes abound, where litigation is extremely expensive, and indeed most economic dealings go on without contracts. In such a world, there are often implicit contracts, understandings, norms, which enable society to function well. What makes economic systems work, by and large, is trust. Individuals do what they say they are going to do. In recent years, in failed societies, we see the disastrous consequences for the economy of the breakdown of trust. Because such implicit contracts cannot typically be enforced in court, they can be torn up at will. There can be short-run gains, but potentially enormous long-run costs. In the 1990s, essential pieces of the social contract were torn to pieces. And as one firm tore up its contract, bottom-line economics put pressures on others to do so, just as firms that might have believed in honest accounting were pressured by those that wanted to maximize today's bottom line. Competition does not always lead to efficient outcomes: here, it led to a race to the bottom.

Modern economics has shown the limitations of the invisible hand and unfettered markets. In the Roaring Nineties, we put aside these lessons of modern economics, just as we ignored the lessons of earlier decades, such as those that should have emerged from the S&L debacle. Instead, we provided both new incentives and better tools for corporate executives to enrich themselves at the expense of others.

The myth of finance

Among our heroes of the Roaring Nineties were the leaders of finance, who themselves became the most ardent missionaries for market economics and the invisible hand. Finance was elevated to new heights. We told ourselves, and we told others, to heed the discipline of financial markets. Finance knew what was best for the economy, and accordingly, by paying heed to financial markets, we would increase growth and prosperity. The rich rewards that financial markets were reaping for themselves all seemed well deserved, for they were taking but a small share of what they were contributing to all of us.

But all of this was shortsighted hype—a shortsighted hype promoted by financial markets themselves. Financial markets are more interested in the short run than in the long. They pushed policies that may have made the accounts look better in the short run, but which often weakened the economy in the long run. They pushed policies which served their interests more than the general interests; in some cases these policies increased instability and actually decreased longterm growth.

Charles E. Wilson, president of GM in the heyday of the automobile, the fifties, famously argued that what was good for the United States was good for GM, *and vice versa*. The new mantra was what is good for Goldman Sachs, or Wall Street, is good for America and the world. The Roaring Nineties was good for Wall Street. It made money on the mergers. It would make money as the mergers had to be taken apart. It made money as capital flowed into the emerging markets. It made money with the restructurings that followed the economic chaos resulting from its pulling its money out. It made money as it gave advice, whether that advice was good or bad, whether it was followed or not.

Many of the policies of the nineties helped financial markets make more money. Deregulation gave Wall Street new opportunities, which it quickly seized. Bad accounting and lower capital gains taxes fed the bubble, and the bubble fed Wall Street. Abroad, the big bailouts meant that the public picked up the pieces when things didn't go as planned abroad, just as the big bailout of the S&Ls, after deregulation, did at home.

If the sheen has been taken off, the more basic lessons have yet to be learned: financial markets are not the font of wisdom; what is good for Wall Street may or may not be good for the rest of the society; and financial markets are shortsighted. A country subjects itself single-mindedly to the discipline of financial markets only at its peril.

The big, bad government myth

Our new finance heroes joined others in propagating another myth: the problems of the economy arise from big government, forcing us to pay high taxes, and regulating us to the point of strangulation. The implication was clear: downsize government, lower taxes, deregulate. Deregulation did not always unleash powerful forces that led to robust *long-term* growth; rather, it often unleashed new sources of conflicts of interest, new ways of manipulating markets. As we have seen, markets managed to waste hundreds of billions of dollars. Many of the corporate CEOs who managed these fêtes walked off with billions, leaving shareholders and workers alike in the lurch. Ordinary taxpayers have had to pick up part of the tab—in California, as a result of electricity deregulation, and almost surely, in the looming defaults of corporate pension schemes; but, fortunately, far less so than in the last episode of deregulation, during the Reagan years.

Among those who propagated the myth of the too-large government were those that were simultaneously benefiting from the lax regulations (in accounting), from deregulation (for instance, in electricity and natural gas), from government subsidies and help in promoting themselves abroad, and from the government's investments in research and development. Much of the New Economy which gave rise to the boom itself rested on the Internet, which government research had created; on the myriad of other innovations derived from basic research; and on biotechnology, which was based on government-funded advances in medicine and biology.

The myth that lower taxes would unleash huge increases in savings and work effort has proved remarkably resistant to evidence. Reagan lowered taxes markedly, but neither savings nor work effort increased, and indeed, productivity growth hardly budged. Clinton raised taxes on the rich, and dire consequences did not emerge.

The myth of global capitalism

America never fully bought the myth that big government is bad. Most Americans continue to believe that there is a role for government, not only in regulating but in providing essential services—education, Social Security, Medicare. Abroad America preached a version of capitalism, based on a minimalist role for the state, which America had itself rejected. Rather than encouraging countries to adopt institutions like those that had served America so well—such as a Federal Reserve with a mandate to promote employment and growth, and not just price stability—America pushed them toward a market fundamentalist version of capitalism. While we worried about the dangers of media concentration at home, we pushed those abroad to privatize without regard to these concerns.

With the U.S. Treasury at the center of international economic policy, it was no wonder that the free flow of capital became the centerpiece. It provided new opportunities for profits for Wall Street—but it exposed the developing countries to enormous risks, without reward. Growth was slightly enhanced as capital flowed in, yet the devastation that was brought about as capital flowed out, or as the interest rates that they had to pay to keep it in, far exceeded those temporary benefits. The countries that grew the fastest over the long run—even the countries that attracted the most foreign direct investment—were those that intervened to stabilize these flows.

The myth of triumphant capitalism, American style

Americans had always had a faith in capitalism and the market economy, but our success, and the demise of communism, renewed that faith and brought it to new heights. There have always been a number of different flavors of capitalism; American capitalism is different from Japanese and European capitalism, and America's success relative to these other versions reinforced the belief that America's system was not just right for America but right for everyone else. Believing it had discovered the answer to the world's economic ills, America pushed its version of the market economy onto other countries.

The American economic system has enormous merit, but it is not the only system that works; other systems may work better for other nations. The Swedes, for example, though they have modified their traditional welfare system, have not abandoned it; the security that it provides reduces extremes of poverty—still so prevalent in America—and also encourages the kind of risk taking that is essential in the New Economy. Living standards have improved every bit as much, new technologies have spread every bit as fast, in Sweden as in the United States. And the Swedes have in fact weathered the latest global slowdown better than America has.[2]

There are other countries which believe that their economic system is better, at least for them. They may have lower incomes, but they have more job and health security; they enjoy longer vacations, and lower stress may be reflected in longer lives. There is less inequality, less poverty, lower crime, a smaller fraction of their population spends a large part of their lives behind bars. There are choices, there are trade-offs.

The collapse of the bubble economy, the uncovering of the accounting and other scandals, has brought the expected response from the rest of the world: a crowing at America's problems, at the sudden turnaround in its standing, at the pride that preceded the fall. But more important, it has revived the real debate about alternative versions of the market economy.

Because America is the strongest country in the world, others are looking for us to falter; our hubris, the overselling of American-style capitalism, fed their hostility. The cracks in our system that have now been exposed have provided ample opportunity for America's critics to say, "I told you so." If the selling of U.S. capitalism and democracy was one of the primary objectives of American foreign policy, our conduct was self-defeating.

Long-Run Strategy

The United States focused so much on its own economic mythology, and on managing globalization to its own short-term benefit, that it did not see what it was doing to itself and the world.

What gave passion to most of those who worked hard to get Bill Clinton elected was not trade liberalization, deregulation of the banking system, deficit reduction, or even tax reductions for the rich (the 1997 capital gains tax cut). But somehow, these were the issues that marked the success, that dominated our agenda. Some, like deficit reduction, were issues that had to be attended to before we could turn to others. Some represented the common ground between the New Democrats and the conservatives who came to dominate Congress after the 1994 election, but who were already important before 1994.

In the beginning of the Clinton administration, a small group of us met once a week to discuss our vision of the U.S. economy, and the global economy, as it would likely unfold over the coming decades. We depicted alternative scenarios, and what we might do to make it more likely that those scenarios that comported with our interests and values would emerge. But it was not long before day-to-day matters came to predominate, the fight for one bill or initiative or another. Even with a more clearly articulated vision, it is unlikely we would have avoided all of the mistakes. Politics matter—and self-interest was at play. But I do believe that without such a vision, mistakes, big mistakes, are much more likely to occur. The conservatives had a vision, an oversimplified vision of rugged individualism, of government engaged in taking away individuals' hard-earned money, a Horatio Alger optimism that allowed every poor American the prospect that, if only he worked hard, and the government did not take from him what was duly his, he too would be able to enjoy the life of wealth that was every American's birthright. This vision may have been based on myths and not on reality; but it was a powerful vision. The challenge today is to formulate an alternative vision, based not on these myths but on the realities of today's economy, and on embracing the lessons that we have learned from the nineties.

CHAPTER 12

Toward a New Democratic Idealism

VISION AND VALUES

G EORGE H. W. BUSH was quite open about not being into the "vision thing." By contrast, Bill Clinton was impressive in articulating a sense of where America should be going. He wanted to reshape America, and the occasion of the new millennium provided ample rhetorical opportunity. The economic message underlying that vision was simple. We were groping for a third way, a way between socialism and its overly intrusive government and the Reagan-Thatcherite minimalist governments of the right. Of course, there is not a single, third way, but a multiplicity of third ways. We were seeking a third way that was right for America.[1]

As we have seen, that quest was distorted: we did not achieve the balance that we sought. We pushed deregulation and deficit reduction too far, not arguing as forcefully as we should have for the important roles that government can, and should, play.

I believe that had we had our goals—and how they might best be achieved in today's economy—better in focus, we might have been able to avoid some of the excesses of the 1990s, and we would have been better able to manage the problems that followed. A clearer vision should also give us guidance in going forward: how, for instance, we should address the problems posed by the recent corporate scandals.

In the discussion below, I try to describe more fully a vision for America. I call it Democratic Idealism, to reflect that it is a vision, an ideal, toward which we should be striving. But it is not utopian. It reflects the selfishness of individuals and the imperfections of our institutions, including our public institutions. I was tempted to call it a New Democratic vision, but that term has already been pre-empted—and as I have suggested in this book, the New Democrats have perhaps moved too far away from the idealism that should constitute a vision. At the very least, their vision has been blurred at times. I hope that this discussion will help them see more clearly what they could be striving for.

It is a vision which lies somewhere between those who see government having a dominant role in the economy and those who argue for a minimalist role; but also between the critics who see capitalism as a system that is rotten to the core, and those who see the market economy as unblemished, a miraculous invention of man that brings unprecedented prosperity to all. I see the market as a powerful instrument for doing good—but one which has not only not lived up to its potential, but has, in the process, left some behind, and actually made some worse off.

This vision entails a balanced role for government, an attempt to achieve social justice *at all levels*—at the global level as well as at the local—at the same time that it promotes a sense of individual and national responsibility. It envisions strengthening individual opportunity at the same time that it enhances democratic collective action. It is a vision and agenda that takes into account the links between the economy and political processes, and between these and the kind of society—and the kinds of individuals—we create.

What We Were Against

It is always easier to define what one is against than what one is for, and the years of Ronald Reagan and George H. W. Bush had given us ample opportunity to see what it was that we were against.

The conservative mantra holds that the smaller the government and the lower the taxes, the better: money spent by the government is, by and large, wasted, whereas that spent by the private sector is well spent. The events of the 1990s should have laid rest to such claims: the private sector wasted money at a pace and in a manner that was beyond even the dreams of most government officials; the CEOs managed their empires in ways that were unchecked, rivaling the least democratic of governments.

By contrast, Democratic Idealism holds that there are legitimate areas for government activity—from education to the promotion of technology to social protection for the aged and the disadvantaged. There is a role for both government expenditures and regulation. Without the government, markets sometimes produce too much of some goods—like pollution—and too little of other goods—like research. At the heart of every successful economy is the market, but successful market economies require a balance between the government and the market. The particular balance may differ from country to country and over time; it will differ from sector to sector, and from problem to problem. Striking that balance requires asking what each should do, and how it should do it.

To take one example: over the last thirty years, there has been increasing concern about the environment. Markets, by themselves, will lead to excessive air and water pollution, too many toxic wastes will be produced, and there will be insufficient care in their disposal. Government intervention is required to ensure that these public concerns are attended to. Today, because of government programs, our air is cleaner, our lakes are purer than they otherwise would have been; and in some cases, the environment is actually better off than it has been in a long time. All citizens have benefited.

Underlying the views in favor of a minimalist government was a simplistic ideology, one I referred to earlier as "market fundamentalism," which said that by and large markets by themselves are both stable and efficient. I call it an ideology because it is a matter of faith: it rests on no acceptable economic theory, and is contradicted by a host of experiences (it would be true, for instance, if there were perfect information, perfect competition, complete markets, etc.—conditions that are simply not true even in the most advanced of countries). The fact is that markets often do not work well; that they often result in unemployment; that, by themselves, they do not provide insurance against many of the important risks which individuals face, including the risk of unemployment;[2] that much of the growth of recent years has been based on government-funded research. The growth of government has largely come in response to the failures of markets. The conservatives have tried to claim that government is more often part of the problem than the solution. But that is simply wrong: The fact of the matter is that before government intervention to regulate the overall macroeconomy—systematic efforts under the influence of Keynes's ideas began after World War II—economic fluctuations were far worse than they are today. Downturns were longer, and booms were shorter.[3]

Even the argument that government is necessarily inefficient is based more on ideology than science. The late Herbert Simon of Carnegie Mellon University, who received his Nobel Prize for important contributions to understanding how organizations behave, recently put the matter this way:

Most producers are employees, not owners of firms. . . . Viewed from the vantage point of classical [economic] theory, they have no reason to maximize the profits of the firms, except to the extent that they can be controlled by owners. . . . Moreover, there is no difference, in this respect, among profit-making firms, non-profit organizations, and bureaucratic organizations. All have exactly the same problem of inducing their employees to work toward the organizational goals. There is no reason, *a priori*, why it should be easier (or harder) to produce this motivation in organizations aimed at maximizing profits than in organizations with different goals. *The conclusion that organizations motivated by profits will be more efficient than other organizations does not follow in an organizational economy from the neo-classical assumptions. If it is empirically true, other axioms will have to be introduced to account for it.* (emphasis added)[4]

There was more to the Reagan-Bush conservative economic agenda, though, than just cutting back on government. Even Reagan and Bush realized that there were some things you needed government for. They pushed, for instance, for an increase in defense expenditures and the conservatives had a particular view on how best to raise the required taxes. Reagan's supply-side economics held that any tax on the rich would so enervate incentives that they would work less hard and save less, so the poor would actually be worse off. This kind of reasoning provided the basis of the 1981 tax cut. Arthur Laffer, President Reagan, and others who argued that tax revenue would increase were proved wrong—disastrously wrong for the country's fiscal health.[5] Savings and labor supply simply did not increase as they had predicted. (By the same token, those who predicted dire consequences from Clinton's increase in the tax rate on the rich in 1993 also were proved wrong.)[6]

There is a suspicion that not even Reagan was so foolish as to believe that cutting taxes would increase tax revenue; there was a longer-term agenda to downsize the government, and especially social expenditures. Looming deficits would force these cutbacks. If this was what Reagan had wanted, he won; even better, from this perspective, was that Clinton was forced to do the hard and dirty work of figuring out how to make the cuts. It was only the enormous growth of the economy and the peace dividend from the end of the Cold War that made the cutbacks in non-defense expenditures tolerable.

Reagan's agenda of cutting taxes for the rich was partly based on a misguided model of the economy. In the Reagan view, not only would tax cuts for the rich pay for themselves in terms of economic growth—which they did not—but even the poor would benefit. This was an old idea in economics, and one that had already been widely discredited. It was called "trickle-down economics." It held that the best way to help the poor was to give money to the rich; the benefits would eventually "trickle down." Those at the bottom saw their incomes actually fall in real terms during the two decades from 1973 to 1993.[7] The Reagan view had no support either in economic theory or in history. Even those who believe that markets are efficient should know that they do not solve all problems. The demand for unskilled labor may be so low, for instance, that unskilled wages drop below subsistence levels. There is a role for government in reducing inequality—for example, by providing education and supplementing the income of low-wage workers.[8]

The Reagan tax agenda, however, was not just based on a misguided economic model. It often seemed there was a different set of values from those later espoused by the Clinton administration: the Reaganites may not have really believed that tax cuts would truly lead to an increase in tax revenue; they may not have really believed in trickle-down economics; it may have been that they were simply not very concerned about the consequences to the poor.

As much as we objected to the *principles* which underlay much of what Reagan had advocated, even more, it was the *practices* which gave rise to our ire. Words are cheap; today, everyone pays lip service to "compassion." It is actions that count. Certain actions, for instance, become emblematic: at one point during the Reagan administration, the two vegetable requirements for nutritious school lunches came to be satisfied by mustard and ketchup. Similarly, early on in George W. Bush's administration, the allowable level of arsenic in the water skyrocketed. These actions stand for a host of other decisions, each of which might themselves be viewed as unimportant—decisions about affirmative action, spending on Project Head Start (the preschool program for disadvantaged children), standards for disallowing disability payments, policies toward unemployment insurance—but when added up, they evince a clear pattern, a reflection of differences in values and judgments, a pattern which exhibited frugality to the poor and generosity to the well-off, and which often belied a true commitment to free market principles.

How could one reconcile massive airline and agriculture subsidies, huge bailouts for banks, with the free market principles that they *seemed* to advocate? With the growth of corporate welfare, protectionism (by one estimate, by the middle of Reagan's term in office, a quarter of all imports were covered by some trade restriction), and tax preferences, the free market rhetoric seemed simply a facade for a political agenda that included help for oil companies, lower taxes for the wealthy, and lower benefits for the poor. This double standard was not lost on many "true" conservatives.

The Challenges Facing Liberal Democracies

As Clinton came to office, he faced multiple challenges. The conservatives had been enormously successful in pushing their ideology, and in painting Democrats as "liberals"—in favor of big government and high taxes. It was unfair. Even before the fall of the Berlin Wall and the demise of communism, Democrats had recognized that the regulatory framework of the New Deal was not working, and with the continual changes in the economy, it seemed more and more out of date. Our first challenge was thus to explain what was wrong with the conservative ideology, and to present an alternative vision. But rather than attacking the premises, the ideology, we accepted the terms of the debate as they had been framed. We sought to show that they were wrong by deregulating as enthusiastically as any conservative, by cutting spending more ruthlessly than they had ever done.

The conservatives had had another major political success: by a seeming sleight of hand, they managed to convince much of the middle class that they are all, or are about to be, upper class, so that any tax even on the well-off is looked at askance. There was widespread support for the repeal of the inheritance tax, even though very few actually pay it, and even fewer would pay with a slight adjustment of the threshold (the level of bequest below which no tax is due). Democracy means that it is the will of the "median voter"—the middle class—which will predominate; and so politics will reflect their values and perceptions. Traditional Democratic politics had focused on the "underdog," that is, helping the poor. These perceptions made it increasingly difficult for Democrats to pursue this "redistributive" agenda. But even had the conservatives not succeeded in convincing most of the middle classes that they were, or might be, in the upper 2 percent of the income distribution, changes in the economy would have required a change in the redistributive agenda. The increasing share of income earned by the middle class has meant that the middle class will, in some way or another, have to contribute to addressing the problems of the poor: in many countries, even if all of the income were taken from the very rich and given to the very poor, the problem of poverty would not be solved.

Making the task of formulating a redistributive agenda all the harder was that the conservatives—including some inside the Clinton administration, especially at Treasury—tried to characterize redistributive politics in "class terms." The battle against corporate welfare was seen as a battle against the rich, one which if waged by Clinton would cost the administration its stripes as advocates for the market. The irony was that those who took this position were themselves using class analysis, trying to suggest that those pushing for redistributive policies were fomenting class warfare. It is a simple fact that different policies affect different groups differently, and it has long been a principle of good and open government that those effects be identified; it is one of the few ways that those who attempt to subvert public policy for their private interests can be stopped.

We did less about the problems of inequality plaguing our society than we could have—and with some of the policies discussed in this book, such as the capital gains tax cut, we made matters worse (unless you subscribed to the trickle-down theory). We recognized that one of the causes of poverty was lack of education, and we recognized too that in many parts of the country schools are deficient. Urban ghetto schools, with large and unruly classes, make learning difficult even for well-motivated children. When the Council of Economic Advisers proposed a revolving loan program that would have allowed small federal expenditures to be multiplied into large improvements, as I mentioned in chapter 2, Treasury opposed the initiative, worrying about the impact on the deficit and whether the money would be well spent. But the same concerns could be raised against almost every government program. Similarly, we knew that in coming years, Americans would increasingly need to have more than twelve years of schooling. This led us to push for tuition tax cuts and credits, but this was a program that benefited the middle class—though most of the middle-class children who were able, and wanted to, were managing to go on to college; it was the children of the poor, whose parents were so badly off that they paid little or no income tax, who really needed help.

A second challenge, then, that we only partially lived up to, was to formulate an agenda of "social justice," of how to treat the disadvantaged in our society, that would be well received by the average voter. To a large extent, the response was to deemphasize these issues, and to look for programs that helped all Americans, and in helping all Americans, the poor too were helped. Social Security was a program not for the poor but for all Americans. All Americans benefited from technology programs—like that which developed the Internet—and from health programs that provide treatments for cancer and heart diseases, or that make it easier for individuals to buy homes through the Fannie Mae. Indeed, a stance of many Democrats has been that a means-tested program—a program aimed only at the poor—will be a mean program, that is, it will provide inadequate benefits.

The programs I have just described *simultaneously* address market failures and issues of redistribution. Private insurance companies simply do not provide annuities that offer the same level of old-age security, for instance, because they do not provide insurance against inflation.

But as we compromised the redistributive part of the agenda, a third challenge was posed. If we—Democrats and Republicans—are all for the middle class, if we are all for the market economy, unfettered by regulation, then what is it that separates the left from the right, the Democrats from the Republicans? What is it that Democrats stood for? Was it the end of politics, at least as we knew it, at least so far as the economy is concerned?

The Efficiency and Growth Agendas

One could think of the two parties as two management teams, each claiming that they know better how to run the economy. The Democrats would like to convince voters that they could do a better job in promoting growth, getting the deficit down, downsizing government, deregulating. The Democrats could try to describe themselves as the "honest" management team, unbeholden to the special interests which held such sway over the Republicans. The contrast in economic performance provided some support to these contentions, and that might have been a vision, but there were two problems. First, as we did little about corporate welfare, as we allowed special interests to prevail in one area or another, that vision became blurred. We could only attempt to persuade voters that we were *less* beholden (which I think was true), but all too often, the voters despaired of making such fine distinctions.

The second, more fundamental problem is that it is not an inspiring vision. I, and most of those who joined the Clinton administration, came with a more ambitious one. As an economist, I focused on redefining the role of government and collective action in the economy. Modern economic theory had identified the myriad of situations where markets failed and where government intervention might make a positive difference, and as Americans, we took many of these examples almost for granted. Americans supported the view that government was needed to protect the environment and to provide education. By and large, they favored Social Security and Medicare, and supported basic government research. As an economist, I welcomed the opportunity of seeing how these ideas might be put into practice. I believed that, in fact, policies based not on free market ideology but on an understanding of the limitations of markets and the government would most likely produce sustained economic prosperity. Growth would be higher, and unemployment would be lower. I believed that the balanced course, recognizing both the strengths and limitations of markets and government, was not only consistent with the teaching of modern economic theory but also with the lessons of economic history, and not only in the United States but elsewhere. And having watched what happened in the nineties, and the aftermath, I believe this even more strongly: it is one of the primary lessons to emerge from that episode.

Markets are *means* to obtain certain ends—most notably, higher living standards. They are not ends in themselves.[9] Even more so, many of the specific policy measures that have been advocated in recent decades by conservatives, such as privatization and liberalization, should not be viewed as ends in themselves but as means. While the goals of markets are narrow—they are concerned with material well-being, and not with broader values like social justice—unfettered markets often fail to achieve even these limited objectives. The nineties showed that they did not ensure stability, the seventies and eighties that they need not produce high growth, and that poverty may increase even as the economy grows. The years after the beginning of the new millennium have shown that markets may not only not create enough jobs to keep up with new entrants to the labor force; they may not even keep pace with the destruction of jobs brought about by greater productivity.

I want to stress the importance of maintaining the economy at as close to full employment as possible; unemployment represents the most dramatic failure of markets, a wastage of our most valuable resource. It is a primary responsibility of government to maintain the economy at full employment. The problem is not that we do not know how to do better, but that we have not been fully committed to the pursuit of full employment. As I noted in chapter 3, William Jennings Bryan, in the election of 1896, argued for a movement off the gold standard, toward a bimetallic (gold and silver) standard, as a means of reversing the deflation that was hurting the economy, and especially hurting the farmers. The advocates of the gold standard were concerned with the possibility that rampant inflation would follow were we to abandon the gold standard. Nothing of the sort happened. But today, in too many countries, the pursuit of full employment has been sacrificed on the cross of inflation fears. In the fight against inflation, to the central bankers, the unemployment numbers are just statistics, the body counts—the unintended but inevitable collateral damage. Treating them as cold statistics dehumanizes the fight: one doesn't have to think of them as people, real people with families and children; one can ignore the suffering—and the suffering goes well beyond the loss of income; those without jobs lose a sense of worth; they are more likely to get divorced; their children are more likely to have their education interrupted.

We should learn from the successes of the nineties as well as the failures; and one of the successes is that unemployment fell, and productivity and growth rose. These successes were closely related. For by getting the unemployment rate down, we made it possible for people to undertake risk, and risk is the basis of the entrepreneurship, which was at the core of the real success of the decade. Young people didn't have to worry if the company they worked for failed, for they knew that they could get another job. As the unemployment rate has crept up, their spirit of risk taking has waned, and in the long run, the economy will suffer. Conversely, during the nineties, as more and more workers were brought into the labor force, their skills improved: a virtuous cycle was set in motion.

To me, then, achieving the right balance between government and the market is the best way to achieved sustained growth and long-run efficiency. The right balance would mean strengthening the role of government in some areas and weakening it in others. It would mean eliminating, or at the very least, restructuring agricultural subsidies, looking far more askance at government bailouts of large corporations (such as airlines) and at market interventions that restrict competition (as we did for aluminum). It also would mean, however, taking a more active role in protecting consumers (against unsafe products and monopoly practices) and investors (against the kinds of misbehavior that we have described so amply in previous chapters). It would mean supporting research and education and working to protect the environment better. It would mean recognizing that there are many market failures—individuals, for instance, face enormous risks for which they cannot obtain insurance—and that government needs to think hard about how to deal with the consequences. There is much that can be done to improve Americans' sense of security, whether it is in the area of health or old-age income or unemployment. America needs, for instance, a better system of unemployment insurance, as we recognize every time we go into a recession and the numbers of long-term unemployed soar.

But I and most of my colleagues in the Clinton administration were concerned to do more than just increase the economy's growth rate and improve efficiency—though we believed the policies that we pushed would do that. The intensity of the conflicts between conservatives and liberals, Democrats and Republicans, cannot be explained simply in terms of economic efficiency. It is inequality and poverty, politics and power, values and the very nature of society and where it is going that provide the emotional force for the debate. That is, for instance, why tax reforms so often give rise to such emotional intensity: the capital gains tax cut gave a few people a lot more money to spend, the dividend tax cut would give even more money to those at the very top. As I suggested earlier, tax policy can be viewed as a statement, in concrete, of our values. Clinton's 1993 tax changes, by contrast, were concentrated on those who were most able to pay, those who had seen their incomes increase the most during the previous twenty-five years, the upper 2 percent. We had proposed a tax to discourage greenhouse gases, to improve the environment.

The Values of Democratic Idealism

While policies based not on ideology but on a balanced perspective of the role of markets and the government are more likely to promote growth and efficiency, there is a broader vision which I would like to try to articulate. It is based not just on an understanding of our economy but of our society, and it goes beyond the materialistic values that are paramount in the growth and efficiency agenda. There are three cornerstones: social justice—views about equality and poverty; political values, particularly democracy and freedom; and views about the relationship between individuals and the communities in which they live. As we shall see, all three are intricately interlinked.

Social Justice

This is not the place to defend basic values of social justice.[10] I shall merely assert: We should be concerned with the plight of the poor. It is a moral obligation, one that has been recognized by every religion. It is an ingrained American value: the Declaration of Independence begins with "We hold these truths to be self-evident, that all men are created equal, that they are endowed by their creator with certain unalienable rights, that among these are life, liberty, and the pursuit of happiness. . . ." The first phrase captures the commitment to equality (regardless of race, ethnicity, gender, etc.), and without a basic level of income, the "pursuit of happiness" is meaningless.

I also believe that we all benefit from a society which is less divided. America has one of the largest proportions of its population behind prison bars, and part of the reason is surely the huge inequalities in its society. It seems outrageous that in the richest country of the world, many of the poor still do not have adequate access to health care, that infant mortality rates in some places in America should be higher than those of some of the less developed countries. East Asia has shown that, among developing countries, those that have been successful in limiting inequality have grown faster—partly because they have made better use of their human resources, partly because greater equality has been associated with greater social and political stability.

While the principles of social justice are longstanding, the foci of concern, and the instruments by which social justice should be pursued, have altered. In the discussion below, I touch on only a couple of the key issues. There are others, such as affirmative action, which are of no less importance.

Equality of opportunity

Increasingly, attention has, I think rightly, focused on *equality of opportunities*, particularly opportunities for children. Politically, this makes enormous sense, in America especially, which thinks of itself as the land of opportunity. Everyone should agree that a child's prospects should not depend on how well off his or her parents are. Focusing on opportunity also provides a way of sidestepping some of the issues of trade-offs upon which economists so often focus. In the old-fashioned redistributive politics, if the poor were to gain, or at least gain significantly, it had to be partly at the expense of the middle class. The left believed that they could continue to appeal to the middle class's higher moral values, but the right won: not only did they appeal to a baser selfishness, they made the further argument that even if you wanted to help the poor, giving money to the government was not the best way to do it, since government inevitably wasted most of the money. The right emphasized private charity ("a thousand points of light"), an idea which sounded well in a speech or two of Bush I, but then floundered.

Greater equality of opportunity means that the country would be using its basic human resources better, by ensuring that everyone lives up to his or her potential. There would be greater efficiency and equity. Who could oppose that? We have yet to explore the full ramifications of equality of opportunity. We recognize that if disadvantaged children are to have an equal opportunity in school, they must be provided pre-school education, but Project Head Start, which is supposed to do that, remains underfunded. We recognize that if poor children are to learn, they have to have adequate nutrition, and that permanent damage can be done from malnourishment at early ages. Yet programs aimed at addressing these problems also remain underfunded.

Notice the difference between this stance—which says that we can get both more equality and faster growth—and trickle-down economics, which says that everyone can benefit by giving resources to the rich. Both are seeming attempts to avoid trade-offs. But trickle-down theories, even were they to work, do not ask, do the poor benefit as much as the rich? Or, are there other ways of more directly benefiting the poor that might even have greater benefits for economic growth?

Employment

No opportunity is more important than the opportunity to work. Unfortunately, as I noted earlier, in many countries of the world, today many are deprived of this opportunity; and in almost all countries of the world, there are extended episodes for which that is true.

Today, we have the economic tools and, in the more developed countries, the resources with which to enhance the opportunity of employment, particularly in the recessions that periodically mark all market economies. America in the post–World War II era has enjoyed longer expansions and shorter downturns, and we have been fortunate to have been spared the extremes of unemployment that marked the Great Depression. But there have still been long periods in which unemployment has been unnecessarily high. During the nineties, we showed that the economy could operate with less than 4 percent unemployment without inflation rising. In parts of the country and among some groups, the unemployment rate was below 2 percent. America could probably do even better—if it turned its mind to it.

In much of Europe, the employment statistics are far more dismal than in America, and have been so for a long time. But the solution requires more than just more "labor market flexibility"—which has become almost a code word for saying lower wages and less job security. In some countries, lower minimum wages might lead to slightly higher employment levels of the most unskilled workers. And slightly less job security might translate into slightly higher wages for higher skilled workers, as employers would be willing to pay for the right to redeploy them more easily. Still, it is clear: in earlier decades, labor market protections were if anything stronger, and yet unemployment was far lower, and countries with some of the best labor market protections, like Sweden, have far better performing labor markets. Even more than America, Europe needs to reaffirm a commitment to full employment, to providing a job for everyone who is willing to work, taking measures like the development of education and training programs that facilitate job mobility and, most important, the adoption of macroeconomic policies that sustain full employment. Unfortunately, the economic framework in Europe is fighting the battles of the last generation; it is worried more about inflation than about employment creation and growth, with a Central Bank whose mandate focuses on inflation and with a Stability Pact which impairs the ability to engage in stimulative fiscal policy. (Of course, Europe is, as a consequence, spared the huge deficits which provide only minimal stimulus that Bush has pushed through, though many on the right in Europe seemingly would like to follow his lead.) While Clinton successfully pushed back the Republican attempt, with a balanced-budget amendment to the Constitution, to end the era of Keynesian economics, the Europeans almost enthusiastically agreed to have their hands tied. The consequences of this choice began to be felt in the years after the beginning of the new millennium.

Empowerment

The shift in focus from outcomes to opportunity reflects a parallel shift of attention from income to assets, empowering individuals so that they can shape their lives and make the most of their potential.

Some have suggested giving every individual an endowment at birth to be invested for their future.[11] This would not only provide a modicum of economic security but allow individuals greater freedom in making critical choices; today, too many young Americans leave college and graduate school burdened down by a high level of indebtedness, which constrains them, for instance, from choosing a life of public service.

Empowerment, of course, is a political as well as an economic issue, and I shall briefly comment on the political aspects later.

Intergenerational equity and sustainability

We need to be concerned with fairness and justice among those living today, but also across generations. Our growth today should not be at the expense of the well-being of future generations. That is one of the reasons that we worry about the degradation of the environment. If we pollute the atmosphere, if we change the climate by increasing the concentrations of greenhouse gases, as we have been doing for the past two hundred years, then we may compromise the well-being of our children and grandchildren.

That is why we should be concerned not only with social justice today but with *sustainability*, with the well-being of future generations, including the preservation of the environment, the conservation of our natural resources, the maintenance of our infrastructure, and the strengthening of our culture.

Politics and Power

There has long been a concern in America and elsewhere about the ties between wealth and politics. Our democracies are imperfect. Ostensibly, we have a system of one person one vote. Only a few extreme conservatives believe that individuals should be able to sell their vote. (After all, such sales, when freely undertaken, make both the seller and the buyer better off; otherwise they would not have undertaken the transaction.) But indirectly, through the media, votes are bought and sold. People have to become informed, convinced to go to the trouble of voting, even taken to the voting booth, and all of this costs money. That is why campaign contributions are so important. But individuals, and even more so corporations that contribute, expect something in return. They are buying government support— not in the crass way that politicians may be bribed in some countries, yet the link between policy and money is unmistakable. That is why campaign finance reform is so important for those who seek to break the nexus between money and politics; and unless that link is broken, we will continue to have policies that advance special interests over general interests, corporate interests over those of the average citizen.

Today, information is more important than ever. If the Internet has been, in some ways, a strongly democratizing force, the increase in media concentration in one country after another has weakened effective democracy. In Russia, we saw the extreme: state-controlled TV being replaced by oligarch-controlled TV, replaced in turn by state-controlled TV. Yet, during the nineties, restrictions on media concentration were weakened. In the United States, we had the opportunity to demand of the TV and radio stations, in return for their use of the public airwaves, that they provide extensive campaign support, in an equitable way; this could have been done in such a way as to reduce significantly the role of campaign contributions. But such reforms were in the interests neither of the media, who profited from the advertisements, nor of the corporations, who profited from the power that came from campaign contributions. Though we don't buy and sell votes explicitly, those who wanted there to be *political markets*, the buying and selling of politicians, won the day.

Over the past thirty years, there have been major strides in achieving greater electoral democracy.[12] It is partly because of our successes that we know how far we must go. African-Americans who were excluded from voting in large parts of the United States can now vote—but even today, there are places where they face obstacles to casting their ballots. We should be making voter registration easier—and Clinton tried—but there are those who would like to make it more difficult. Yet democracy means more than just periodic elections. It includes meaningful participation in decision making, a deliberative process in which different views and voices are heard and taken into account. Strengthening our democracy is an ongoing process. Non-governmental organizations (NGOs) play a more important role than they did a half century ago, and the Internet has strengthened civil society, not only in the United States but around the world. Civil society has had some striking achievements—for instance, getting the Land Mines Treaty adopted in 1997, even over the opposition of the United States and its Defense Department; and in 2000 the Jubilee movement succeeded in getting debt relief for more than twenty countries, when the IMF had significantly blocked debt relief during the preceding three years. Meaningful participation in decision making requires an educated and informed citizenry. The Freedom of Information Act (1966), though imperfect, gives ordinary American citizens information about what their government is doing which they otherwise would not have. Yet there still remain important realms of secrecy, and as the late Senator Daniel Patrick Moynihan argued, far more than is necessary for the interests of national security. Freedom of speech and the press are well-recognized basic rights; but these rights can only play the role that they should if individuals know what it is that their government is doing. There is a fundamental *right to know*. Unfortunately, in the last couple of years, government secrecy has increased.

Even as the bubble burst, it left one legacy: unprecedented inequality, a new and larger cohort of multi-billionaires. Societies in which there is much greater inequality function differently from those in which there is more equality—if only because differences in economic power inevitably get translated into differences in political power. We have already seen some of the manifestations of this, with the tax cut of 2001, and particularly the repeal of the inheritance tax, which was part of that 2001 tax cut. Public interest arguments were put forward for the repeal, which upon closer scrutiny make little sense; it is clear that the tax cut was simply an attempt by the wealthy to keep more of the wealth for themselves. For instance, it was argued that the inheritance tax was particularly hard on owners of small businesses, who were forced to sell their enterprises. But this problem could have been easily dealt with: increasing the deduction for a married couple from the current level of $1.2 million to, say, $10 million, would have exempted all but the very richest Americans—and virtually all small businesses. The argument that the inheritance tax destroyed incentives was patently self-serving. How many of the dot-com billionaires would have said, I will not create my company if the government takes, say, 40 percent of my wealth in excess of $10 million? The gains—and losses—were beyond their wildest dreams; what drove them was the excitement of creation. In their greed, wealthy conservative forces pushed for—and succeeded in getting—the complete repeal. But more than that was at stake, as many of even America's wealthiest recognized. The nature of our society would be affected if there were a new class of superrich, who inherited their wealth from their parents and grandparents. Already, data showed that the American dream of rags to riches, the Horatio Alger story, was largely a myth. Economic mobility was extremely limited. The abolition of the estate tax could solidify these changes, creating a new "class" society, based not on ancient nobility as in Europe, but on the bonanza of the Roaring Nineties. The inheritance tax had in fact been a positive force in shaping American society, encouraging the creation of foundations and private universities, which have played such an important role in civic life and the country's success.

The abolition occurred just as it became clear that much of the wealth that had been seemingly created in the Roaring Nineties was nothing more than a phantasm, that much of the wealth was "stolen" property, acquired through misleading accounting and tax scams, in an economy where corporate governance had failed, and failed badly. But for the lucky few who had cashed in, there was the basis to found a new set of dynasties. At least the railroad barons of the nineteenth century, who used political influence to attain their riches, left behind a legacy of railroads, of hard capital, which bound the country together and energized its growth. What was the legacy of so many of the dot-com millionaires and billionaires, the executives of Enron, Global Crossing, WorldCom, and Adelphi, other than the horror stories which would regale future generations?

The Individual and Society

The fights about taxes, about government programs, sometimes even about redistribution, are, in some ways, skirmishes. The real battle is more profound: it is about the nature of society, and the relationship between the individual and the society.

Western philosophy puts the individual at the center: society is created to help individuals reach their fulfillment. Other non-Western societies have given greater primacy to the community. But even with Western individualism, today, we recognize our interdependence; it is hard to imagine life as a hermit, without goods that we receive, somehow, from others. We live in communities, and how those communities function has a major impact on the well-being of each of us. Today, the conservative "ideal" is based on a kind of rugged individualism, in which each individual's success is the result of his own efforts, and his efforts alone. The reality, of course, is far different. The government, both in what it does and what it does not do, has played a key role in many of the successes. For instance, where would the recent technology fortunes, such as those in the Internet New Economy, be, if the government had not funded the research that underlay the Internet? Intuitively, of course, many grasp this: the drug companies encourage government support for the basic research that underlies so many of their patents and so much of their profits.

At the very least, without some *collective action*, we would be exposed to others taking our property.[13] Maintaining law and order is the first order of any government. But modern society requires far more than that. We buy and sell goods and services with each other, and government plays a central role in regulating those exchanges, a role that goes well beyond just ensuring the enforcement of contracts.[14] Modern economics has helped delineate the arenas in which collective action may be desirable, for instance, in the myriad of circumstances in which markets fail to work well—such as when they do not produce enough jobs. And as we noted earlier, even when markets are efficient, some individuals may have an insufficient income on which to live.

Government, of course, does not always solve the problems it sets out to address. There are government failures just as there are market failures. Over time, firms have learned to be more efficient; at least in some areas there have been marked improvements in the efficiency of government, though obviously, there is enormous scope for further improvements. It should be one of our objectives to continue to improve the efficiency and effectiveness of government; for unless we do so, there will be less confidence in government, and less scope for addressing those needs that can only be dealt with by collective action.

Rights as constraints and objectives

One of the most important areas in which collective action is required is the preservation of our freedom and our basic rights. The words of Franklin Roosevelt still resonate: we have to work not only for our basic freedoms, freedom of religion, speech, and the press, but also for the freedom from fear, and the freedom from want. The extension of traditional civil rights to include economic rights was incorporated in the Universal Declaration of Human Rights, adopted by the United Nations on December 10, 1948. Outside the United States these rights are increasingly recognized: of what value is the freedom of speech to a man who is so starved that he can hardly speak, freedom of press to a woman who has not had an education and cannot read?[15]

In America, we have typically thought of rights as restraints on government: the government cannot intrude on any individual's basic rights. But as the list of basic rights expands—from the right to privacy, the right to know what the government is doing, the right to choose, to the right to decent work, or the right to basic health care—government is also required if individuals are to achieve these basic rights.

Beyond markets and government

The debate over the role of the government has, in recent decades, been broadened and enriched. There is clearly a need for collective action, but government is not the only way by which we act collectively. What is distinctive about government, as opposed to other bases for collective action, is its power of compulsion. All individuals in a community *have* to belong, have to pay taxes, and are proscribed from doing certain things, like taking drugs or committing murder. Other forms of collective action are *voluntary*. It would be nice if we could rely totally on voluntary actions, but economic theory has provided insights into why we cannot. There is a need to provide public goods, goods from which we all benefit, but individuals have an incentive to take a free ride on the contributions of others. Instead, they must be forced to pay their fair share. Individuals can inflict harm on others, for instance, by polluting the atmosphere, and they must be stopped from doing so. Sometimes social pressures work; but in large, anonymous societies, they typically fail to do so, at least when a great deal of money is at stake.

While there is a need for government, however, government, and the political processes that govern it, have their limitations. Non-governmental organizations (NGOs) play a critical role, not only in providing a voice (a kind of collective action of certain groups within the political process) but also in providing services. There is a long tradition of health and education services being provided by NGOs, and provided efficiently. Competition among private universities in the United States has improved the quality of higher education; but the universities are not-for-profit institutions. There are for-profit schools, but they have not fared well in the competition in the education market, proving that there are some arenas in which the profit motive patently falls short.

How large that arena is may differ across countries and over time. In Sweden, cooperative grocery stores are every bit as efficient as for-profit stores. In agriculture, throughout the world, cooperatives have, and continue to play, an important role, both in providing credit and in marketing. In the United States, the most capitalist of countries, the marketing of raisins, almonds, and cranberries is dominated by cooperatives. Often the cooperatives have arisen out of a failure of markets—either because markets were absent, or because markets were dominated by profit-making firms with monopoly power that exploited the farmers.

In short, the market/government dichotomy is an oversimplification. There is a need to go beyond markets. There is a need for collective action. But there are a variety of ways of doing this. Free market advocates have not only overemphasized the role of markets; they have underemphasized the potential for non-governmental forms of cooperative activity as well as the need for government.

Beyond selfishness

Adam Smith argued that individuals by pursuing their own interests contribute to the public good. But we have seen in this book that this is often not the case. We have underestimated the importance of traditional virtues such as trust and loyalty in making our economic system work. Earlier, firms and their workers were bound by loyalty and trust, so that firms often retained workers through an economic downturn—and in some countries that is still the case. But bottom-line economics in the United States has changed that; today, workers who are not needed are quickly discarded—never mind the cost to society or to their families. Of course, in the future, firms that act with such ruthlessness to their workers may find it more difficult to recruit staff, but companies focusing on today's profits pay little attention to these long-run consequences.

This is but one example of the broad class of phenomena where individuals' actions have effects on others. Those impacts are not appropriately taken into account in markets. The gains of the executives described in earlier chapters were partly at the expense of shareholders and bondholders. When individual actions affect others, for which compensation is not rendered, the effects that arise are referred to as "externalities." An individual's right to pursue his or her own interests is, or should be, circumscribed by potential adverse effects on others. "Freedom" entails individuals' rights to live as they will—provided it does not have adverse effects on others. The problem is that increasingly, in our integrated complex society, individual action can have further consequences for others. Smoking can give rise to secondhand cancer. So in some states smoking in the workplace has been banned. But what then of smoking in the privacy of one's home? It gives rise to increased medical costs, and with Medicare, the government provision of health care for the aged, taxpayers in general bear the cost.

Although government regulations and other policies are intended to limit the extent of adverse externalities, for the most part "good behavior" is ensured through norms and ethics—attitudes about what is "right" and "wrong." Implicitly, both conservatives and liberals agree we have a responsibility to try to shape our community, and the individuals who comprise it, and that we must be sensitive to these broader impacts of public policy. They differ only in how they want to shape it. Conservatives are attracted to the Smithian view that individuals in pursuit of their own self-interest lead to the general betterment of the community—a remarkable conception, which allows you to eat your cake and have it too. Were it true generally, morality would be devoid of content. We would never need to ask, what is the *right* thing to do? We would only need to ask, what do we *want* to do, what will make us happier?

In a way, businesses have been nurtured on double-speak: if making money and acting selfishly was supposed to be the same as serving the community, then it followed that lobbying for deregulation, or enhancing opportunities for profits, was an act of public-spiritedness—even if part of that lobbying entailed arguing to legislators that markets were inherently competitive (so profits would be quickly dissipated) and arguing to shareholders, at the same time, that the (hoped-for) profits would be sustainable, because these markets were inherently uncompetitive. And the same *morality* that affected (or infected) business leaders affected (or infected) our political leaders. They were doing good by doing well. They could argue for deregulation, believing that in so doing they were helping the economy and the society more generally, and at the same time receive hefty campaign contributions, which enabled them to get reelected. Morality in both the private and the public sector took on a new meaning: increasing profits.

Unfortunately, as convenient as it would be, there is no basis for these Smithian beliefs.[16] This book has, I hope, helped show how wrong, and dangerous, such ideas are. The captains of industry—the leaders to whom all Americans were told to look up to, those who served as the aspiration for others—have, it turns out, acted in ways which benefited themselves at the expense of others. At least in retrospect, their actions look deeply immoral.

It was clear that the problem was not just a couple of bad apples. As time went on, more and more apples seemed rotten. There had, of course, always been some executives who were less than virtuous. What stunned America was the number of bad apples, and the number of prominent companies that acted badly. Was it that that had always been there, but hidden from view? Or had capitalism itself changed—and changed the people who headed it? A central tenet of this book is that behavior is affected by incentives. There are always judgment calls in business. Matters are often not black and white. Accountants have hard decisions to make, and they try to make them in a professional way. But when there are large amounts of money at stake—at first large tax dollars, then large bonuses from increased share values—judgments get distorted, at first a little, but over time, more and more. In the nineties, incentives got distorted, and accordingly, so did behavior, in a vicious, self-reinforcing way.

In the nineties, norms and ethics changed. What is considered acceptable is affected by what others do, what they find acceptable. If CEOs normally get paid three times as much as an ordinary worker, it might be acceptable for an exceptional CEO to get paid four times, but not forty times. If CEOs normally get paid ten times as much as an ordinary worker, it might be acceptable for an exceptional CEO to get paid fifteen times more than an ordinary worker, but not a hundred times. In America in the nineties, there were no bounds; everything became acceptable. Strong incentives were in place to break out of previous bounds, and those incentives worked. You were worth what you could get. Period. There were incentives to change views of right and wrong, of what was acceptable and unacceptable. And those incentives worked.

Shaping Individuals

The vision of the role of the government that I have put forward begins where most economists begin: *given the preferences, the values, of individuals*, what is the best economic arrangement for meeting the desires of individuals? But underlying the debate about what happened to America in the Roaring Nineties was concern about how our values and our society were being altered. Those of my generation were perhaps particularly sensitive to these changes. We had grown up in the era that prompted John F. Kennedy to urge: " . . . ask not what your country can do for you—ask what you can do for your country." Lyndon B. Johnson had begun the War Against Poverty. And we began the fight for civil rights.

The Roaring Nineties helped reshape Americans. When I was a student at Amherst College, large numbers of my classmates went on to graduate school in the arts and humanities. Many who went to law school went on to practice public interest law, and many who went to medical school took up careers in research. In the nineties, far more of the best students went on to business and law schools. The best and the brightest were not interested in public service; they were attracted to the thrill of mergers and acquisitions, and the rich material rewards. That work became interesting partly because the stakes were so high.

There was another, more positive side to the bubble, that perhaps represented the best of American traditions. It unleashed an unparalleled level of innovation in the economy, an excitement among young people—they held the keys to the New Economy. Like the Wall Street traders, their "burnout rate" was high; an expert in one technology became obsolete as that technology was succeeded by another. At thirty-five, you were destined for the dustbin—or for a senior management job shuffling paper, raising cash, putting together deals so that other young people might exercise their wits.

But there was a curious contradiction in America: The success of the nineties was based on science and technology. Yet, to a large extent, America was borrowing ideas and people from abroad, just as it was borrowing from abroad to finance its boom. Silicon Valley exhibited an unparalleled openness to foreign talent. Indian immigrants, engineers who excelled in our universities, became the highest income ethnic group in America, joined by Chinese and a host of others. But Americans themselves did not value science and technology—the very basis of the New Economy. American students made up less than 50 percent of the graduate students in science and technology at our best universities.

It was not just America, however, that was affected by the changes in morals and behavior. In Europe, at first the dominant sentiment was that America's corporate scandals confirmed prejudices that Americans were selfish and immoral, and that the consequent travails through which the U.S. economy was suffering were simply justice being done. But as events unfolded, more than one European executive was found to have engaged in similar practices. Again, at first, it seemed to be directly related to the Americanization of European business: those like Messier at Vivendi Universal who were the first to fall had been the most outspoken advocates of American-style capitalism, focusing on shareholder value (by which was meant profits today), rather than the more inclusive European approach, in which explicit attention was paid to the concerns of other stakeholders. But then it turned out that the problems in Europe too were more pervasive, involving many of the same industries, the Swiss banks, the French and German telecoms, but others too—Swissair and Sabena, and even a Dutch grocery company.

I remain hopeful: from the reactions already observed, I suspect we are in another episode of what Albert Hirschman of Princeton's Institute for Advanced Studies called *Shifting Involvements*.[17] He argued that each episode of public-spiritedness is followed by one in which there is a focus on the private level, which in turn is followed by another episode of public-spiritedness. Each has its disappointments, and only by living through one do we come to understand the limitations. The events of the past few years have affected the young people I see in my classroom; more are thinking about once again joining the War on Poverty, the War on Terrorism. Applications for Americorp and the Peace Corps are on the rise, and probably more than simply can be accounted for by the economic slowdown.

Globalization

Globalization has meant that the issues we have discussed here—about the appropriate role of the government, about the limitations of markets, about how economics shapes individuals and society—are being debated on a global scale. We are now writing the rules of the game, but those rules are being written by international economic institutions in which particular countries and special interests—and particular ideologies—have large sway. And while America often speaks of the "rule of law," its pursuit of unilateralist policies reflects a rejection of the rule of law at the international level. It is in favor of global rules of the game, but worries that the World Trade Organization, or the International Criminal Court, might infringe its own sovereignty. In short, it is in favor of the rule of law, as long as the outcomes conform with what it wants. A moment's reflection should show that if the United States worries about the infringement of its sovereignty by global institutions, how must other countries feel, and especially poor developing countries, who see the global institutions dominated by the United States and the other advanced industrial countries?

The problem is that economic globalization has outpaced political globalization. The United States has been successful in selling the idea of democracy around the world. Democracy means that no single individual can dictate the outcome: only in dictatorships does anyone always get his way. And in democracies, each party tries to persuade others of the merits of what it advocates; leadership typically entails a process of consensus formation, finding approaches that represent an acceptable compromise among competing viewpoints and interests. But in the global arena, the United States has repeatedly made it clear that it must get its way. If it can do so through using whatever power it has, including its economic power, all the better; if it cannot, it will go its own way. For instance, under George W. Bush, the United States, the largest polluter in the world in 2001, unilaterally withdrew from the international agreement intended to reduce greenhouse gas emissions, which are having palpable effects on climate through global warming.

Globalization has meant that the countries of the world are more closely integrated, and with closer integration inevitably comes a greater need for collective action, to solve common problems. The entire world shares the same atmosphere, so that the emissions in one country—the United States—can have significant consequences for others; they may lead to flooding in Bangladesh, or even the submersion of some Pacific Islands states. Yet America has been reluctant to accept that decisions that affect the whole world ought to be made in a way which is consonant with democratic principles.

Nor have we yet come to a clear view of which decisions ought to be made at the global level, which at the national level. There are a myriad of levels at which collective action can, and does, take place. Economics has provided a set of principles that guide what should be conducted at each level. Global public goods and externalities—actions which affect others throughout the world—need to be dealt with at the global level; local public goods and externalities—those which affect only those within the local community—should be dealt with at the local level.

More than economics is involved in the discussion about decentralization, regionalization, and globalization. Political forces are calling both for greater decentralization—putting government closer to the people—and greater globalization—setting global standards to facilitate global commerce, with all the *economic* gains that might accrue (at least to some) from the creation of a global marketplace. These two forces are at odds with one another; yet both are going on at the same time, and undermining the traditional focus of political power, the nation-state. As I have observed, these battles are driven as often by interests as by principles: the question is posed, at what level of government are the particular views that I advocate more likely to succeed? In the United States, conservatives have pushed for the delegation of responsibility for welfare to the states mainly, I believe, because they believe that the advocacy groups for the poor are not as strong at the state level as they are at the federal level, and at least in many states, this will imply cutbacks in the provision of welfare. Similarly, some of the protections for investment and intellectual property rights that have been embedded in international agreements are stronger than business groups could have achieved even in the pro-business environment of the United States. But there is no legitimate economic reason why some of the codes and standards should be set internationally; there should be scope for each country to make its own decisions. There may be trade-offs, and different countries may have different views about those trade-offs. Recent trade agreements have gone well beyond trade.

Nor has the United States really accepted the principle of reciprocity (the golden rule). For instance, we have insisted (I think legitimately) that Thailand use fishing nets for catching shrimp that do not endanger turtles. Our reason: conservation of endangered species is a global concern. But that same reasoning implies that the rest of the world could insist that we not pollute the atmosphere with our greenhouse gases.

Globalization also forces us to address issues of social justice at the global level. Principles of fairness and justice guide our attitudes toward how we treat members of our family, our community, and our nation. Of course, at each level, we think about our own interests. But in *collective* decision making, individuals seemingly try to go beyond their own interests, at least rhetorically. Positions are always defended in terms of what is in the general interest. With globalization, principles of fairness and justice will increasingly need to guide our attitudes towards how we treat members of our global community. At the global level, many in the United States continue to argue for positions simply in terms of what is in America's narrow self-interest; but in recent years, there is increasing effort to couch policies which are in America's interest *as if* they were in the interests of others, including the developing countries. We have said: "If they would only subscribe to the principles of globalization that we advocate, to market fundamentalism, they too would share in the prosperity that has come to America!" The problem is that as we pushed policies abroad that we would not countenance at home, as we acted hypocritically, our arguments have been hollow, and the results have been dismal.

While I think it is morally right for us to begin to think about "fairness" from a global perspective—and not just in our own self-interest—in the long run, I also think such a stance is in the interests of the United States. Globalization has meant that we cannot isolate ourselves from what is happening elsewhere in the world, as the events of September 11 brought home so forcefully. Terrorism can move easily across borders, as can the money that is used to finance it.

We may, in the short run, be able to make progress in winning the physical war on terrorism. But in the long run, the battle is for the hearts and minds of the young people around the world. If they are confronted by a world of despair, of unemployment and poverty, of global hypocrisy and inequity, of global rules that are patently designed to advance the interests of the advanced industrial countries—or more accurately, special interests within those countries—and disadvantage those who are already disadvantaged, then the young will turn their energies from constructive activities, to building a better world for themselves and their children, to destructive activities. And we will all suffer as a consequence.

Conclusion

Some thought that with the end of the Cold War, there would be an end to ideology. The free enterprise system had won the day. We could all go about the task of perfecting that system. The defeat of communism was a defeat of a pathology, of a perversion, of an authoritarian regime, and the fight against that perversion diverted attention from the broader and deeper issues of what kind of society we wish to create.

In much of the world today, however, there is a debate about whether there is a crisis in capitalism. The series of scandals, from Enron on, made clear that the problems went deep: had Enron not gone bankrupt, no one would have been able to investigate what had gone on, and the company's manipulation of the energy market, which was long suspected, might never have been uncovered. Each investigation turned up more evidence of wrongdoing. The CEOs, who had shown such cleverness in some of the ways that they manipulated accounting, had shown equal cleverness in the ways in which they hid what they had done. It is easy in a bubble economy to hide pyramids. With the economic downturn, the pyramids and scams became exposed. The bursting of the bubble exposed the weaknesses—it not only exposed the bubble for what it was, but exposed all the chicanery that went on under cover of the bubble, chicanery that had, at the same time, served to reinforce the bubble.

To critics of the market economy, the scandals that have rocked America—and to a lesser extent Europe as well—some of which I have described in this book, have reinforced their doubts about globalization. If the corporate world is driving globalization, and if the corporate world is as corrupt as it appears to be, we need something else. Yet supporters of the market economy point to the unprecedented prosperity that it has brought about, and not just to a few in the advanced industrial economies. They would like to dismiss the crisis in capitalism as an aberration, a slight blip in an otherwise smoothly running machine.

The market economy has been an enormous success. It has brought prosperity beyond the wildest dreams. It has put the middle class at the center of our societies. But it has not, as some claim, ended redistributive politics. Our prosperity means that we have new, unparalleled opportunities. We could, if we wished, end domestic poverty and malnutrition. We could, if we wished, ensure that everyone had a basic modicum of health care. America is the richest country in the world, but the basics of U.S. health care are below those of far poorer countries. The United States chooses not to provide these basic services, because it chooses not to tax itself. Other countries manage to provide these services efficiently and effectively, through a variety of institutional arrangements. There is every reason to believe that, were the United States to choose to do so, so could it.

Some of the policies that have been advocated and adopted in the United States are based on a misreading of economics, and that has been the starting point of this book. Market economies have enormous powers, but they also have their limitations. My own research focused on problems associated with asymmetries of information, problems which have been increasingly important in our information-based economy. Our struggle is to understand the limitations, so that we can make our economy work better. Economies can suffer from an overintrusive government, but so too can they suffer from a government that does not do what needs to be done—that does not regulate the financial sector adequately, that does not promote competition, that does not protect the environment, that does not provide a basic safety net.

I have been most adamant in criticizing the "one-way" view: that there is a single set of policies which will make all of us better off. In the one-way view, we should all favor tax cuts for the rich, we should all favor repeal of the estate tax, we should all favor deregulation, we should all favor strengthened intellectual property rights, and so on.

There is a common ground to which politicians of all persuasions appeal: "democracy, "family values," "community," "opportunity," "equality," "free markets," "freedom," "justice"—but what is meant by these slogans can differ markedly. I have tried to delineate the values that I have stressed, which for want of a better name I referred to as Democratic Idealism, from those that conservatives like Reagan put forward; and behind these slogans and their hidden meanings lie marked differences in policies. There are choices, there are alternatives. And because we cannot know for certain what lies in the future, and there is even much uncertainty about today's economy, there are risks associated with any policy—or even with doing nothing. Who benefits from different policies can differ markedly, just as who bears the risks associated with different policies differs greatly. The right has been enormously successful in selling the "one-way" idea; but it is wrong, and we need to understand both why it is wrong, and why the right has used it so effectively.

Economics has been my starting point, yet I have been forced to go beyond economics. The economic issues are important—people have fought and killed over far less than what is at stake in the battles described in this book. But what has really provided the emotive power behind these battles is the nature of our society—not so much today as a generation from now. The idea of social engineering fills all of us with horror, with visions of *1984*. But like it or not, the policies that we adopt today do shape our society. They are a reflection of our values, and they send important messages to our youth about what we value. Economics and society are inextricably intertwined. A society with massive inequalities will inevitably be far different from a society in which disparities are limited. A society with high unemployment will inevitably be far different from a society in which everyone who wants a job can find one.

Globalization affects the kinds of *societies* that are being created throughout the world. And it is precisely because those in the rest of the world are aware of this that emotions about globalization run so high: we have been pushing a set of policies that is increasing inequality abroad and, in some cases, undermining traditional institutions.

There is an alternative vision, one based on global social justice and a balanced role for the government and the market. It is for that vision that we should be striving.

Further Lessons on How to Mismanage the Economy

THE BUBBLE BURST. The economy went into a recession. It was inevitable that this would happen—that the days of the Roaring Nineties, built on such false premises, would eventually come to an end—just as it was inevitable that a backlash would set in against globalization. But it was not inevitable that the economic downturn be as long and deep as it has been, or that there be as much suffering. For more than two years, the U.S. economy has performed significantly below its potential—a loss of more than a half trillion dollars, a waste to be piled onto the money that was misinvested in the boom. As this book goes to press, the economy is still performing well below its potential. Just as there are important lessons to be learned from policy mistakes of the nineties, there are important lessons to be learned from the policy mistakes of the new millennium.

We saw in chapter 1 how Clinton had inherited a set of problems from Bush I: an economy in recession, with slow productivity growth, growing inequality, and huge and growing fiscal and trade deficits. Some of these problems he solved—the economy emerged from the recession and, most important, the huge deficit was eliminated. In some areas, such as the increase in productivity, the success was beyond what anyone expected. In other areas, such as the increasing inequality, there was some limited progress: poverty was reduced, and those at the bottom of the income distribution at last saw their incomes rise. But the huge increases in inequality that had marked the preceding two decades, including the Reagan and Bush I years, were not reversed. In still other areas, like the huge trade deficit, there was little if any progress.

The Clinton administration would have liked to have done more to address the long-run problems of America but was stymied by lack of resources—sacrificed, like so much else, in the name of deficit reduction—and lack of cooperation from Congress. We knew that as productivity increased, we were living off a base of previous investments in research and development in science and technology; we wanted to expand those investments, but budgets limited us, as did the conservative ideology that government should not support technology. We knew that there were great weaknesses in our infrastructure, that we had to invest more in education and in improving the environment. We even put forward ideas that would have gone a long way toward putting Social Security on a sound financial footing.

Though we did not do as much as we would have liked, the economy that was bequeathed to George W. Bush had enormous strengths. The government's deficit had been turned into a huge surplus, and unemployment was lower than it had been in decades.

The New Economy is real, even if its significance has been exaggerated—the economy today is markedly different from what it was a decade ago; new technologies, like the Internet and cell phones, have changed the way we do business and communicate. New technology has engendered increases in productivity that have continued—and will continue—to make an enormous difference in our living standards. These transformations in our economy have enabled us to have lower unemployment without inflation. Conditions that sustain low rates of unemployment have both fueled economic growth and given us an opportunity to address important social problems—particularly those involving the exclusion of less skilled laborers from the job market. America has a highly educated labor force, and in recent years, it has become even better educated, enhancing the ability to move from job to job. The strategy of facilitating that movement, through, for instance, the increased portability of pensions and a focus on lifetime employability, rather than job security as it has traditionally been defined, has paid off.

While a number of weaknesses in our financial institutions have been exposed, their underlying strength—their ability to get capital out to new enterprises, to support innovation—is the envy of the rest of the world.

But these strengths, although they serve us in good stead, are not enough to ensure our continued economic success, and are particularly not enough to ensure that the fruits of that success are widely shared. We should have learned from the successes and failures of the nineties and the first years of the new millennium that more is needed. And we should have learned more about *what* is needed.

George W. Bush inherited a country with enormous strengths, but some problems as well: the economy was going into recession; deregulation, ill-advised tax changes, bad accounting, corporate greed, and an insufficiently adroit monetary policy had all worked to inflate an unsustainable bubble. In some areas, America had seized the opportunity afforded by the end of the Cold War to exercise true leadership—pushing an agenda of human rights and democracy—but in other areas, it had behaved less well, putting special economic and financial interests above principle, so much so that confidence in globalization had been badly eroded.

Bush faced some hard choices. He could try to learn the lessons of the Roaring Nineties and address the remaining problems; or he could ignore those lessons and take up the Bush I–Reagan agenda where it had been interrupted. Regrettably, he chose the latter course, with results that were bad for the economy, bad for the country, bad for the world. It is not just that the economic downturn has been far longer and far deeper than necessary. The problems of inequality and poverty in which we had made some, but limited progress, became worse, as unemployment increased but unemployment benefits did not keep pace, and as tax cuts were directed at those who had benefited so much (and in some cases, effectively "stolen" so much) during the nineties, while expenditure cuts were directed at those who had not shared fully in that boom. Investments in some areas of R&D were cut back, and the trade deficit increased. The discontent with globalization, already evident as the nineties drew to a close, reached new peaks.

None of this needed to have happened. And I say this not just with 20-20 hindsight. The course that should have been taken was clear as the economy first slipped into a downturn. Even with the inevitable uncertainties of policy, in early 2001 I and others advocated policies that would have spared the economy much of the travails of the succeeding years. It was not so much that the Bush administration had not learned the lessons of the nineties, had not learned how to manage the risks of the New Economy; they had, I believe, another agenda.

Mismanaging the Overall Economy

As Bush took office, he pushed a tax cut that was not designed as a stimulus, and did not work as a stimulus. The economy languished. The tax cut gave huge breaks to the well-off, but did little for those who would spend the money to make the economy go. While he seized on Keynesian arguments to sell his tax cut, he and his advisers should have known that its impact would be minimal and would not suffice. Perhaps he was hoping that monetary policy would do the trick. But the experience of the nineties should have taught him that it was risky to rely on this. In the end, monetary policy did not pull the country out of its doldrums; lower interest rates did not rejuvenate investment: firms with excess capacity did not start building even more fiber optics just because the cost of borrowing was lower. Lower interest rates did induce many homeowners to refinance their mortgages, and the money sustained consumption; but this left the economy in an even more precarious position for the future, with households heavily indebted.

Rather than giving large tax cuts to the rich, there were policies which would have stimulated the economy—more quickly, more surely, and providing more bang for the buck. We know how to create a powerful and effective tax stimulus. Give money to those who will spend it, and spend it quickly: the unemployed, the cities and states that are starving for funds, and lower income workers. An incremental investment tax credit, for instance, only goes to corporations and individuals who increase their investments.[1] A strong stimulus is also an equitable stimulus: for the money, by and large, goes to the poorest Americans, those who have benefited least from the growth of the last quarter century. Giving money to cities and states will prevent cutbacks in educational and health expenditures, which can hit particularly hard at the poor.

Although even in early 2001 it seemed to me, and to most other close observers of the economy, that the economy was in for a serious downturn, given the level of excess capacity in those sectors which had played such a large role in the boom, there are always uncertainties. Given the uncertainties, I and others warned: put into place some automatic stabilizers—extend unemployment insurance and provide assistance to make up for the shortfall in tax revenues resulting from recession; for the states and localities, if the downturn continued, would be forced to cut back on their expenditures and raise taxes, prolonging and worsening the downturn. If the downturn proved as bad as we feared, these would help rejuvenate the economy. If it did not, then there would be no extra expenditures.

We also warned: don't count your chickens before they hatch. Budget numbers can't be relied upon. The surpluses could change magically before your eyes into deficits. Having worked with budget projections during my years at the Clinton Council of Economic Advisers, I knew how precarious such projections are, how slight changes in assumptions, or economic conditions, could change a large surplus into a large deficit. Rosy projections during the Reagan and Bush I administrations had brought discredit on the government and the reliance on its claims; we wanted to change that, which is why we were deliberately conservative in our projections. We turned out to be more accurate than others, more accurate in particular than the Republican Congressional Budget Office, but when we erred, it was systematically on the conservative side. Bush had some good economists working for him, and they must have known what we knew. Indeed, with so much of the revenue due to capital gains tax revenues—themselves due to the bubble—and the bubble already bursting before the tax cuts were passed, it was clear that that source of revenue would quickly dry up. It was obvious that the budget forecasts would have to be revised downwards, perhaps dramatically so.

Bush's father had warned against voodoo economics, the idea that by cutting taxes one could raise revenue, because there would be such large "supply-side" responses. And the country had learned the hard way of the dangers of accounting trickery in the private sector. But George W. pushed for "dynamic scoring," claiming that the actual deficits would be smaller than projected, because of the dynamism to which the tax cuts would give rise.

Bush chose to ignore the advice of the past. He was interested in one thing, and one thing only: a tax cut, one that not only helped those who had already done so well in the Roaring Nineties but was beyond what the country could afford. He had evidently learned from fellow CEOs during the nineties how to use projections—no matter how flimsily based—to sell his wares. He was not selling over-inflated stocks, but a tax cut that was beyond the means of even the richest country of the world.

As predicted, the tax cut did not provide the stimulus that the country needed, nor, in spite of record cuts in the interest rate, did monetary policy suffice. The economy continued to operate substantially below its potential. As the downturn continued, the other problems about which he had been warned manifested themselves. Cities and states were forced to raise taxes and cut back expenditures, as they too faced increasing deficits. The economic downturn led to increasing unemployment, which in turn led to increasing welfare roles and increased violence.

Bush's budget forecasts proved even rosier than Reagan's two decades earlier. Within eighteen months, Clinton's legacy of huge surpluses was turned into huge deficits. The ten-year fiscal position changed by an astonishing $5 trillion—a large number even in a large economy. Some of the turnaround was because the surpluses that had been counted upon were not there; some of the turnaround was because the tax cut did not adequately stimulate the economy—just as had been predicted; and some was because of the tax cut itself. On all three counts, Bush was to be faulted: he had been warned about spending money that was not there; he had been warned that his tax plan was not a good stimulus; and he had been warned that his tax cut was expensive.

The tax cut, however, was not a temporary one designed just to stimulate the economy. It is a permanent one, with long-term effects. For the year 2008 alone (hopefully, even with misguided economic policy, we will recover by then), there is a projected $190 billion deficit, and by the time 2008 roles around, that number will undoubtedly be much, much larger.[2]

But even these numbers underestimated the dire state of the U.S. fiscal position. Bush took budget duplicity to a new height when he persuaded Congress to repeal the death duties (the estate and gift tax) for only one year. At first glance, this appears to be an absurd idea. Why should those whose rich relatives die in that particular year, rather than the year before or the year after, receive so much more? Obviously, Bush could not have meant to create a perverse incentive for families to knock off their soon-to-be-departed rich relatives in order to save possibly millions of dollars. Instead, Bush was betting on the fact that no one really expected the repeal to last for only one year. It was simply budget gimmickry. The president did not want anyone to know the full cost of the tax cut—a cost that would be felt over decades. By eliminating the estate tax for one year, and one year only, it appeared that the cost of the tax cut was much lower than it would in reality be if, as he was sure would happen, Congress was forced to extend the repeal.

When the Bush tax cut prescription failed, and the economy continued with its weak performance, Bush came forward with the same failed solution: more tax cuts for the rich. Except this time, he outdid himself, with an audacious proposal to eliminate the dividend tax—audacious in its cost, in its inequity, and in its likely ineffectiveness in stimulating the economy. As I wrote in an article on the dividend tax cut in *The New York Review of Books*: "Never have so few received so much from so many."[3] The 226,000 American tax filers with incomes in excess of $1 million would have received, in total, roughly the same benefit as the 120 million filers with incomes of less than $100,000. While 50 percent of all tax filers would receive $100 or less, two thirds $500 or less, at least one very senior member of the administration was reported to receive $600,000. The calculations of the Urban Institute–Brookings Institution Tax Policy Center show that more than half of the benefits of exempting corporate dividends from the individual income tax would flow to the top 5 percent of the population—a group of people all of whom earn more than $140,000, with an average income of $350,000. While more and more Americans today own stock, most of their holdings are in tax-exempt pension and IRA accounts; it is only the very rich that would benefit. Bush's theory was that these few people would demand more stock, and this would drive up share prices, and this in turn would lead to more investment. But each of the links in this chain of reasoning is questionable. Why, for instance, should anyone expect higher share prices to lead to increased investment, and especially in the short run, when lower interest rates had failed so miserably? Firms that have excess capacity are not going to build more excess capacity simply because their share prices were higher. And there is concern that share prices and investment may actually fall, as the looming larger deficits drive medium- and long-term interest rates up (the basic law of supply and demand says that increased government borrowing should drive up rates; and higher interest rates should lead to lower share prices).

Bush tried to sell the tax cut as a growth and stimulus package. But if growth and stimulus were his objectives, there were policies that would be more certain to work—and would have been far fairer. With the crash of the dot-com and hi-tech world, many of our scientists were out of work, and it would have made sense to expand government spending on research. By contrast, the benefits of the dividend tax cut went to the "old economy" firms—for instance, the aluminum and railroad industry from which Bush had chosen his secretaries of Treasury—not to the dynamic New Economy firms, which typically pay out little if anything in dividends, and which rely far more heavily on capital gains. The proposal would tilt the economy to the slow-growing industrial sectors.

If one wanted a quick stimulus, aid to the unemployed and the states and localities would have been extremely effective. As we have noted, just as predicted two years earlier, when the downturn persisted, the number of long-term unemployed soared, more than doubling; an increasing number of Americans faced hardship as their unemployment benefits ran out; and the states and localities were facing huge deficits, and as they cut back expenditures and raised taxes, that in turn put large downward pressure on the economy.

If I were drawing up a short list of tax policies to stimulate the economy, the dividend tax cut and the other measures pushed by Bush would not have made it even onto the list, let alone to the top. If I were drawing up a short list of reforms to our tax code that would stimulate growth, the dividend tax cut and the other measures pushed by Bush would also not have been anywhere near the top. But even if one thought it important to end the double taxation of dividends (the problem was that, as we saw in earlier chapters, all too often corporations and their executives had found ways of avoiding taxation; the problem was not double taxation, but zero taxation), there were easier and more equitable ways of doing so, for instance, by allowing the deduction of dividends from the corporate income tax (just as interest payments are tax-deductible) or by imputing the income of a corporation back to the shareholders.[4] It was evident that the proposal to eliminate the dividend tax was not motivated either to promote growth or to stimulate the economy. It was an attempt to help those who had helped Bush get elected, to reduce the taxes on the very rich.

Although the benefits of the proposal were dubious at best, the costs were enormous. The United States would have to borrow enormous amounts. Most of this likely would come from abroad. America would become even more indebted. Its trade deficit would continue to soar—and even as these proposals were being made, new records were being set. It was not just a matter of bad luck. It was the result of bad policy. Since Reagan had set the country on a path of high deficits a quarter century earlier, the United States had gone from being the world's largest creditor country to being the largest debtor country. And these new proposals would only make matters worse.

Some of the increased borrowing, however, would come from Americans; and as the United States returned eventually to full employment—every recession eventually comes to an end—some of the money spent to finance the increasing deficit would come out of funds that otherwise would have been spent on investment. As a result, the proposal more likely would lead in the long run to lower incomes, not to higher growth. However the deficits are financed, whether by borrowing from Americans or by borrowing from abroad, the incomes of Americans will be lower—according to one estimate, in 2012 by 1.8 percent, or $1,000 per capita[5]—and although the tax largesse goes to a few rich, the burden of this lower income will be felt by all Americans.[6]

In the nineties, I sometimes thought we pushed deficit reduction too far, but there was enormous pressure from the financial markets and the conservatives. Suddenly in 2002 and 2003, with deficits looming, many of the conservatives changed their tune. Just as Reagan had tried to repeal the laws of economics, so too did Bush II and some of his advisers. Normally, with the law of supply and demand, if demand goes up, price goes up. If the demand for borrowed funds goes up, interest rates go up. In the New Economics of Bush, this evidently is not the case. Supply-side economics had once again reared its head: this time there was no claim that lower taxes would lead to more tax revenues—that claim had been too thoroughly discredited. To the extent that one could figure out what was entailed in the so-called New Economics, it was that the tax cut would so stimulate savings that the supply of funds would more than match the government's multi-trillion-dollar increased demand for funds, and interest rates would not rise, an idea as sure to be discredited as the supply-side mysticism of the Reagan years.

Even more moderate Republicans could not countenance the tax cut proposal—even if they did not focus on its unfairness, they recognized the serious risk to the country's economic future posed by the soaring deficits, and they recognized that, as structured, it provided little stimulus to the economy. The compromise passed by Congress in May 2003 was, by official reckoning, $318 billion over ten years, less than half the $726 billion Bush had asked for. And the bill included $20 billion in aid to the states and $12 billion in help to low-income families with children that Bush had not asked for—money that likely would provide some needed stimulus to the economy. But in reducing the cost to $318 billion, Congress had engaged in even more budget chicanery than it had two years earlier, with the dividend tax cut gradually increasing, but then suddenly abolished.[7] As dividend and capital gains taxes got cut, there was little evidence in support of Bush's "theory" that the dividend tax cut would lead to high stock prices and higher stock prices to more investment: stock prices reacted to the passage, as they had reacted to the earlier announcements when it was proposed, with hardly a whimper. *The New York Times* headlines for its articles on the reactions tell the whole story: "No Big Rush to Stocks After Cuts in Two Taxes" and "Expectations of a Jump-Start Are Countered by Wait-and-See."[8] And there were no indications from the business community of a direct response through increased investment.

The economy will undoubtedly recover from its current downturn, and when it does, Bush will undoubtedly claim credit for his tax plan. The lesson for the future from this episode—that any kind of deficit increase will stimulate the economy—would be every bit as wrong as the lesson drawn from the last—that any kind of deficit reduction will bring about recovery. We draw our economic lessons from our politicians only at our peril.

Mismanaging the Corporate Scandals

One of the reasons that the economy continued to perform so much below its potential in the new millennium was the seeming lack of resolve in addressing the host of problems that had become manifest as a result of the auditing, corporate, and banking scandals. Shareholders knew that the numbers they had been provided in the past could not be trusted, and unless substantial reforms were made, what reason did they have to trust the new numbers? What was required was a return to more balanced regulation; what the Bush administration wanted was more of the same, more deregulation. As we noted in chapter 10, as the California electricity problems mounted, the administration steadfastly maintained a hands-off policy, and steadfastly maintained that the trouble had nothing to do with deregulation or market manipulation. It was caused by excessive regulation, they said, especially environmental regulation. The result was a disaster, both for users and for California taxpayers. And with the Enron bankruptcy, eventually the truth won out. Brazil had shown that careful government intervention could prevent price gouging of consumers and yet maintain overall market efficiency; but this was the road that the Bush administration chose not to take.

There were perhaps other reasons for the reluctance to take strong action: with so many in the Bush administration and their friends having themselves been implicated as beneficiaries of these scams, there was little desire to rush to their condemnation. Eventually, popular pressure succeeded in getting a reluctant Bush to endorse some of the reforms, but even then, the worry was that they would go "too far" rather than not far enough. For instance, nothing was done about what I have argued was one of the underlying problems, the treatment of stock options, though many within the corporate community finally decided to take action themselves—to disclose, for instance, more than was required, and to expense stock options. As the Bush administration thrashed around for someone with respectability that they could trust not to go "too far," their first pick turned out himself to have been not just a director, but on the auditing committee of one of the firms that had engaged in these aberrant practices.

Mismanaging Globalization

But as badly as the Bush administration may have managed the economy, the way it managed globalization was even worse. America was the sole superpower, both economically and militarily. Globalization meant that there was need for the countries of the world to work together, to cooperate to address common problems. The Clinton administration was sometimes ambivalent in the manner it approached globalization. It strongly supported the UN, finally addressing the longstanding problem of America's arrears in its dues. But at the same time, in the economic arena it changed Teddy Roosevelt's dictum: Speak softly, and carry a big stick, to: Speak loudly, and carry a heavy club. When, during the East Asia crisis, Japan proposed an Asia Monetary Fund, it quickly squelched the idea, worried what such an institution might do to America's economic hegemony in the region—but in doing so, paid scant attention to the hardship that it imposed on the region. U.S. Treasury worked hard to suppress dissension to its views, and with its effective veto at the IMF—the single country with the veto—it succeeded in imposing its will in many areas. There was no sense of multilaterialism; others were cajoled and badgered to do what America wanted.

But as critical as one might be of the Clinton administration's approach to globalization, Bush's was a thousand times worse. He walked away from treaty after treaty—from that governing global warming to strategic arms treaties. While speaking of the rule of law, the administration showed an utter disdain for the rule of law at the international level and shunned the International Criminal Court. No wonder then that when the Bush administration turned to others for help in matters of concern to them, they found a decided lack of enthusiasm.

Even in the areas of economic globalization, where during the Roaring Nineties we had mismanaged matters, the Bush administration built on this discontent to make matters worse. To earlier charges of hypocrisy new ones were added: agricultural subsidies and steel tariffs reached new heights. All of us urban dwellers could, for instance, agree that agricultural subsidies should be cut. Today (unlike when the farm subsidies were originally passed), average farm income exceeded those off the farm, with most of the subsidies going to high-income farmers and, increasingly, corporate farms. The farm subsidies are not only encouraging excessive use of fertilizer—the more the farmer produces, the larger the check he receives from the government—and contributing to the degradation of the environment; they are also hurting poor farmers in the developing world, who could have competed in a world of fair competition, but not with subsidies of over 100 percent. When I was at the Council of Economic Advisers, knowing that a new farm bill had to be passed in 1995, we carefully laid the groundwork, presenting the evidence systematically to the president. In spite of the difficult politics, we put together a farm bill that was designed to wean farmers off the subsidies to which they had become addicted over the preceding seventy years—a marked contrast to Bush's new farm bill, which more than doubled the subsidies, raising them to $190 billion over ten years.

It is inconsistent for free market Republicans to push for agriculture subsidies, and the inconsistency between Bush rhetoric and reality was striking in other areas. In one instance, at least, the administration quickly came to rue the position they had taken.

As we saw in chapter 9, before September 11, Bush's Secretary of

Treasury Paul O'Neill opposed the OECD (the "club" of the advanced industrial countries) effort to increase transparency of the offshore banking centers. The centers should have been suspect. Why did a half trillion dollars of banking occur in the Cayman Islands? Clearly, those in the Bahamas or the Cayman Islands do not know more about banking than do bankers on Wall Street. It is not that their weather provided better natural conditions for banking. They had one product: secrecy, and the avoidance of regulations. They enabled many well-off Americans to avoid taxes, if not to engage in more nefarious activities. And, of course, the business of transferring money to these centers and arranging deals through these tax havens generated good fees for those in the financial community. These secret offshore banks existed at our sufferance. If we did not allow our banks to do deals with them, in all likelihood they would have quickly withered. We had passed tax laws and regulations, and then, seemingly, opened up a major loophole through which the rules could be avoided, at least by large corporations and very rich individuals.

But like so many other things, this changed on September 11, 2001. It was soon discovered that the terrorists were at least partly funded through secret offshore bank accounts, and unless something was done, there would be no way of controlling their access to a ready supply of funds. Suddenly what had seemed so hard, so impossible, and so undesirable, took on a new urgency. The United States became the advocate of transparency—although only as it related to the finance of terrorism. Secrecy that helped conceal tax evasion, corruption, and other nefarious activities still seemed perfectly acceptable.

The Clinton administration may have faltered in managing globalization in the early days after the end of the Cold War, but it was groping honestly to find the right path in a complicated new world. There was an attempt to balance hard bargaining with diplomacy, with building long-run goodwill. We may have got the balance wrong—I think we did—but I think we were prepared to learn from our mistakes. The intellectual property regime we established was condemning thousands, perhaps millions, in the developing world to a premature death, and when this was pointed out, after brief vacillation, we worked to change the policy, worked to get the drug companies to make drugs available voluntarily. But the Bush administration, after reluctantly allowing the matter to be raised in what was called the Development Round, stood adamant against the world in agreeing to reform. It continued to put the interests of the drug companies above the suffering of those in the developing world.

The Roaring Nineties—the first decade of the new era after the end of the Cold War—may not have been the fabulous decade that it seemed at the time. We were sowing some of the seeds that would lead to the destruction of the very boom of which we were so proud. But growth was increased, and poverty was reduced.

In this new era of globalization, not only do goods move more freely around the world, but so do ideas. The seeming triumph of American capitalism has had enormous influence in Europe, Latin America, in Asia and all around the world. Other countries wanted to know to what should America's success be attributed, so that they might better imitate it. And some in America have not been reticent in sharing their perspectives: the U.S. Treasury has, for instance, freely lectured East Asian countries on how they should follow America's principles of accounting and corporate governance, Latin America had (willingly or unwillingly) to adopt the "Washington Consensus" policies, which were *supposed* to make their economies more like their neighbor to the North.

Some in Europe were happy to provide their own interpretations: it was *bottom line* corporate behavior, dynamic CEOs incentivized by high pay that made the difference—this was an interpretation that European CEOs, looking on with envy at their American counterparts who received tens or hundreds times higher pay, for no better performance. A few seized upon the new tricks that American ingenuity had uncovered—stock options, hidden multimillion dollar pensions—to enrich themselves. But others were more skeptical; in Europe there was a debate about the nature of corporate governance, there was at least a discussion about the extent to which the interests of workers ought to be taken into account. It should be clear: I have argued that it was not that American CEOs at this particular juncture in history were particularly villainous or that, on average, European CEOs were more virtuous; but rather American CEOs were subject to temptations they could not resist—financial innovations gave them new ways to cheat their shareholders and provided them with enhanced incentives to do so; and the problems in corporations in general spread to auditors and banks, in a self-reinforcing way. There was a strong incentive for norms to change, and change they did. It became *acceptable*, even *necessary*, to pay amounts that in earlier times or other places would seem outrageous. The same pressures were at play in Europe and elsewhere. In Europe, they were checked by perhaps stronger norms, and an accounting system that emphasized not just abiding by the details of the rules but giving an accurate overall picture of the financial health of the firm. But I have little doubt that had America's boom been prolonged, the pressures would have been irresistible. Today, the market for CEOs is a global market, and so eventually American norms about "fair pay," and "meeting the competition" (a first-rate company has to have a first-rate CEO, which means it has to pay top dollar!) would, I think, have prevailed. Fortunately for Europe, America's problems came to light before more permanent damage was done. Today, many in Europe are working hard to ensure that there are stronger corporate governance and accounting standards, but as in America, there is resistance. Just as many in America opposed the requirements for better information concerning stock options, fearing that it would erode stock market value (as it should), so too in Europe. And while, in many respects, Europe starts from an advantage over America, in others it is weaker: America's legal framework, including common law principles which protect minority shareholders, and an overlapping of jurisdictions allowing actions both at the federal level, by the Securities and Exchange Commission (SEC), and at the state levels, by the attorney generals, arguably provides better enforcement of what rules are on the books. It was not the SEC, captured by George Bush and his friends, many of whom had made their fortunes by not dissimilar methods, and who saw little wrong in such behavior (so long as you could get away with it), but New York State's attorney general, Eliot Spitzer, who uncovered and prosecuted the most egregious examples of wrong doing.

There is, in this, a lesson for Europe: in this arena, as in others touching on corporate behavior, it is better to have duplication of oversight; there are real risks of concentration in Brussels *and* of leaving the matter exclusively to the separate countries. Italy illustrates neatly the latter concern: just as the rest of the world's attention is focused on the necessity of strong accounting standards, Italy's center-right government has decriminalized false accounting, making it a misdemeanor. It has sent a signal to Italian firms that it is of little moment to cheat your shareholders a small amount—say by 5 per cent of the company's value (which can be an enormous sum)—nothing worse than going 40 kilometers in a 30 kilometer speed zone.

Elsewhere, there has been perhaps closer study of the tricks of American corporations, banks, and accountants, by those who would profit by using them, than there has been of the legal structures designed to curb them. This has been particularly disturbing in the developing world and the former Communist countries making a transition to capitalism, each striving to figure out what makes for success. In some cases, as in the Czech Republic, the links are clear, with some of the American malefactors serving almost as teachers to the country as it embarked on the road to a market economy. In Russia, allegedly American "experts" from Harvard financed by the

American aid agency were providing "assistance" on the rule of law, at the same time they were using their own connections to enrich themselves.

For many in the developing world and the economies in transition, all of this has been most confusing. On the one hand, they are told to deregulate, to get government out of the way. Moreover, America seemed to have succeeded *in spite of bad corporate governance*; some in the "Wild East" (the name sometimes given to the ersatz capitalism of Russia and some of its neighbors) seem to claim that it may have succeeded *because* of its "freedom," (read: lack of rules and regulations preventing these abuses). They have watched the Bush administration as it equivocated over what to do about the scandals. On the other hand, they have been lectured *ad nauseum* about transparency and the need for good accounting and corporate governance.

The good news is that at last issues of corporate governance are beginning to receive the attention they deserve around the world, even if some of those in the business community worry that it will lead to excessive regulations. The fact is that capitalism requires trust: savers have to turn over their hard-earned money to others, and to do so there must be an expectation that at least they will not be swindled. Strong regulations make for a strong capitalism. As long as the regulations are well designed, those who are honest, who are not abusing their positions of power and trust to cheat on their shareholders and bondholders, should welcome them.

The most successful countries, like Korea, Hong Kong, and China have, again fortunately, been able to draw the right lessons; they have recognized that there will always be some strong interests pushing for lax regulations and weak corporate governance, but they have also recognized that the country as a whole will benefit from getting the balance right. In Korea, a strong democracy, the opponents have mustered political clout, and reform has not been easy, just as it has not been easy in the United States.

In other arenas the news is less positive. The same senior executives, having enriched themselves with bonuses of hundreds of millions of dollars, speak ardently of the need for more labor market flexibility—meaning less job protections and lower wages and incomes for workers. That there is a need for some reforms in many European countries is clear; but it is also clear that firms or society more broadly are usually in a better position to bear the risks of a changing market place than are workers. In some cases, the job security provisions have been so unbalanced that workers are better off when they retire than when they worked, or when they are sick than when they are well, and job protections are so great that a worker can shirk with impunity. The challenge is to provide security and equity with incentives; the sometimes intense conflict between management and workers, exacerbated by management's lush treatment of itself and the contrast between the harsh words used to describe labor, has not created an atmosphere which is hospitable in the search for solutions which are broadly beneficial.

In macro-economics, the Bush administration has been setting the worst possible example to center-right governments around the world. It is a cruel irony that the center-left has become the guardian of fiscal responsibility, both in the United States and Europe. In arguing for tax cuts to stimulate the economy, the center-right has adopted Keynesian rhetoric, but only the rhetoric. The tax cuts are not designed to stimulate the economy, but to give more money to those who are already doing well. No European country has approached the audacity of Bush—either in the size of the deficits stretching out into the future or in their inequity. Here, the stability pact has played a mixed role: it has prevented the excesses, but it has also prevented Europe from undertaking the actions which *should* have been undertaken to maintain its economic strength. (At least now there is the recognition that labor market flexibility is not the *only* problem facing Europe.)

A curious debate has broken out in some parts of Europe, as in America: are tax cuts better than expenditure increases for rekindling the economy? The center-right, with neither theory nor evidence to support it, claim that it is tax cuts. The correct answer is: it depends on what kind of tax cut. Expenditure increases are far more effective than tax cuts for the rich (especially America's dividend tax cut); and, if directed at health and education, can provide the basis for greater equity and stronger future growth. On the other hand, a targeted investment tax credit or a tax cut on the poor can be just as effective as an expenditure increase. In some cases, to limit the deficits associated with the tax cuts, expenditures have been cut; such changes can actually depress the economy.

As this book goes to press, Europe is going through a downturn, which has resulted in high unemployment rates. In some circles, the unemployment rate seems to have been so high for so long that little notice is taken of these fluctuations. But there is still a huge cost to these fluctuations, for they reduce further the prospects of re-employment of those laid off, and they contribute to a social malaise and disaffection. In Europe, as in America, it is the unskilled and un-educated that bear the brunt, and in many European countries, as in America, the problems are concentrated in certain ethnic groups. In some cases, the problem can be partly transferred abroad: reduced demand for workers in Spain shows up as increased unemployment in Ecuador. But from a global perspective, the costs cannot be ignored.

There is another side to the policies of the Roaring Nineties, which perhaps got less attention than the stock market boom, but which may be more relevant for Europe in trying to solve its problems of persistent unemployment. This entails not an eliminating of job protections but reshaping them; a greater reliance, for instance, on the earned income tax credit, under which the government encouraged hiring low wage workers, supplementing the wages from the firm by up to 40 per cent; active labor market policies that helped train workers for the new jobs that were being created and helped move workers off of welfare into work; and reforms to the welfare system that ensured that individuals would not be *worse off* by going to work.

The response of the European Central Bank to the downturn illustrates an aspect of policy highlighted in the discussion of globalization: sometimes, by pushing decision making to "higher levels" they become less attuned to the local concerns, and a democratic deficit is created. As I have noted, I suspect that if the citizens of Europe and America had been asked if they supported a level of intellectual property protection that would result in those dying of AIDS in Botswana being denied access to lifesaving generic drugs at affordable prices, there would have been close to unanimous rejection. Yet they were not asked that question; it was left to trade ministers, who, under pressure from the drug companies, gave precisely the opposite answer. Similarly, I suspect that if the citizens of Europe were asked if they cared about jobs and growth, and if their Central Bank should pay at least some attention to these concerns, they too would have said yes. But that was not the answer provided by those who set up the European Central Bank, instructing that it focus only on inflation.

All of this raises for Europe, Asia, and Latin America the fundamental question, *what kind of market economy do they want to create?* Is it capitalism American style? Or is it capitalism with a more human face, a gentler, more humane capitalism? A Swedish-style capitalism? In a world of globalization, do we all have to march to the same drum? What is the scope for diversity?

In Latin America, there is a gradual awakening to the fact that the kind of capitalism that they were sold—namely, the Washington consensus—may have been the kind of capitalism that the U.S. Treasury preached, but it was not the kind that the U.S. itself practiced. In some areas, there was a consensus in Washington that the Washington consensus was *wrong* for America—whatever its virtues for the rest of the world, or however it might serve America's interests for others to do something different from what America did at home. There was, for instance, a consensus at home that the Fed should continue focusing on employment and growth; there was a consensus in support of our public social security system, though many in the private sector drooled at the profits that they might be able to make were it to be privatized. There was no consensus in favor of privatizing the publicly owned power companies; measures to do so made no headway in Congress. There was a consensus that, even with unemployment low, American workers needed somehow to be protected against a surge of imports from abroad, though some wanted the help to come more in the form of assistance in finding another job than in protectionist measures.

In short, while in Europe there has been extensive discussion of *convergence*, that the countries should adopt similar if not identical rules, regulations, and practices, the Latin Americans are gradually realizing that while they have *thought* that the reforms were leading them to converge to the kind of market economy found in the U.S., they were in fact not doing so. They were being forced to adopt a form of the market economy that might have been some conservative's dream, but did not comport to the reality of any successful democratic country. The failures are already apparent; and the backlash has already begun. Market economies are not self-regulating, they are buffeted by shocks beyond their control, they are prone to manias and panics, to irrational exuberance and pessimism, to swindles and risk-taking that verges on gambling, and many of the costs of their mistakes and malfeasances are borne by society as a whole. In recent years in Latin America and East Asia, short-term capital flows, hedge funds, and speculation were the mechanisms through which these problems manifested themselves, with effects most manifest in stock markets and real estate. In the past, there have been other mechanisms (as Kindleberger has so vividly described); in the future, undoubtedly, there will be still others.

In this book, I have been somewhat critical about how America has handled globalization: both about American unilateralism and its lack of concern about global social justice. On the first, over the past two years, Europe has seen the consequences of this new form of dominance, just as the developing countries had long experienced it, with the rejection of the treaty on global warming, the International Criminal Court, the Strategic Arms Treaties, and, most recently, in connection with the Iraq War. On the latter, Europe's rhetoric has been far better, but that has meant that the gap between its rhetoric and reality has been even greater. The initiative to allow all commodities from the poorest countries of the world in free from duty ("Everything but Arms") is clearly a move in the right direction, but so long as subsidies remain at the level they have been, the developing countries cannot compete. In other arenas, it would be hair splitting to try to decide who has the better claim on virtue: the U.S. has used its economic muscle to push destabilizing short-term capital flows and to block efforts to reduce bank secrecy, Europe has been pushing the investment protections in the last round of trade negotiations that the developing countries have looked at with deep skepticism. Neither side is willing to even discuss the idea that in judging what should be an "unfair" trade practice, it should make no difference whether the good is produced at home or abroad. Both wanted to continue to have the right to use such protectionist measures.

However blame is shared, it is the developing countries who have suffered; both from what has been done and from what has not been done that should have been, both from the policy reforms that have been urged on them that were largely ideological in nature to those that should have been pushed, but were not, lest too much of the established order be disturbed. If we democratize globalization so that the voices of the developing countries are heard more clearly, the agenda of globalization will change.

Among the greatest challenges facing Europe as well as its relations between the developing and developed countries, is the role of standards and standardization (or to use a more loaded term, homogenization). It should be clear: there is no reason, for example, that we have to consume the same food or spend our incomes the same way. The great virtue of the market economy is that it allows at least those with adequate incomes the freedom to choose. In the Roaring Nineties, at times, it seemed that countries were about to lose their freedom to choose the kind of society that they would like to become: everyone was to adopt the American style of capitalism. We now know that that was wrong. There are certain areas where standards are absolutely essential: consumers have to be confident, for instance, that the food they are eating is safe, regardless of where it is produced. Where there is doubt, they should at least have the right to know how it was produced, so they can make a judgment for themselves. I believe banks and securities markets provide another arena where standards are essential: depositors have to be confident that they can get their money back, and investors that they will not be defrauded. In some arenas, especially where what is required may not be certain, competition among standards and legal frameworks may be valuable; there is evidence that investors will gravitate to markets with the strongest investor protections. But sometimes, especially where one side of the market is very poorly informed, competition among regulators can result in a race to the bottom. It makes sense, too, to have international agreements to regulate situations where what happens inside one country has effects everywhere around the world. America's excessive use of energy, and the resulting greenhouse gas emissions, is the single largest man-made contributor to global warming. There should be international standards in this arena, and trade sanctions should be allowed to enforce such standards. There is, however, no reason why every country has to open itself fully to short-term speculative capital flows. Some countries may decide to have stronger worker protections, stronger health and safety laws, or stronger zoning restrictions. There are costs and benefits—borne by those within the country—and it is these populations who should make the decisions.

In this book, I have presented an alternative perspective to the view that there is a single form of market economy. I have tried to go beyond what went wrong (and right) in the Roaring Nineties, to give an alternative vision.

It should be evident from the unfortunate turn of events in the first years of the new millennium that we have yet to learn fully the lessons both of the successes and the failures. My modest hope is that this book will contribute something to our understanding of these tumultuous years. Perhaps the next American administration will avoid the pitfalls into which America has fallen. Perhaps the next administration will have more success in addressing the long-term needs of America and the world. At the very least, perhaps citizens in the rest of the world will be more wary about succumbing to the myths that have guided so much thinking about economic policy over recent years. Perhaps together, America and Europe, and the developed and the developing world, can forge a new form of global democracy, and a new set of economic policies—policies which will ensure a new-found prosperity, a prosperity which will be shared by all the citizens of the world.

Notes

1. The fixation with financial markets did not manifest itself only in deficit reduction. For instance, in trade policy, we worried about what would happen to the exchange rate. And even in thinking about exchange rates, the perspective of finance dominated. Lower exchange rates (fewer yen to the dollar) mean that American firms can export more, and American producers face less competition from foreign producers. America grows faster, jobs are created—or at least not lost. But the lower exchange rate means losses to Wall Street speculators who have placed their bets on the "strong dollar," and may mean slightly higher inflation, as imported goods become more expensive. As always, there are trade-offs, yet the debate was dominated by Finance, which saw only the negatives—so much so that when a Treasury official was once asked by a reporter to respond to Detroit's worries that as the dollar strengthened, the automobile industry would find it increasingly hard to sell abroad and to compete against Japanese imports, he argued in effect that the strong dollar would spur them to compete even more strongly, to sell even more: his argument if taken seriously meant the repeal of the law of downward sloping demand curves.

2. For a particularly thoughtful exposition, see that of Arthur Levitt (former chairman of the SEC), with Paula Dwyer (contributor), *Take On the Street: What Wall Street and Corporate America Don't Want You to Know. What You Can Do to Fight Back* (New York: Pantheon Books, 2002).

   The Enron scandal has already produced several book-length treatments, cited in note 1 to chapter 10. Arianna Huffington in her book *Pigs at the Trough: How*

Corporate Greed ad Political Corruption Are Undermining America (New York: Crown, 2003) provides a particularly scathing and entertaining attack on corporate America. Even the financial and business press has joined the attack. See, for instance, Jerry Useem, "Have They No Shame?," *Fortune*, April 14, 2003, pp. 56–64, and Janice Revell, "CEO Pensions: The Latest Way to Hide Millions," *Fortune*, April 14, 2003, p. 68.

3. In writing this book, I have had the good fortune to benefit from the large number of books that have been written by former members of the Clinton administration reflecting upon their experiences, as well as some excellent journalistic accounts. These have enabled me to juxtapose my recollections and interpretations of the events with those of other participants in these events. While they are largely congruent, not surprisingly, there are some differences, particularly in interpretation.

   I should particularly mention the excellent book, *The Fabulous Decade* (New York: Century Foundation Press, 2001) by my fellow Council member, Alan Blinder, and by my successor as chairman of the Council, Janet Yellen, who put more emphasis on the classic interpretation of the role of deficit reduction in the recovery. For somewhat more academic studies, see Jeffrey A. Frankel and Peter R. Orszag, eds., *American Economic Policy in the 1990s* (Cambridge, MA: MIT, 2002). Among the memoirs that I found most helpful were those of Arthur Levitt, *Take On the Street* (with Paula Dwyer), and Reed Hundt, formerly chairman of the Federal Communications Commission, *You Say You Want a Revolution: A Story of Information Age Politics* (New Haven: Yale University Press, 2000), as well as Robert Reich's *Locked in the Cabinet* (New York: Knopf, 1997) and George Stephanopoulos's *All Too Human: A Political Education* (Boston: Little, Brown, 1999). Among the accounts of the Clinton presidency, Bob Woodward's *The Agenda* provides detailed discussion of the budget battles and his book *Maestro: Greenspan's Fed and the American Boom* (New York: Simon & Schuster, 2000) gives a quite different interpretation of the boom. Elizabeth Drew provides a comprehensive discussion of the first few years in *On the Edge* (New York: Simon & Schuster, 1994) and *Showdown: The Struggle Between the Gingrich Congress and the Clinton White House* (New York: Simon & Schuster, 1995). Other books include Joel Klein et al., *A Day with the Department of Justice: Leading Business Issues* (Washington, DC: National Legal Center for the Public Interest, 1997), and Steven E. Schier, ed., *The Postmodern Presidency: Bill Clinton's Legacy in U.S. Politics* (Pittsburgh: Pittsburgh University Press, 2000).

ACKNOWLEDGMENTS

1. The last edition of his book *Manias, Panics, and Crashes: A History of Financial Crises,* 4th ed. (New York: John Wiley & Sons, 2000) was published before the cycle of events described here were completed, but any reader of his book will notice the extent to which the current events fall within an almost classical pattern. He writes: "What happens, basically, is that some event changes the economic outlook. New opportunities for profits are seized, and overdone, in ways so closely resembling irrationality as to constitute a mania. Once the excessive character of the upswing is realized, the financial system experiences a sort of 'distress,' in the course of which the rush to reverse the expansion process may become so precipitous as to resemble panic" (p. 2). While his historical list of sectors that can set off a mania unsurprisingly does not include telecommunications, he goes on to point out that "a particular recent form of displacement that shocks the system has been financial deregulation, or liberalization" (p. 5).

2. And with whom I delivered a paper at the American Acocunting Association's meetings in 1987, touching on some of the issues discussed below, subsequently published as "Taxation, Information, and Economic Organization," *Journal of the American Taxation Association*, vol. 9, no. 2 (Spring 1988), pp. 7–18.

3. Readers are referred to that earlier book for a list of those to whom I am particularly indebted.

4. In listing these members of the staff of the Council I do not intend to shortchange others who worked hard in other areas, such as environment, labor market policies, health care, agriculture, and natural resources. The Council acted collaboratively, and the various branches of economics cannot be compartmentalized. One of the great pleasures of being at the Council was to watch some of the junior economists—some of the best graduate students in economics from around the country—grow during their year in the Council, so by the end they too were more than just research assistants: they were making important contributions to policy analysis. Lack of space makes it impossible to name them all here, but they are listed in the annual *Economic Report of the President*.

5. Dickens's important research with George Akerlof and Janet Yellen on inflation is cited later in this book.

6. Alan Krueger spelled out those ideas, together with his Princeton colleague David Card, in *Myths and Measurement: The New Economics of the Minimum Wage* (Princeton: Princeton University Press, 1995). Later, together with Robert Solow

of MIT, he edited *The Roaring Nineties: Can Full Employment Be Sustained?* (New York: Russell Sage Foundation, 2002).

7. For an interesting overview of the functioning of the National Economic Council, see Kenneth I. Juster and Simon Lazarus, *Making Economic Policy Work: An Assessment of the National Economic Council* (Washington, DC: Brookings Institution Press, 1996).

8. Alan S. Blinder and Janet L. Yellen, "The Fabulous Decade: Macroeconomic Lessons from the 1990s," in Krueger and Solow, eds., *Roaring Nineties*, p. 166.

9. Though it does not play much role in the discussion of this book, I was moved by his deep commitment to the environment, his insistence that policy be based on sound science, and his bringing top scientists into the White House for discussions of environmental policy—these made especially the early years of the Clinton administration often seem like an exciting university seminar, but one in which policy was not just discussed, it was made.

CHAPTER 1

1. See Charles P. Kindleberger, *Manias, Panics, and Crashes: A History of Financial Crises* (NewYork: John Wiley & Sons, 1978).

2. To borrow Alan Greenspan's famous phrase from his December 6, 1996, speech. For a discussion of irrational exuberance in the stock market, see Robert Shiller, *Irrational Exuberance* (Princeton: Princeton University Press, 2000).

3. At least during the Clinton years borrowing went to finance investment, rather than—as in the Reagan and first Bush administrations—a national consumption binge. Borrowing cheaply for high-return investments makes sense, of course, if all goes well: returns are more than sufficient to pay what is owed, with interest.

4. There was even some concern that it could have an adverse effect, as some states might respond by increasing tuition, leaving those whose parents did not benefit from the tax credits less able to afford college.

5. These topics are elaborated on at greater length in Joseph E. Stiglitz, *Globalization and Its Discontents* (New York: W. W. Norton & Company, 2002).

6. John Lloyd, "Who Lost Russia?," *New York Times Magazine*, August 15, 1999.

7. We could get by with such reckless economic behavior because the dollar was the de facto global currency. The problem with the global reserve system was one of the fundamental problems that we did not even discuss, let alone attempt to address.

8. In Russia, when the elected parliament resisted what we thought were the reforms that were right, we encouraged Boris Yeltsin to use presidential decrees, circumventing parliament; and when Yeltsin looked to be defeated, we looked the other way as Russia gave away its rich resources to the oligarchs, who paid him back by working to get him reelected. Similarly, we paid little attention to how private media concentration might result in a lack of diversity in viewpoints that was little better than a state-run media. The speed of privatization seemed at times the only thing we cared about.

CHAPTER 2

1. A theme we will strike repeatedly is that the numbers must be treated with care: the growth rates reported then have since been substantially revised downwards.

2. Woodward, *Maestro: Greenspan's Fed and the American Boom*, p. 196.

3. Ibid., p. 13.

4. To borrow E. Kane's memorable phrase. See *The S&L Insurance Crisis: How Did It Happen?* (Washington, DC: Urban Institute Press, 1989).

5. See Alexander Theberge's unpublished paper, "The Latin American Debt Crisis of the 1980s and Its Historical Precursors," April 8, 1999. See www.columbia.edu/~ad245/theberge.pdf.

6. There are surveys, and there is little evidence that *measured* confidence is much affected by deficits; it is much more sensitive to variables like unemployment and growth itself. But those who allude to "confidence" have scant interest in testing their assertions with statistics.

7. While Reagan and the congressional democrats disagreed on what to spend money on (Reagan wanting more on defense, less on social programs), there was really little differences in the *levels* of expenditure that they advocated.

8. This story is told at great length in Nurith Aizenman, "National Security for Sale: How Our Obsession with Privatizing Government Has Left Us Vulnerable to Nuclear Terrorism," *Washington Monthly*, December 17–23, 1997, and Stiglitz, *Globalization and Its Discontents,* op cit.

CHAPTER 3

1. For the minutes of the Federal Open Market Committee, see www.federalreserve.gov.//FOMC/transcripts/1996/19960924meeting.pdf.

2. John Maynard Keynes, *The General Theory of Employment, Interest and Money* (London: Macmillan, 1936).

3. For an excellent exposition of these ideas, see Burton Malkiel, *A Random Walk Down Wall Street* (New York: W. W. Norton & Company, 1974; rev. ed., 2002).

4. My research with Sanford Grossman, later to become Trustee Professor of Finance and Director, Center for Quantitative Finance at the Wharton School at the University of Pennsylvania, then a colleague of mine at Stanford, had shown that there was, in a sense, an internal contradiction in the idea of a perfectly efficient market. As we put it, there was an equilibrium amount of disequilibrium. See Stiglitz with Grossman, "On the Impossibility of Informationally Efficient Markets," *American Economic Review*, vol. 70, no. 3 (June 1980), pp. 393–408.

5. The importance of this line of research was recognized by the award of the Nobel Prize to Danny Kahneman of Princeton University in 2002. The *Journal of Economic Perspectives* ran a regular column by Richard H. Thaler describing these market "anomalies."

6. The Federal Reserve, Remarks by Chairman Alan Greenspan, August 30, 2002: www.federalreserve.gov/BoardDocs/Speeches/2002/20020830/default.htm.

7. Federal Open Market Committee meeting transcripts, Meeting of the Federal Open Market Committee, September 24, 1996, p. 31; www.federalreserve.gov// transcripts/1996/19960924meeting.pdf.

8. See Milton Friedman and Anna Schwartz, *A Monetary History of the United States, 1857–1960* (Princeton: Princeton University Press, 1963).

9. See the Economic Report of the President, 1995 and 1996, at http://w3.access. gpo.gov/eop/.

10. Of course, in many of these episodes Greenspan had allies, who could do some of the work for him. And in a few cases, when the Fed's turf was in danger of being touched, he would be much more open. Early in the Clinton administration, there was an attempt to reform banking regulation. Banks came under the jurisdiction of three, four, or sometimes even five regulators, and in our attempt to streamline government, we wanted to simplify bank regulation, which had evolved in a more or less hodge-podge way. The comptroller of the currency, who reported to the secretary of Treasury, was the main (and oldest—dating back to 1863) regulator, but the Fed also had jurisdiction. Naturally, Treasury wanted to consolidate regulation under its control, and naturally the Fed resisted. We (the Council, working with Treasury and the White House) proposed a compromise, one that would rationalize regulation and also provide more of the kind of infor-

mation the Fed needed to perform its macroeconomic responsibilities. The Fed resisted—and won. It was easy to see through the specious arguments it put forward: it didn't like its turf being intruded upon, and, as inefficient as the old system might be, it liked things the way they were.

11. There is one perverse possibility: lower short-term interest rates could lead to higher long-term interest rates, if the lower short-term interest rates led to a burst of inflationary expectations; but as we have said, there was no reason to expect that.

12. In fact, the term is misleading. It should be called the non-*increasing* inflation rate of unemployment, NIIRU.

13. The recent examples of very high inflation have mostly occurred in Latin America. Argentina, Bolivia, Brazil, Chile, Peru, and Uruguay together experienced an average annual inflation rate of 121 percent between 1970 and 1987. One true hyperinflation occurred during this period. In Bolivia, prices increased by 12,000 percent in 1985. In Peru in 1988, a near hyperinflation occurred as prices rose by about 2,000 percent for the year, or by 30 percent per month. See www.econlib.org/library/Enc/Hyperinflation.html.

14. John Cassidy provides an unusually frank insight into the inside machinations. See his *New Yorker* article: "Fleeing the Fed," February 19, 1996.

15. Another more liberal appointment to the Fed, that of Alicia Munnell, a distinguished economist who had served as assistant secretary of Treasury, was also quashed. Later, she was to join the Council of Economic Advisers, where she made particularly important contributions to the debate on Social Security reform.

CHAPTER 4

1. Paul Starr, "The Great Telecom Implosion," *The American Prospect*, September 9, 2002.

2. Reed E. Hundt, *You Say You Want a Revolution: A Story of Information Age Politics* (New Haven: Yale University Press, 2000).

3. Chairman Michael K. Powell, in a speech before the Goldman Sachs Communicopia Conference, FCC, on October 2, 2002.

4. Peter W. Huber, "Telecom Undone—A Cautionary Tale," *Commentary*, January 1, 2003. See www.manhattan-institute.org/html/_comm-telecom.htm.

5. Ibid.

6. This set of ideas was referred to as "contestability." Even as experience demon-

strated that the central tenet, that all that was required to ensure zero profits and low prices was *potential competition*, economic theory was explaining the limitations of the theory. For a discussion of the doctrine of contestability, see, e.g., William Baumol, "Contestable Markets: An Uprising in the Theory of Industry Structure," *American Economic Review*, vol. 72, no. 1 (March 1982), pp. 1–15; for a critique, see D. McFadden, S. Peltzman, and J. Stiglitz, "Technological Change, Sunk Costs, and Competition," *Brooking Papers on Economic Activity*, vol. 3, Special Issue on Microeconomics (1987), pp. 883–947.

7. Or corporatization, in which a government corporation, like Amtrak, is set up. The proposal we actually sent to Congress asked to establish a new government corporation, rather than privatization. We thought privatization might seem too "radical" to the pro-business corporate jet advocates.

8. There was another element to this story, one of our few forays into cutting corporate welfare: corporate jets just happened to be manufactured in Nebraska, the home of the Republican Senate Leader, Bob Dole, and Georgia, the home of the House Leader, Newt Gingrich. Corporate jets were symbolic of corporate welfare; but perhaps politics played a role in our initiative as well?

9. Nevertheless, in November 2000, just nine months after the new legislation was passed, the WTO ruled that it, too, was not compliant. The trade conflict began in January 2000 when a different WTO court ruled that the Foreign Sales Corporation (FSC) Act was illegal under the same WTO rules. Congress replaced this law with the Extraterritorial Income Exclusion (ETI) Act, but that was also ruled illegal. (The case is ongoing in April 2003.)

10. The Ninth Annual Report of the FCC, December 31, 2002. See Katherine Reynolds Lewis, "Cable's Share of Market Slips As Satellite Picks Up," *Los Angeles Times*, January 1, 2003.

CHAPTER 5

1. See Arthur Levitt, with Paula Dwyer, *Take On the Street: What Wall Street and Corporate America Don't Want You to Know. What You Can Do to Fight Back*, and Julie Kosterlitz and Neil Munro, "Full Disclosure," *The National Journal*, February 23, 2002.

2. Arthur Levitt, with Paula Dwyer, op cit.

3. It was a political judgement: Levitt worried that the consequences of not backing off, encountering Congress's wrath, would be even more dire, and in the end, the option proposal would be sunk in any case.

4. Disclosure requirements in the United States were far stronger than in many other countries, and as executive compensation soared, there were frequent articles in the business press highlighting the seemingly exorbitant pay of one executive or another. But the information was not presented systematically, in ways which enabled investors to assess the impact on share value, and with all the distortions in accounting (to be described below), investors had little idea of the value of the compensation relative to the *true* increase in the value of the firm. So long as share prices were soaring, nothing mattered much; but when the boom came to an end, investors decided they needed to take a close look at what was going on.

5. After Enron's bankruptcy, all the analysts who had recommended its stocks, and the banks that had lent it money, argued that no one, not even the experts, could have figured out their footnotes.

6. Some firms that use stock options have argued there is a difference between paying a CEO $10 million and giving him a stock option worth $10 million; though both mean there is less left over for other shareholders, they have different implications for the cash position of the firm. In industries in which firms often face strong liquidity constraints, this difference can be important. The appropriate way to deal with this is to have accounting frameworks that provide comprehensive information about the firm's liquidity position.

7. There are some technical limits, which need not detain us here.

8. The preceding paragraph discusses the tax treatment of incentive stock options (qualified options), which were used in about half of all firms granting options in the late 1990s. With non-qualified options, companies could deduct from their taxes the gains of their employees when they exercised their options, but the companies didn't have to report this expense on their income statements to shareholders. As a result, non-qualified options allowed companies simultaneously to exaggerate their reported profits while minimizing their taxes. For a further discussion, see Myron S. Scholes et al., *Taxes and Business Strategy*, 2nd ed. (Englewood Cliffs, NJ: Prentice Hall, 2001).

9. See, for instance, Jerry Useem, "Have They No Shame?," op cit.

10. See Adolf A. Berle and Gardiner C. Means, *Modern Corporation and Private Property* (New York: Commerce Clearing House, 1932).

11. The work on the economics of information, for which George Akerlof, A. Michael Spence, and Joseph Stiglitz received the Nobel Prize in Economics in 2001, focused on these problems of information asymmetries, where one party (here the manager) knows more than another party (here the shareholder).

12. There is no simple definition of derivatives. They are assets (or gambles) that are

derived from other assets—hence their name. An option—the right to buy a share at a fixed price (called the strike price)—is a derivative, in the sense that its value derives from the underlying share; the buyer of the option gets all the gain in excess of the strike price. A put—the right to sell a share at a fixed price—gives the buyer of the put the difference between the strike price and the actual price, when the value of the share falls below the strike price. Derivatives can be based on interest rates, prices of oil, or combinations of two or more prices.

13. "Andersen is no stranger to fraudulent business schemes. It has been an enabler for other companies that made a practice of fleecing the public," said [Connecticut attorney general Richard] Blumenthal. "Andersen was deeply involved in the Waste Management scandal, resulting in . . . a recovery of millions of dollars for victim investors . . . [and] a key player in the Colonial Realty fraud that . . . ultimately [led to] payments by the firm and bans on certain activities"—Connecticut Attorney General's Office press release, February 5, 2002. See www.cslib.org/attygenl/press/2002/other/aasubp.htm.

CHAPTER 6

1. IPOs stand for "Initial Public Offerings"—the first offerings of a share on the market; typically, they are sold at a price considerably below the value to which they rise almost immediately after being issued, which is why getting IPO shares is so valuable. IPOs are discussed at greater length below.

2. Readers interested in a more extensive description of the misconduct by almost every leading investment and commercial bank in America should turn to the findings of the New York State Attorney General at www.oag.state.ny.us/press/statements/global_resolution.html.

3. The issues discussed in this paragraph relate to what is more broadly called the problem of corporate governance, which I discuss at greater length later in this chapter. The modern discussion of corporate governance is traced to Berle and Means, *Modern Corporation and Private Property*, though cogent discussion occurred earlier, e.g., Alfred Marshall (see Alfred Marshall, *Principles of Economics*, [London: Macmillan, 1928]). His survey of the challenges facing economic science in the coming century focuses on issues that today are referred to as corporate governance. In the early and mid-80s, I began to look at the problem of corporate governance through the lens of asymmetric information and public goods. See J. E. Stiglitz, "Credit Markets and the Control of Capital,"

Journal of Money, Banking and Credit, vol. 17, no. 2 (May 1985), pp. 133–52. See also Andrei Shleifer and Robert Vishney, "A Survey of Corporate Governance," *Journal of Finance*, vol. LII, no. 2 (June 1997).

4. In a settlement in April 2003, Jack Grubman and Henry Blodget agreed to lifetime bans from the industry along with fines of almost $20 million, though without admitting guilt. In the same settlement, the chairman and chief executive of Citigroup, Sanford I. Weill, agreed to be barred from communicating with his firm's stock analysts about the companies they cover, unless a lawyer is present. Before his downfall, Grubman had been rated by *Institutional Investor* as the telecom sector's best analyst. Only Meeker remains on her job.

5. Goldman Sachs's reputation had not always seemed so untarnished; in the years leading up to the Great Depression, it seems to have been caught engaged in some unsavory practices. See John K. Galbraith, *The Great Crash, 1929* (Cambridge, MA: Riverside Press, 1954). A brief summary of some of what Goldman Sachs did can be found at http://politics.guardian.co.uk/columnist/story/0,9321,901295,00.html.

6. Though neither UrbanFetch.com nor Kozmo.com was publicly traded, their sheer existence is an example of the overexuberance of the market.

7. Among the important contributors to this line of research are Roman Frydman of New York University and Michael Woodford of Princeton University.

8. Gift exchanges are exchanges in which one party gives a "gift" to the other, normally in the expectation that the gift will be reciprocated. The analysts give a gift to the company—bloated reports—and the company gives a gift to the analyst—information that it makes available to the analyst but not more widely. Gift exchanges can be analyzed much like a market (there is usually an implicit understanding concerning the value of the gifts being exchanged). Gift exchanges are often used when formal, market exchanges would be unseemly, as in social relations, or illegal or improper. It would be illegal, or certainly improper, for the analyst to ask for a bribe for providing a good report.

9. The magnitude of the "theft" was enormous. Three hundred and nine mostly high-tech IPOs generated over *$50 billion* in first-day trading profits, more than the actual amount raised by the issuers, and twenty times the amount of underwriting fees on thse issues—meaning that if only 5 percent of this amount wended its way back to the investment banks, it would have doubled their revenues from the deals.

10. Of course, if information were perfect, this might not matter. Shareholders,

knowing of the banks' largesse, might even decide to seek a corresponding reduction in the size of the paychecks going to a company's executives. In competitive markets, managers are paid what they need to be paid to recruit them. They don't care about the form of payment. If they get more in IPO allocations, they ask for less in the form of salary, bonuses, and stock options. But in the world of greed and lack of transparency that marked America in the Roaring Nineties, managers did not disclose their IPO allocations, and their total compensation was not adjusted to offset what they received from the investment banks.

11. The Reconstruction Finance Corporation (RFC) Bank was established during the Hoover administration to provide liquidity and restore confidence in the banking system. In February 1933, when there were banking problems in Detroit, the RFC agreed to help a troubled bank, the United Guardian Trust. President Roosevelt inherited the RFC. He and his colleagues, as well as Congress, found the independence and flexibility of the RFC to be particularly useful. The RFC was an executive agency with the ability to obtain funding through the Treasury outside the normal legislative process. Thus, the bank could be used to finance a variety of favored projects and programs without obtaining legislative approval. RFC lending did not count toward budgetary expenditures, so the expansion of the role and influence of the government through the RFC was not reflected in the federal budget.

12. It is perhaps no accident that the two investment banks, Citigroup and J. P. Morgan Chase, most involved in the Enron scandal both had significant commercial banking operations and were created only as a result of the repeal of Glass-Steagall. (See July 2002 Senate Government Affairs Committee hearings and John. R. Emshwiller, Anita Raghavan, and Jathon Sapsford, "How Wall Street Greased Enron's Money Machine," *Wall Street Journal*, January 14, 2002.) That said, it is worth noting that even had Glass-Steagall not been repealed, there would have been all of the other problems we have discussed; the repeal was not at the center of the story, but it did make a bad situation even worse.

13. U.S. Bankruptcy Court Southern District of New York, "First Interim Report of Dick Thornburgh, Bankruptcy Court Examiner," November 4, 2002, p. 8.

14. Gretchen Morgenson, "More Clouds Over Citigroup in Its Dealings with Ebbers," *New York Times*, November 3, 2002, sec. 3, p. 1.

15. Jack Grubman's letter of resignation from Salomon Smith Barney, August 15, 2002, available at www.citigroup.com/citigroup/press/2002/data/020815d1.pdf.

16. Of course, as we note elsewhere in this book, Smith was more aware of the lim-

itations of this argument—that when individuals pursue their own interests, they advance the general well-being of society—than are many of the modern followers of his doctrines. But Smith did not fully grasp the limitations imposed by imperfect information.

17. The advocates of options as ways of rewarding managers often implicitly assumed markets were rational and well informed, for in that case, market value would increase if, and only if, managers would increase the long-term profitability of the firm. Managers were given the responsibility of providing information that would enable the market to value accurately the firm—but also were provided incentives not to do so.

18. There are some complicated subtleties involving *which* shareholders do and should bear the costs.

CHAPTER 7

1. The two parties each blamed the other for the failure to cut expenditures. The fact is that the Reagan and Bush administrations did not propose expenditure cuts that would have brought the budget in balance; the disagreement between the administration and Congress was not so much about the level of expenditure as about what the money should be spent on, for instance, defense versus social services.

2. In his presidential campaign, the Republican candidate, Robert Dole, was to advocate another dose of voodoo economics in 1996. The Democrats, and the American people more generally, wanted no part of it.

3. Technically, this is referred to as a step-up of basis at death.

4. Similarly, even some attempts to improve accounting (given the compromise form that they took) backfired. Firms were gven the right *not to expense* certain options—"fixed-plan options," which are options with a fixed exercise price. Introducing almost any kind of complexity into the option design, including basing options on *relative* performance, results in an option plan which *must be expensed*. Expensing was required for those forms of options for which valuation was most difficult. The desire to avoid disclosure contributed to the use of option plans that were far from optimal. (At the same time, it should be recognized that a firm could provide the same incentive structures *without* using options—and sometimes with greater tax advantages. Moreover, the failure to use well-designed option schemes predated the new accounting rule.)

CHAPTER 8

1. As this book was being completed, the deficiencies in the private pension system became increasingly a subject of scrutiny, with widespread journalistic coverage.

2. The worry that inflation would return did exist—part of the reason that long-term bonds were typically so much higher than short-term bonds was the concern that, over the long term, there would be some bout with high inflation, leading to high short-term interest rates.

3. Some central bankers had put forward still another argument. If enough people had indexed bonds, too few would feel large losses from inflation; thus, the crusade against inflation would be undermined. In short, they *wanted* people to suffer from inflation. The argument that indexed bonds insulated retirees against inflation was not an argument for the bonds, but against. I thought this illustrated the gulf that separated the mind-set of so many central bankers from that of the rest of the economy, and illustrated the themes of chapter 3 about central bank independence.

4. The Council put forward other ideas, such as inflation "puts," that would particularly address the fears of some market participants who felt that they could manage small variations in inflation—it was the small possibility of a large increase in the inflation rate that led the long-term rate often to be so much higher than the short. Inflation puts were a form of government insurance, which our calculations showed would have generated substantial income, making it unnecessary to undertake some of the shenanigans to balance the budget that may prove so costly, especially in the long run (such as the sale of the government corporation making the core ingredient of nuclear weapons, enriched uranium).

5. A recent evaluation of the quality of the Social Security system's telephone responses, for instance, gave it ratings comparable to that of the top three large private corporations.

6. Mamta Murthi, J. Michael Orszag, and Peter R. Orszag, "The Charge Ratio on Individual Accounts: Lessons from the U.K. Experience," Birkbeck College Working Paper 99-2. March 1999.

7. Intellectual consistency has, as we have repeatedly noted, not been the high-water mark of political discourse. George W. Bush pretended to take seriously budget projections, based on high growth, for his tax cuts. If the projections of faster growth that were used for Bush II's huge tax cut had much validity, then the fiscal problem of Social Security—the problem that originally motivated reform—would have been limited, undermining the argument for privatization.

8. There are a host of other imperfections in capital markets. For instance, one cannot obtain insurance against important risks that one cares about, and there is often credit and equity rationing. While some of these seeming market imperfections can be explained by asymmetric information, some (such as the inability to buy insurance against inflation) cannot.

9. Thaler has described a host of other anomalies in markets that can only, or best, be explained by market irrationalities. See Daniel Kahneman, Jack Knetsch, and Richard Thaler, "Anomalies: The Endowment Effect, Loss Aversion, and Status Quo Bias, *Journal of Economic Perspectives*, vol. 5, no. 1 (Winter 1991), pp. 193–206. See also the regular columns on financial market anomalies in the *Journal of Economic Perspectives* and Shiller, *Irrational Exuberance*.

CHAPTER 9

1. In *Globalization and Its Discontents*, I explain at much greater length the often well-justified sources of this discontent with globalization, *as it has been managed*, and how the rules and institutions which govern globalization can be reformed in ways that will enable globalization to live up to its promise. I argue that with these reforms, globalization can enhance growth and reduce poverty in the less developed countries; but without these reforms, poverty may increase, growth may be stymied, and democracy may be undermined.

2. Especially full capital market liberalization, which allowed the rush of speculative short-term capital into and out of a country. See the discussion below and *Globalization and Its Discontents*.

3. In several visits to Argentina in the years immediately before the crisis, I repeatedly heard these complaints. The Argentinian government itself was concerned, and set up a special lending program, but it appears to have been of limited effectiveness. More recently, on a visit to Mexico in 2002, with only one large bank remaining in the hands of Mexicans, I heard similar concerns expressed, even by senior officials in the normally conservative Central Bank. Studies conducted by the World Bank suggest that the evidence on these effects of foreign bank entry is ambiguous.

4. In 2001, the value of the cotton the farmers produced at international prices was approximately $3.5 billion, but they received an additional $4 billion from the government. U.S. subsidies are twice the $1.9 billion allowed under WTO. Oxfam estimates that the total cost to African cotton farmers in 2001 was $301 million. See www.oxfam.org/eng/pdfs/pp020925_cotton.pdf.

5. The argument that without such restrictions the drug companies would have no incentive to produce drugs was unconvincing. At the high prices, they made few sales in, say, Africa. With most of the expensive drugs highly regulated, largely sold through hospitals and prescriptions, and covered by third party insurance, it would be relatively easy to limit the extent of resale.

6. The concern about rich countries trying to use unequal treaties to kick away the ladder with which they climbed to the top had been raised in the nineteenth century by Friedrich List, one of Germany's leading economists. See Ha-Joon Chang, "History Debunks the Free Trade Myth," *The Guardian*, June 24, 2002.

7. For an excellent discussion of these intellectual property rights issues, see Michael Perleman, *Steal This Idea: Intellectual Property and the Corporate Confiscation of Creativity* (New York: Palgrave, 2002).

8. See "International Competition Policy" at www.ids.ac.uk/tradebriefings/ti5.pdf.

9. As we noted in chapter 2, dumping was only part of the problem. Excess zeal for deficit reduction (based on faulty accounting), ideology, and special interests had combined to drive the privatization of USEC. It was clear, however, that the privatized firm would have every incentive to keep out the Russian material, which depressed prices and profits. Unfortunately, these concerns proved only too accurate. One magazine labeled this venture "National Security for Sale"—see Nurith Aizenman, "National Security for Sale: How Our Obsession with Privatizing Government Has Left Us Vulnerable to Nuclear Terrorism," op cit.

10. See Daniel Lederman, Anna María Menéndez, Guillermo Perry, and Joseph E. Stiglitz, "Mexico Five Years after the Crisis," in *Annual Bank Conference on Development Economics 2000* (Washington, DC: World Bank, 2001), pp. 263–82.

11. They were also called "neo-liberal" reforms, or "market fundamentalist reforms," because they were predicated on the conservative free market ideology of Reagan and Thatcher, who were in office at the time the ideas were developed.

12. These were known as the moral hazard problem.

13. The only major emerging markets not to have crises were those in China and in India, which had not followed the IMF/Treasury advice to liberalize their capital markets.

14. This discussion is based upon and expanded in Joseph Stiglitz, "A Fair Deal for the World," *New York Review of Books*, vol. 49, no. 9, May 23, 2002.

15. This was not the only instance in which, in retrospect, Treasury clearly put the interests of financial markets above national security. In note 9 above, I described

how Treasury pushed for privatization of the U.S. Enrichment Corporation, responsible for the production of the enriched uranium used in atomic weapons, and for the importation of nuclear material from Russia's warheads—a policy that clearly risked nuclear proliferation. Even the head of the CIA at the time sided with the Council of Economic Advisers about the lack of wisdom; but privatization was Treasury's province, and it prevailed. Later, after concerns about terrorism grew with the attack on the U.S. Embassy in Kenya, ways of choking off funds to the terrorists were explored. I had left the Clinton administration by then, but according to Joe Klein, Samuel (Sandy) Berger, the head of the National Security Council, said it was impossible to move Treasury. Klein reports that Treasury secretaries Rubin and Summers worried that strong measures, like cyberwarfare, would threaten the stability of the international financial system, and quotes one official as saying: "This was a neuralgic issue for Treasury"—see Joe Klein, *The Natural: The Misunderstood Presidency of Bill Clinton* (New York: Doubleday, 2002), p. 190.

16. Though the World Bank is an international institution with a membership of 184 countries, Europe and the United States have a majority of the votes, and they have agreed among themselves always to have an American head the World Bank and a European to head the IMF. This clubby arrangement has increasingly come under attack.

17. The percentage of the population living below $2 a day rose in Latin America from 35.5 percent in 1987 to 36.4 percent in 1998.

18. This was part of the Publish What You Pay Initiative, launched in June 2002 by George Soros, Global Witness, and Save the Children UK. Tony Blair announced in September 2002 that the U.K. government intended to lead an international initiative to prevent mismanagement of revenues paid by oil, gas, and mining companies.

19. The good news is that though the program was limited, those that have been able to avail themselves have benefited with significant increases in exports (from an often admittedly very low base).

CHAPTER 10

1. Loren Fox's *Enron: The Rise and Fall* (New York: John Wiley & Sons, 2003) offers a detailed and thoughtful examination of the case of Enron. For the story of former Enron executive and whistle-blower Sherron Watkins, see Mimi

Swartz's book (written with Watkins) *Power Failure: The Inside Story of the Collapse of Enron* (New York: Doubleday, 2003). See also Brian Cruver's *Anatomy of Greed: The Unshredded Truth from an Enron Insider* (New York: Carroll & Graf, 2002).

2. For a discussion of Ponzi and other such schemes, see Charles P. Kindleberger, *Manias, Panics, and Crashes*, op cit.

3. As we saw in chapter 4, some economists went further—even if there is a single firm in an industry, a monopolist, we need not worry about the exercise of market power, for if he charges ever so much greater than the lowest price that he could survive at, some other potential entrant will enter. Potential competition is all that is required. This argument had less sway in electricity deregulation than in airline deregulation (and even there it proved wrong).

4. Pacific Gas & Electric, California's largest utility, went bankrupt on April 6, 2001. It claimed that the power crisis had led to debts of $9 billion.

5. The fact that the electricity companies went bankrupt did not totally remove them from the suspect list. After all, they could have begun by thinking that they could enhance their profits, but as matters got out of control, they wound up losing. But it suggested that there were other guilty parties.

6. Fox, *Enron: The Rise and Fall*, p. 200.

7. See Paul Krugman, "Frank Thoughts on the California Crisis," www.wws .princeton.edu/~pkrugman/wolak.html.

8. The experience in California illustrates the difficulty of doing deregulation "right." Part of the reason is that, even in a large state like California, competition in general can be limited. Deregulation advocates recognized that there would not likely be competition in transmission but assumed that there would be intense competition in generation and retailing, and many underestimated the problems of making a competitive market work when a central piece—transmission—was essentially a monopoly. Part of the reason too had to do with "political economy": while critics of regulation complain about politicization of the regulatory process (with similar complaints about government ownership), they fail to note that the deregulatory process (like the privitization process) is fraught with similar problems, and with potentially even worse outcomes. Some interpret the flaws in California as arsing as much from political battles between the distribution firms and the generation firms (and the worries of the electricity providers about stranded costs) as from the desire to protect consumers.

Some deregulation efforts (Pennsylvani, New Jersey) appear to be much more successful—so far—than California's. In any case, it is worth emphasizing that Enron and the other firms manipulating prices were only part of the problem; it is conceivable that the generating firms themselves would have caused almost as much disruption on their own without Enron's help.

9. Fox, *Enron: The Rise and Fall*, p. 210

10. see www.house.gov/reform/min/pdfs/pdf_inves/pdf_admin_enron_jan_16_let.pdf.

CHAPTER 11

1. There is by now a large literature on these issues. See, e.g., Alan J. Auerbach, ed., *Corporate Takeovers: Causes and Consequences* (Chicago: University of Chicago Press, 1988), including the article by Andrei Shleifer and Lawrence H. Summers, "Breach of Trust in Hostile Takeovers."

2. Growth in 2000–02 in Sweden was 4.4, 0.8, 1.5 percent; for the United States, 3.8, 0.3, 2.4 percent—from EIU Country Data.

CHAPTER 12

1. The term "third way" has attained different, and in some cases, quite specific, connotations in different countries. In using it, I do not wish to invoke any of these former debates or the passions which they provoked. I mean nothing other than what I say: a third way between socialism, where government plays an intrusive role in the economy, and laissez-faire economics, where government plays no role.

2. My own research helps explain why markets provide inadequate insurance, and identifies the high costs of the absence of insurance. But it also shows that whenever there is insurance, the insurer attempts to "regulate behavior," to reduce the risk of the insured against the event occurring. From these perspectives, deposit insurance is welfare-enhancing; but deposit insurance needs to be accompanied by supervision to ensure that the risks which deposit insurance covers become less likely to occur.

3. Similarly, some conservatives blame government deposit insurance for financial crises. Even countries without deposit insurance—and without adequate regulation—have faced financial crises (Sweden providing the most recent example in early 1990s), and these crises have occurred repeatedly, well before deposit insurance became part of the scene.

4. H. Simon, "Organizations and Markets," *Journal of Economic Perspectives*, vol. 5, no. 2 (1991), p. 28.

5. See chapter 2.

6. There was a third doctrine, which held some sway among economists but never had much influence with the general public. This held that one could separate out issues of efficiency from equity; economists, in this view, should focus just on efficiency, leaving it to the political process to discuss distributive issues.

7. This was not the first such episode. Karl Polanyi in *The Great Transformation* (Beacon Hills, MA: Beacon Hill Press, 1944) describes the immiseration of the working class during the nineteenth century; worsening living conditions resulted in shorter lives—and by some accounts shorter individuals. More recently, in Latin America, those in poverty (at the $2 a day standard) have increased, even while GDP has increased.

8. Through the earned income tax credit.

9. Markets are also related to political ends; conservatives have rightly emphasized the importance of the freedom of choice associated with markets—see Milton and Rose Friedman, *Free to Choose: A Personal Statement* (New York: Harcourt Brace Jovanovich, 1980). But, as I shall point out later, often one person's actions encroach on another person's well-being, and sometimes even on his or her freedom to choose; and markets often lead to such poverty that many individuals' freedom to choose is greatly circumscribed. Here, I limit myself to the economic dimensions.

10. See, e.g., John Rawls, *A Theory of Justice* (Cambridge, MA: Belknap Press, 1971), and the huge literature to which his book gave rise.

11. Tony Blair proposed the Child Trust Fund or "Baby Bond" in 2001.

12. There are further questions about electoral democracy, brought home by the American election of 2000, where a candidate who got a minority of the popular vote became the president. Gerrymandering may result in minorities controlling the political process, even when there are free elections. Different electoral rules (e.g., proportional representation) may provide for greater voice of minorities a higher probability that the will of the majority be heard.

13. These notions can be traced at least back to David Hume, *A Treatise of Human Nature* (1739–40).

14. There is a large philosophical literature which attempts to link the extent of admissible redistributions with what individuals might be able to achieve on their own, without collective action, e.g., in the enforcement of property rights. See, e.g., Robert Nozick, *Anarchy, State, and Utopia* (New York: Basic Books, 1974).

As a practical matter, what an individual could achieve on his own is probably sufficiently limited that this does not impose significant constraints.

15. See, for instance, the 1993 constitution of the Republic of South Africa.

16. Smith himself would not have subscribed to such beliefs. He was much more aware of the limitations of the market than his latter-day followers.

17. Albert Hirschman, *Shifting Involvements: Private Interest and Public Action* (Princeton: Princeton University Press, 1982).

EPILOGUE

1. When I was at the Council, we devised a variety of other "low-cost" stimuli— e.g., allowing firms that invest more to carry back profits and losses more years, which even increases overall economic efficiency. By contrast, the Bush proposal restricts carryback provisions for firms that want to qualify for tax-free dividends.

2. See William Gale and Peter Orszag, "A Reckless Budget," *Financial Times*, February 3, 2003.

3. Joseph E. Stiglitz, "Bush's Tax Plan—The Dangers," *New York Review of Books,* vol. 50, no. 4, March 13, 2003.

4. This is what is done in the case of some European countries and is used for the treatment of some small corporations. The earnings of the corporation would be treated *as if* they had been fully distributed to shareholders. Any retained earnings then would be treated *as if* the shareholder had reinvested those earnings. The result would be that each individual would have paid a tax corresponding to his own tax rate, upper-income individuals paying a rate of close to 40 percent, low-income individuals paying low or no taxes. But under the Bush scheme, high- and low-income individuals both pay the same 35 percent tax rate.

5. See William G. Gale and Peter R. Orszag, "The Economic Effects of Long-Term Fiscal Discipline," Urban Institute–Brookings Institution Tax Policy Center Discussion Paper, December 17, 2002, and Gale and Orszag, "A Reckless Budget."

6. Even the Bush administration was aware of these weaknesses, though they did not advertise them. While the administration claimed that growth between 2003 and 2008 would increase an average of a mere 0.1 percent per year, the longer-run prospect was for an actual decline in growth, relative to what it would otherwise have been.

7. Because of the budget chicanery, many believed that the true costs of the tax cut

might well exceed Bush's original $726 billion, as Congress would find itself loath to reinstate taxes once abolished. Of course, this was all part of the Bush strategy, just as the resulting deficits were part of a strategy to force roll backs in government expenditures. Some thought there was an even more nefarious agenda: surpluses could have been used to put Social Security on a sound footing; without these surpluses, Social Security might look more precarious, and this might advance Bush's plans to privatize Social Security.

8. Alex Berenson, *New York Times*, May 24, 2003, p. B1, and Daniel Altman, *New York Times*, May 24, 2003, p. B1. Because the tax cuts were allegedly temporary, many economists thought that the stimulus effect would be much smaller than had been earlier calculated. According to standard economic theory, households base their consumption on their *permanent income*, the amount they have to spend in the long run. A temporary tax cut, in this view, does not do much to long-run spending power, and hence most of the tax cut will be saved. More recent theories have stressed that the result depends critically on who gets the tax cut. If low-income individuals, whose spending is constrained by their income, get a tax cut, they will spend the money, but if high-income individuals get the tax cut, there will be only a modest increase in spending.

Index